Controlled Burn:

Exposing Child Sex Abuse and Corruption at
America's Largest Private Catholic High School

Controlled Burn:

Exposing Child Sex Abuse and Corruption at America's Largest Private Catholic High School

by
Elizabeth Cucinotta Sorvillo

with a Foreword by
Felicia Mooradian

DEMAND IT
MEDIA

Published by
Demand It Media, Inc.
2647 Gateway Road., Suite 105-159
Carlsbad, CA 92009
USA

ISBN 978-0-9973151-0-3

Printed in the United States of America

*To my wife, Josephine, who is my light,
to my son, Andrew, who has been my greatest
teacher, and to Felicia Mooradian, whose
courage and passion for the truth opened a door
to healing for so many.*

*And to my dear friend,
Marla Krolikowski – Rest in peace, Marla.
We did it.*

Foreword

What does it mean to be a survivor of child sexual abuse? The word "molested" is used to describe the act of sexually abusing a child- a word that simply means to bother. We use this word to sterilize what it means to endure sexual abuse as a child, perhaps because it is incomprehensible to those who have not lived it.

As survivors of child sexual abuse, we are forever changed. Someone we trusted perverted the gift of our childhood innocence. Maybe we were happy kids and slowly began to lose the joy that other children felt. All of a sudden, we were no longer children. We were introduced far too soon to the world of sexual exploitation and forced to grow up in an instant. We felt different and alone. We started to do poorly in school and hate ourselves. We didn't sleep well anymore. We began to hurt our own bodies, taught by abusers that we were inherently bad. Maybe we stopped eating, maybe we took razors to our skin, maybe we turned to drinking and drugging. Maybe we found that the high from the needle was the only vehicle to return to the happiness we felt before we were abused, or the numbness from the bottle was the only thing to turn off the self-loathing for a few precious, fleeting moments.

As we entered adulthood, the world seemed to pass us by. While our friends were successful in college, we failed out. While our peers embarked on careers, we couldn't hold down a job. While everyone else was in love, we couldn't maintain healthy relationships, because in everyone we tried to get close to, there was the abuse like a ghost waiting to destroy all that is good. No matter how much we told ourselves we weren't to blame, there was always a part of us that believed we were.

Maybe eventually we sought help and managed to recover from the abuse, or maybe we didn't. Maybe some of us were too ashamed to ever tell, crushed by the weight of the secret. Maybe some of us felt that if the people who knew didn't say anything, we shouldn't either. Maybe some of us tried to disclose what was happening and weren't believed. Maybe some of us are still living shackled to the abuse, going through the motions of life, just getting by. Maybe some of us couldn't take the pain anymore and ended our lives. It never had to be this way for us.

In my case, and in the case of every survivor I know, there was someone who knew that the abuse was going on and did nothing to stop it. Sometimes it's a family member who turns a blind eye, or sometimes it is an institution, such as a church or school that has engaged in a systematic cover up of sexual abuse, enabling child predators to destroy soul after soul. Many survivors never seek justice, and the ones who do are faced with archaic laws, such as absurdly inadequate statutes of limitation, designed to shield sexual predators and those that conspire to cover their tracks.

By the grace of God, I chose the path of recovery. I know that for every one like me, there are a thousand who don't make it. Through the aid of therapy, self-help groups, and organizations for sexual abuse survivors, I have made it. There was a time when I could not function without some intoxicating substance to carry me through the day- now I am sober. I dropped out of four colleges, accumulating credits here and there, and now I am entering my final semester at Queens College. I will graduate with a degree in psychology and pursue a career in mental health counseling. Life is not perfect. There are days when I am depressed and can't get out of bed. There are nights that I wake up screaming, terrorized by nightmares. There are times when I panic and feel as though the world is closing in on me. There are times when the disease of addiction beckons to me, lying in wait to relieve the pain. There are times that I feel I will never shake the darkness or the persisting mark left upon me by the abuse. What keeps me going through those episodes is the knowledge that I am not alone and that I have taken the power back from my abusers and their accomplices by fighting for justice.

If you are reading this book and you have not lived through child sexual abuse, I pray that this book will elucidate for you what it is to be sexually abused as a child and, most importantly, that you will feel implored to fight for survivors with the relentless ardor that the author of this book has.

If you are one of the 1 in 3 girls or 1 in 5 boys who is a survivor of child sexual abuse and you are reading this, **you are not alone**. We are united by a common bond that no one else can possibly understand. It is my hope that this book will give you faith and comfort. What happened to you does not have to define you. **It wasn't your fault**.

Child sexual abuse is an epidemic. The contents of this book represent a microcosm of a tremendous problem. It is an obligation we all share to prevent child sexual abuse and to crusade on behalf of survivors. When children are sexually abused, they are robbed of their voices. It is about time we started speaking up for them. We must fight to end child sexual abuse. The time has come to stop protecting the predators and start protecting the survivors.

—Felicia Mooradian

CONTENTS

PROLOGUE

Many psychics say buildings hold energy, both positive and negative. The theory is, the sturdier the building material, the more psychic energy the building holds.

The largest private Catholic high school in the United States is St. Francis Preparatory School in Fresh Meadows, NY. It is constructed of steel and concrete block, through and through. Many memories have been made there, and that building holds them all.

St. Francis Preparatory School began as St. Francis Academy, founded in 1858 by two Franciscan Brothers from Galway, Ireland. These two men had been summoned by the Bishop of the Brooklyn Diocese, John Loughlin, to undertake the work of educating the male youth of the community. The school's first location at 300 Baltic Street was staffed by these two Brothers and three additional teachers.

The Brothers used the basement as their monastery, and generously dedicated the upper floors as classrooms. Thus started the long St. Francis tradition of the Brothers living in the school itself.

Over the years, St. Francis Academy grew into both a college and a high school, under one roof. As the high school grew to include more than 600 students, it became evident it could no longer function as part of a single entity. On June 21, 1935, the Board of Regents of the State of New York conferred upon St. Francis Academy a new charter establishing St. Francis Preparatory School as a separate and distinct educational institution.

In 1952, St. Francis Preparatory School was relocated to Williamsburg, Brooklyn, where it continued to flourish. It remained at its famous North 6th Street location until 1974, when the Brothers decided it was time for a major shift. The school was relocated to a modern facility in Fresh Meadows, Queens, which was the former site of Bishop Reilly High School. It is at this point that St. Francis Prep became co-ed, and doubled in size to nearly three thousand students.

Throughout its history, St. Francis Prep has been considered a school of distinction. In 1999, it was recognized by U.S. News & World Report as an "Outstanding American High School." In the following years, the school experienced a decade long streak during which its students were named semi-finalists in the prestigious Intel Science Talent Search.

Graduates include legendary coach Vince Lombardi, world champion NY Yankee manager Joe Torre, "Big Brother" and "The Talk" host Julie Chen, actor Peter Facinelli of the "Twilight" movies, and former "The Walking Dead" showrunner Glen Mazzara. These are just a few names in a plethora of professional athletes, business moguls, politicians, and celebrities who call themselves alumni.

Despite all the accolades, however, St. Francis Prep has had one major failure - a very dark, shameful, and painful failure four decades in length, and no less wide.

This is the story of how two ballsy women used their ingenuity and tenacity to expose it.

CHAPTER ONE

ELIZABETH 1983-1986

When I attended St. Francis Prep, the school was considered one of the best Catholic high schools in the country. Competition was fierce to get into the school – there were four children competing for every seat in the freshman class, which usually consisted of about 2,900 students. To be considered for admission, an applicant had to take a standardized test, and check St. Francis Prep as their top choice on a list of three schools he or she would consider attending.

St. Francis Prep was definitely my first choice. I had several reasons, one being its high academic ranking in NY, another being that it was co-ed (most of my friends were boys), and lastly that I would not have to wear a uniform. The school had an uncomplicated student dress code instead, which consisted of slacks (no jeans), shirts with buttons, and if you were a girl, knee-length skirts. This was very, very appealing to me. I hated having my individuality squashed all through Catholic grammar school by being forced to wear a uniform. They were unflattering and unforgiving, especially if you were a little overweight, like I was. Wearing one for another four years was out of the question.

In fact, I wanted to go to St. Francis Prep, or "Prep" as it was known in Queens, so badly that I stretched my poor mother's nerves to their end worrying about taking the standardized exam. I worried so much, that she internalized my worry and threw up on the way to driving me to the exam. After that unfortunate incident, I learned not to worry so much about exams anymore.

I still have my acceptance letter to Prep. That's how much I cherished it. I know it's weird. I save lots of random things. It's just the way I am. I have the letter in a memory box, it has been there for 30 years, and there it will stay.

My freshman year at St. Francis Prep was a little rough for two reasons. One, it was very academically challenging for me. I was an excellent student in grammar school, especially in math, but we had not covered much algebra. When I saw all these letters in math problems in high school, it threw me for a loop. I barely passed and I was very upset with myself.

I'm partly to blame, but I also blame my teacher, Mrs. Wall. Her teaching style just did not click with me. I didn't understand her, and she was not helpful in offering additional explanation.

In my opinion, she was a little off, too. Something wasn't right in her head. I remember clearly that one day in the cafeteria I started choking on my soda. I was drinking and laughing at the same time, and it went down the wrong pipe, and I couldn't breathe. I was literally dying. Mrs. Wall was two feet away from me and watched me choking. I was gasping for air, and it was obvious. But, she did not make a move to help me. My friend, Anthony, took it upon himself to do the Heimlich maneuver on me. Up came all the soda! He saved my life that day and I will never forget it.

The other reason I didn't do as well as I could have is that I was scared to death of a particular teacher. Brother Richard was my Earth Science teacher. Brother Richard was an enormous man. He was easily 6 foot 3, and he was very overweight. He had a bald head, and in that brown dress the Franciscan Brothers wear, he looked like Buddha. So that's what everyone called him.

Brother Richard had anger management problems. If he was in a bad mood, or he felt a student was putting him in a bad mood, he would throw chairs across the room, and sometimes push the offending student against a wall and yell in his face. I don't recall him pulling the physical stuff with girls – but he would yell at girls in the same way he would yell at boys. I have a young son, and when I think about the things I witnessed when I was a student at St. Francis Prep I get very upset. My son is no giant. Imagine being a high school freshman boy, tiny, and this enormous man is pushing you against a wall and screaming in your face?

I was so afraid of Brother Richard it distracted me quite a bit from the material in his class. I am not making excuses; I'm not into that. And maybe I should have told someone in a position of authority at the school about what I was feeling, but I didn't think it would matter. It was common knowledge that he acted this way, and no one on the faculty seemed to care.

And therein lies the rub.

Brother Ronald was a similar situation. He was my social studies teacher my sophomore year. Brother Ronald spoke so quietly that he was barely audible. He was always calm, but underneath the calm there was an abusive personality. Brother Ronald would hit us quite a bit - boys and girls, all of us, in his class. He would hit in a way so as to make it seem he was emphasizing a point to us. For example, he would make a fist with one hand, hold a child's shoulder with the other, and pound on the child's shoulder while he was explaining something. In my opinion, it was to make it appear that he was emphasizing a point, while the real intent was to inflict pain. Yes, it was painful. When he would hit me, I could hear the thud, and sometimes I even bruised. He was not a nice man, and I am guessing, is still not a nice man. The teachers who try to mask their behavior, the intention to inflict harm, are the most evil of all. At least Buddha was up front about it. He didn't try to pretend he was doing anything else than what it was – physically abusing students, and scaring the shit out of them.

And so it went at St. Francis Prep. There were some good teachers, and some bad teachers, and teachers who were good but weird, and some who were bad and weird. There were some who were so off the mark that they were scary, and they wanted to hurt us.

My sophomore year was much different than my freshman year. I sort of hit my stride, and my braces came off, and I cut my hair very short in a trendy style. I also cut my hair short because I had realized I was a lesbian and I suddenly felt like one. It suited me. My grades improved dramatically because I learned that 80% of getting good grades is telling the teacher what they want to hear on a test, and not necessarily what you think is the correct answer to any particular question.

I learned the rules, I played the game, and on the whole, life was pretty sweet.

I developed many friendships, and my days were pleasant. I liked my courses, and I liked the majority of my teachers. My grades steadily improved my sophomore and junior years. I was looking forward to being a senior in the Fall of 1986, and I thought lots of wonderful things would happen.

It didn't quite work out as I had hoped.

So let's talk about Tom.

CHAPTER TWO

TOM

The Fall semester of 1986 started off in a big way. It was my senior year, I was turning 17 in October, and I would be able to get my driver's license. What was even more important to me was the fact that the New York Mets were going into the National League playoffs. The Mets had won the World Series the year I was born, and now, as I entered my last year of high school, it was possible again.

Growing up in Woodside, Queens right along the 7 train line made Shea Stadium and the Mets a very important part of my life. I took the 7 train to and from the last stop in Queens – Main Street, Flushing – as part of my St. Francis Prep commute. Every school day, I would pass the Willets Point Station twice. Back then you were lucky if there was air conditioning in the train car during the warmer months. So more often than not, the windows of the train car would be open, and I could hear the roar and cheers and (boos) of the crowd inside the stadium during an afternoon game.

The Mets won the World Series in 1986 late into the evening of October 27th. It was nothing short of a miracle. When I woke up the next morning on my 17th birthday, the headline in the New York Daily News was "YES!"

That's the way I should have felt about my life at that point. Everything should have been a big "Yes!" But that's not how I felt, and the main reason for that was my driver's ed teacher, Tom Nuzzi.

Students were randomly assigned driver's ed teachers at Prep in the same fashion that they were randomly assigned teachers for all subjects. When I had first looked at the driver's ed notice board that September and read that I had been assigned Tom as a teacher, my reaction was "Oh god, he's such an asshole."

My frame of reference for making that statement was gym class my freshman year. My very first semester gym course at St. Francis Prep was Square Dancing. You are probably thinking "What the fuck is that?" And yes, all of us thirteen and fourteen year old kids taking that course were thinking that, too. In fact, in 2007 (when I went back to teach at St. Francis Prep), Square Dancing was still the freshman gym course. (The senior gym courses in 2007 were more athletic; in one course the focus was on the students beating each other with swim noodles.)

In square dancing class, each week Tom would assign us a partner for the do-si-do, etc. However, there was one catch to this partnering system: if you were a small boy, or a less masculine boy, he assigned you another equally small or less masculine boy as a partner. It was clearly a bullying tactic for sport.

Square dancing was very uncomfortable for me. I absolutely hated it and I didn't understand what it had to do with physical fitness. We were all required to hold hands with our partner, link arms, etc. I did not understand why I was being forced into physical contact I did not want to have. It's one thing if it is touch football or something like that, but dancing is intimate. Holding hands is intimate. Why would they require this?

I felt very negatively about the class and I was a relatively confident thirteen year old girl. Imagine being a less confident thirteen year old boy who was forced to hold hands with another boy. It was awful for them, and it was awful for us to watch it. But no one in any position of authority seemed to think this odd or something that should be stopped. In fact, the man who is now the Principal of the school, Patrick McLaughlin, was a gym teacher back then who reported to Tom Nuzzi, who at the time was head of the Physical Education and Health Department. McLaughlin was there in the gym with us many times, saw this atrocity with his own eyes, and did nothing in our presence to protect those boys.

What added to the inherent uncomfortableness and humiliation was the fact that we would have square dancing class during what was known as "senior lunch." At St. Francis Prep, different grades would have lunch at different times, and seniors ate when we were square dancing. The gym was on the way to the cafeteria, so of course they thought it appropriate to yell things like "faggots" into the gym as they walked by. Kids will be kids, and even though it was cruel, I don't blame them. I blame the ridiculously incompetent administration who allowed this to continue year after year.

There were two components to the driver's education course when I took it in 1986. One was classroom instruction, and of course, the other was driving. There were always supposed to be four of us in the driver's ed car when we would go out for driving lessons - Tom, me, and two boys.

It was in the car itself that I had my in-depth introduction to Tom's personality. Tom is not a good looking man. He was tall, fit, but not what one would call handsome. He had a thick, big black mustache which hung over his upper lip, and chubby cheeks. However, he was extremely confident, to the point of blatant arrogance. He viewed women as objects and something to conquer. He would often make us drive by the hospital to see if any pretty nurses were outside so he could get his rocks off. He would often make statements about men being smarter than women. He would also comment about me to the boys in the car while I was sitting there. I remember on one occasion he said aloud "Isn't Elizabeth extraordinary guys? She's not your average girl. She's a very special kind of girl."

I had no idea what he meant exactly by "extraordinary" and "special" and I didn't care. I just knew it was inappropriate and made me feel uncomfortable and very embarrassed. I could tell the boys were embarrassed, too. They didn't answer. One just kind of looked at me funny, and we all just kept driving. We always kept driving, no matter what Tom said.

After a few weeks of driver's ed, things took a turn with Tom. He stopped commenting about me in front of the boys and started doing it in the few minutes we were alone, usually while waiting for the boys to arrive at the car for our driving session. One thing he said repeatedly was that his wife had a brain tumor and he was very lonely, and that she would probably die any day. The first time he said it, I told him I was sorry for her and for him, but the more he repeated it, the less of a reaction I showed. I was 17 but not a fool. I knew he was trying to gain my sympathy, but in my mind I was telling him to go fuck himself.

He also on several occasions followed me with the driver's ed car after our sessions and asked me if I wanted a ride home from school. He said we would have to swing by his house first so he could feed his dogs, and then he would take me home. I had no intention of ever being alone with him in his house so the answer was always a resounding, "No, thank you." What is amusing to me now is that by that time I had realized 100% that I am gay, and so I wish I had told Tom Nuzzi he was barking up the wrong tree. I can't imagine what the look on his face might have been. I wonder if he would have backed off or felt I was now even more of a challenge.

In driver's ed our final grade was based in part on a paper we were to write. My assignment was an accident report for a fictitious accident. I was a progressively better student, and by the time I reached my senior year almost all my grades were A's. I did not take driver's ed any less seriously, and so I wrote what I considered a very good paper and handed it in to Tom two weeks before the deadline.

A week before the course was to end Tom told me to meet him after school in his driver's ed office, which was this little room next to the school bookstore that one would never even notice unless she were directed there. In class that day he had handed back assignments to several students, but my paper wasn't in the pile. I should have known what was coming.

When I got to his office, he asked me to come inside and he closed the door. Then he asked me why I hadn't turned in a paper. I responded "What are you talking about? I gave it to you two weeks ago," to which he replied that he had no recollection of having received it. He did, however, have a proposition for me: either fail the course for not having handed in my paper, or have sex with him. I was so disgusted that I made it abundantly clear it would never happen, and I turned around and exited his office. In another week or so, we received our grades, and I had passed. I guess he had found that paper after all.

I never told my parents any of this. In fact, I never told anyone any of this until 2010, when I told the then Dean of Women, Carolyn Szostek, who at the time was a very good friend of mine. When I was a student, I just didn't see the point in discussing it with anyone. It was obvious to several teachers at the school that Tom was a disgusting pig, and I figured if they couldn't do anything about it, neither could I. I also knew that if I had told my father about what Tom had done, he would have taken a baseball bat and driven to Tom's house, and probably have been arrested. My dad was an alcoholic with a bad temper and little self-control, and this was just the type of news that would send him into a rage. So, I handled it on my own.

Not long after that, Tom was "removed" from St. Francis Prep. It was a miracle. However, it wasn't the result of sexually harassing girls. It was for stealing.

Tom and his two friends in the PE department – Steve Hollis and Paul DeCurtis, who is now an adjunct professor in the Family, Nutrition and Exercise Sciences Department of Queens College, organized and chaperoned student ski trips. What had happened was that one student's parents, Anthony and Joanna Longo, had figured out that the price being paid to these men for the trip and the actual price of the trip had a huge disparity. Nuzzi and his pals were pocketing the difference. In addition, on those trips the men would go from room to room and ask the students for money for various things – twenty dollars for this, twenty-five dollars for that – and those amounts went straight into their pockets. They did this for years until they were finally reported by Mr. and Mrs. Longo in the early months of 1987, in what the student body referred to as "Skigate."

What I now know, and what greatly disturbs me, is that Tom and his friends were given a choice: resign and receive a letter of recommendation, or be terminated. This is the way it has gone for many a teacher who has left St.

Francis Prep. Being terminated is rare, no matter what egregious act you have committed.

Why give teachers who have done horrible things a choice? It is very simple. It is a way of deflecting liability for the school. If they say you were a bad teacher, and you were fired for good reason, it could possibly invite a defamation suit by the teacher. So, they would rather you resign. If you resign, they can say you left on amicable terms.

However, the administrators never considered what the aftermath of years of this policy would be. The truth is, bad people don't stop doing bad things. This was the case with Tom. If you Google him today you will see what I can only describe as the 25 year history of a grifter, ending with a lawsuit filed by Tom and his current wife against the Teachers' Retirement System of the State of Illinois. In its decision, the court basically tells the Nuzzis to take a long walk off a short pier, and to reimburse the Teachers' Retirement System approximately $84,000. Sweet justice.

As I mentioned, I kept my secret about what happened with Tom for over 20 years. When I finally told it, I was a teacher at St. Francis Prep.

What a strange twist of fate.

CHAPTER THREE

A TURN TOWARD TEACHING

started working in corporations at age 17 and I hated it. I hated everything about it. I hated the formal dress code, I hated the rules, and I hated the class system. I hated the idea of bloated, arrogant white men telling everyone what to do, and getting paid more for one day of work than many employees would make in a year.

It was Merrill Lynch in 1987. Investment banking was especially awful. Think of the most emotionally constipated person you know, put them in a nice suit, and that was a Merrill Lynch investment banker.

Thus began my corporate career. I started at Merrill as a library assistant in the Investment Banking or "IBK" library the summer after my senior year of high school. The pay was decent, and the hours were decent, but the atmosphere was gross. It was like working for the gestapo. Any kind of joy was severely discouraged there. It wasn't corporate policy to enjoy your day, I guess. I was in trouble often "for goofing around" which basically meant I had either smiled or cracked a joke or two.

I was a complete polar opposite of what they expected personality wise, but I was right on the money brains wise. I was intelligent and efficient, and I got the job done. That was enough to get me by most days.

There was one Assistant Vice President I absolutely could not stand. She was ugly from the inside out, with a horrible bob haircut and a little, cartoonish turned up nose that was the blatant product of a botched nose job. She had nothing better to do than to torture me with nasty comments. Once I wore pants on a Friday because I was going to the South Street Seaport after work, and she complained to the Vice President that I was not dressed appropriately. She just didn't like me for whatever reason, and that's her karma to carry. One would think that in the business world we would be a big sisterhood all trying to help each other get ahead since we make about seventy-seven cents on the male dollar to this day. Nothing could be further from the truth though. Women eat each other alive in the business world, and it's awful. They are catty, and mean, and try to tear each other down. They spread rumors and lies, and do whatever they can to sabotage each other. They would rather the man in the next cubicle get a promotion than their sister. I still can't figure out why.

I worked at Merrill Lynch every summer through college, and almost every winter break, which was usually a month long. I made eleven dollars an hour back then, which is still a lot for many people. (That's what Trader Joe's, ranked one of the best 25 companies to work for in America by Forbes and Businessweek, pays for an entry level position in 2015. Isn't that unbelievable?) I needed to make as much money as possible for school and extras, and at least Merrill Lynch was good for that.

In 1991 I graduated summa cum laude from what was then the Fordham University College of Business Administration, now called the Gabelli School of Business. Fordham business students didn't really have "majors." We all majored in business administration with a "concentration" in something. My concentration was marketing. I actually graduated with the highest GPA in my concentration, a 4.0. I had done a lot of good work there.

Despite my excellent grades, it was hard for me to find a job. 1991 was right in the middle of a recession and all the best jobs went to graduates who had concentrated in accounting. The best job offer I received was to enter the management program at The Gap. Retail wasn't really my thing. I didn't want to have to work on holidays and all sorts of crazy hours. I graciously declined the opportunity hoping something better would come along.

While I was looking for work, a good friend of mine was scheduled to take the LSAT (the law school entrance exam) and she was very nervous about it. She asked me if I would take the exam with her. I registered and paid the fee, and took the test. To my surprise, I did very well without having studied at all. In fact, I had never done so well on a standardized test before, and it got me to thinking. Perhaps I should apply to law school?

My prospects of finding a good job continued to decline as time went on. I took this as a sign from God and I began applying to law schools. What I found most amusing was that despite my 3.98 undergraduate GPA, Fordham Law School had wait-listed me. When I inquired as to why, I was told that the law school was taking a more "national approach" and so New York residents were less likely to be accepted than out-of-state applicants. Gee, Fordham, thanks for taking my $44,000 in tuition and shitting on me. From that point on I threw away every Fordham alumni association donation request that came in the mail.

St. John's University School of Law accepted me right away. I enrolled, studied hard, did well, and found myself working as an associate in the legal department of a major pharmaceutical company my second year of law school. The pay for that position was outrageous. I was making more money than my father. The work was also very interesting, and I actually wrote part of a patent for an artificial ligament. Cool stuff.

On the negative side, the attorney I worked with the most was a skirt chaser. He would chase me around the desk, literally, wanting sexual favors. He had said many horrible things to me, like that I was attending a second rate law school and probably wouldn't find a job afterward. He also told me I needed to go to a conference in London with him, and that we would need to share a hotel room. That's where I drew the line. Maybe a bit late, but I drew it.

I decided to wire myself. I bought a tiny tape recorder that had a microphone on a cord. I tucked the recorder in my waist band, and ran the cord up my shirt and down my sleeve so that the microphone was right by my wrist. Within a few days, I had a tape full of that attorney saying disgusting things to me. So, I marched into the General Counsel's office and I told him what had happened, and that I had taped it. I put the recorder down on the general counsel's desk, but I did not hit play.

What came then surprised me. The General Counsel didn't ask me to hit play. He simply said that he would look into the matter and that I could go home for the day. I was at least expecting him to say something like "You must be joking!" or "That would never happen with Attorney X!" But, he didn't say another word.

On my way to the elevator, I stopped in the ladies room to regroup before I went to my desk to retrieve my handbag so I could leave for the day. On my way out of the ladies room, I saw Attorney X marching down the hall right to the General Counsel's office. I wish I could have been a fly on the wall.

I went back to work for one more week after that, and then I quit. I could tell word was spreading about my situation and it wasn't worth it to me to keep getting strange looks from people and to feel embarrassed when I walked into a room and people suddenly stopped talking.

I guess I must have been home from work about two weeks thinking about what employment complaint to file about Attorney X and with what agency, when I received a phone call from the woman who was the librarian in the corporate library of the pharmaceutical firm. Because of my library work at Merrill Lynch, we had worked closely on a project to find out what improvements the attorneys wanted to see in the library. As soon as she began speaking, I knew that whatever she was going to say, it was good for me. It turned out that Attorney X had done this sort of thing before, and the last female attorney he sexually harassed had sued the pants off the company. They settled with her, and I was told it was enough so that she could retire. That's a lot of money.

So I got myself an attorney, and the pharmaceutical company settled with me for a nice, healthy amount. And my promise to God for helping me was, if ever there was a woman who needed help like I had needed it, I would pay the kindness I had received from my coworker forward.

After law school I eventually wound up at Dean Witter, as a Senior Trust Officer in the new trust company they had just launched. The trust company was in Jersey City, and it was almost a two hour commute each way for me. Dean Witter had actively recruited me from my previous job, and I was glad to come on board on the ground floor of something that I was promised would be big, despite the long days. The immediate team consisted of six trust officers (most of whom were attorneys), a supervisor, and a department head. It was here that I met Barry.

Barry was the supervisor for the department. Barry's management style was such: If I asked him a question about the customer relationship management system, his answer to me was "Figure it out." Sometimes, there is no figuring it out. A math problem, yes, I could figure it out. But the intricacies of a convoluted CRM, no, I needed to be trained and someone needed to show me – once, only once, but once nonetheless.

I was at the company about two years when Barry went on paternity leave. In his absence, I substituted for him and I noticed a lot of customer files under his desk that I did not recognize. There were many names, and no record of them in the CRM. Something was wrong. I reported it to management, and I did not hear about it after that. But, I had reported it, and I felt good about having taken some action in what appeared to be a shady situation. In 2010, twelve years later, I Googled Barry. Barry had gone on to become President of Guardian Trust Company, FSB, which was very impressive. He had also been slapped with a Cease and Desist Order and twenty-five thousand dollar fine by the Office of Thrift Supervision, and sued by his own company for "opening several unrecorded accounts" that did not go through any of Guardian Trust's "standard procedures…including procedures for compliance with the Bank Secrecy Act and regulations of the Office of Foreign Asset Control." The official court complaint states that Guardian Trust had no idea these accounts existed until they showed up on the Bernie Madoff investor list, with Guardian Trust as Trustee. Barry was cold busted.

Back in 1998 when I discovered those files under Barry's desk, I was also thinking seriously about opening up my own practice. I was in a serious relationship, and I was just about to turn thirty. My thoughts were focused on working from home and eventually having a baby.

I decided it was a good time to resign. There's never a great time to make a big move, so when your heart tells you to do it, sometimes you just have to take the plunge.

Well, the years went by, my relationship ended, and at age 36 I found myself with a small, successful trusts and estates law practice in Westchester NY, single, and 8 months pregnant. I had always wanted to become a mother, and I had talked about it often with my mother from when I was a little girl. I just never imagined I would be single when the baby came.

My partner was five years older than me, and she had tried for a few years to get pregnant. The plan was, she would give birth to Baby One, and I would give birth to Baby Two. Despite the fact she was taking fertility drugs, she just could not get pregnant. Sometimes we blamed it on the sperm samples. Sometimes we blamed it on bad timing. Sometimes we blamed it on her stressful job. And other times, we blamed fate.

A year before my son was born, my partner and I had decided I wasn't getting any younger, and I should try to get pregnant. It was easy for me. I had gotten pregnant on my third try with artificial insemination. The moment I found out I was pregnant I was in the middle of a real estate closing, and I couldn't stop crying. It was one of the best days of my life.

Over the next few months, God told me some things. I knew I would have a boy, that he would be huge, and that one thing would be wrong with him. I worried a lot about this last bit of information, even though my amniocentesis had come back normal.

My partner was working in London a lot, so the only emotional support I had locally were my parents. My ex's parents didn't like me, and I didn't like them. They were small, judgmental, and republican, and that didn't mix very well with my liberal tendencies and outspoken personality. They are people who go to church each Sunday, declare their devotion to God, but then come home and insult and belittle their own family at Sunday dinner.

When I was seven months pregnant, my ex came home from London to tell me she didn't love me anymore. I was surprised but not shocked. The more pregnant I got, the more distant she seemed. Was it jealousy because I did what she could not? So I moved out of our home (at her request), taking everything from my son's room with me bit by bit. When I made a trip to retrieve his crib, the locks had been changed. God showed me who my ex really is just in the nick of time, and I am incredibly grateful my boy will never know her.

Sometimes, the worst things that could happen are actually the best things in disguise.

I closed my practice in Westchester and moved back to a multi-family house I had bought with my parents in Queens several years earlier. There was a tenant in my old apartment, so I set myself up in the studio apartment there. It was small, but it was all mine, and I would make it a home for my son in the eleventh hour.

My beautiful little Andrew was born on December 15th, 2005. He was due on Christmas Eve, but he came a bit early. He was big – almost ten pounds. And God was right, there was one thing wrong. His little feet were contorted inward, which I soon learned was a severe case of bilateral clubbed feet.

At two weeks of age, Andrew's legs were put into casts. The casts pointed his feet outward, like a duck's but more extreme. The idea behind this was to stretch the feet out in the opposite direction, as part of an overall treatment to eventually bring his feet back to a neutral position. At twelve weeks of age he had a surgical procedure whereby his doctor cut his achilles tendons to completely release his feet from the pull inward. All this was done with just a topical anesthetic, and my parents and I could hear Andrew screaming from outside the operating room. It was not an easy time.

From that point on, Andrew was in a brace almost twenty-four hours a day. The brace consisted of a metal bar with shoes at the ends, again pointing his feet outward so eventually they would move back to neutral. The brace was awful. If Andrew flipped over on his stomach, he could not flip back. I was up almost all night every night with my baby, because he would flip on his stomach over and over again, with his face buried in his mattress.

By the time Andrew was a little over a year old, his time in the brace had been reduced to about eighteen hours a day. He was learning to walk, and he had started saying a few words. I was very thankful.

It was at this time I reevaluated my life from the ground up. I needed to go back to work, but I wanted to be with my son as much as possible. Ample time off was key for me. I had a house and a nice nest egg. I was not extravagant in my lifestyle. I needed a decent salary, not a huge one. I was focused on needs, and not on wants, and that was good. The needs kept me grounded in my priorities. Wants are the things that can really mess up a person's life.

I decided perhaps teaching was an option, so I could have summers off with my son. Now this you will find odd: For twenty years, about 5 or 6 times a year, I would have a dream that I was teaching at St. Francis Prep. The dream was always vivid, and in it, the halls were very crowded (the way they always were) and I was rushing to get to my classroom. The dream always ended with me just making it to the classroom door as the bell rang.

I took these dreams as another sign from God. For some reason, maybe I was meant to work there. Maybe Tom was a blip in the timeline of the school, and it would be foolish of me to hold that man's actions against them all these years later. Times change, situations change, people and places evolve and grow. Perhaps with Tom gone, that building had become a healthier place. I sent a resume and a cover letter to Br. Mark Waldman, who was the head of the Business and Computers Department, expressing my interest in becoming a business teacher, teaching the very courses I had taken in high school which set me on course for a law degree and a corporate career. Then I waited.

A few months went by and then in the early Spring of 2007 the phone call came. The woman who taught accounting when I was a student in 1987 was retiring. A spot was open for me to teach Accounting, Business Law, and Business Communications, which were all electives for juniors and seniors.

I was very happy about this. I felt it was a new beginning, and my ducks were lining up in a nice little row, and I would have time for my baby, which meant more to me than anything.

Then my maternal grandmother died in April. Then in June, my father had a massive heart attack at Trump Plaza in Atlantic City and died instantaneously. Then my mother had a nervous breakdown, and then I had less than two months to try and stabilize my home life before I started working at Prep. This period turned out to be just about the most stressful time of my entire life.

In July, it became apparent to me that I had no one to watch my son when I went back to work. My parents were supposed to do it. Now my dad was gone, and my mom was completely traumatized. I had no plan as to what to do except to keep talking to her, telling her she had to pull herself together, and that Andrew and I needed her to do it if we were all going to survive. As I am an only child, her recovery was my responsibility. She recovered a little – very little, very slowly, and I think this mantra helped her in that it gave her a sense of purpose moving forward.

In late August, I had my new teacher orientation at the school, and there were no surprises. We went over benefits, hours, some basic rules about dress code, and it was all fine and normal. Brother Mark filled me in about the department, and his plans for the future to add some new courses, and we seemed to be aligned with goals and a good fit. I liked him very much.

The official school year began. The Friday after Labor Day is always the first day of class at St. Francis Prep. I was really excited. Despite the obvious pressures at home, I had come up with what I thought were really good lesson plans, and I was enthusiastic about imparting twenty years of business experience to the group of students I would be teaching. On my first day, I rolled up to the school, parked in the faculty lot, and made my way up to the Business Department on the west side of the second floor of the building.

A religion teacher stopped me there, at the very top of the stairs. She told me something I would never ever forget.

CHAPTER FOUR

FUNDAMENTALLY PHONY SYSTEM

The teacher who stopped me in the hall that day was Sue Vivona. At that time, I didn't even know her name. I just knew she was a religion teacher. She pulled me aside, and asked me, "You're a lawyer, right?" I told her yes, and then she said the following to me: "There was a teacher here last year who had sex with a little Vietnamese freshman girl." I was stunned, and it was a lot to process on my first day teaching, twenty minutes before I was scheduled to teach my very first high school class, ever. I asked her "Well, is he gone?" and she had said yes, and explained to me that he was terminated after the girl had given graphic detail of what had happened. It was at this moment that it occurred to me – maybe things hadn't changed in twenty years? I thanked Sue for telling me, and I walked to the Business Department to settle in before class.

I made a critical mistake that day. I assumed that if a teacher had, in fact, had an inappropriate relationship with a freshman, that the police had been called. However, I found out years later, that wasn't the case. No one had called the police. Not the girl, not her parents, and not a single person from the school who was aware of this situation. Teachers are legally mandated to report any type of suspected student abuse to the authorities in NY under Chapter 193 of the Laws of 2007. Yet, not one teacher or administrator reported the incident. Not one.

That teacher Sue told me about walked out the door, and he is still out there. He and I occasionally butt heads, which is a good thing, because he knows I am watching. He is on my radar, and he knows he will never be off.

My first year teaching at Prep was eye opening, to say the least. Within my first few months Brother Mark had given me an earful of background about the main players at the school. I really enjoyed Brother Mark. He was funny, irreverent, and a true character. He had a desk drawer full of Yankee Candles, and another full of yarn and crochet needles. He loved to dish, and we had many a gab session to the calming scent of gardenia. Here's a short list of what he conveyed to me as a newbie teacher:

1. The Financial Controller of the school, Joseph DiSomma, aka Joe Diamonds, was convicted of conspiracy to commit robbery and served time in prison;
2. The then Assistant Principal of Faculty and Instruction, Patrick McLaughlin, had gotten divorced from his first wife because she decided she's a lesbian and left him for another woman. He also had an affair with the current head of the guidance department, Robyn Armon.
3. The head of the guidance department, Robyn Armon, had started in an entry level position as an Experience Group Leader (Experience Group is a weekly session for students to sit in a circle and discuss their feelings about various topics. It is part of the religion curriculum at the school.) However, a year later she was promoted to Chairperson of the Guidance Department, surpassing others who had worked in the department for decades.
4. The grading system is fake.
5. The whole teacher evaluation system is fake.
6. I was surrounded by numerous assholes and he would protect me.

I am not a big gossip, but if I am presented with information I do listen. I listen very carefully, and then try to form my own opinion based upon what I observe with my own eyes.

I saw a lot in the years that followed. You can Google DiSomma and pull up his court cases. It turns out he was part of a jewelry theft ring that stole over $1.2 million in jewels on an East Coast spree. Here's what my investigation (conducted years later with the help of reporter Sarah Armaghan) turned up:

Joseph Disomma, DOB 1/28/1966, was sentenced to 57 months in prison for conspiracy to commit robbery.
He was convicted on May 11, 1992 in the Southern NY District under Judge Cedarbaum.
His sentence started on Oct. 19, 1993.

He was released on Sept. 19, 1997.
He was at the following facilities in chronological order:
Danbury, CT (minimum security)
Loretto, PA (low security - an UPGRADED security level from min.)
Fort Dix, NJ (low security)
Then to a half-way house under NY Correction supervision.

He had 223 days shaved off his sentence for good behavior, and 79 days credited for time served during the trial.

U.S. v. FRIEDMAN - Argued November 30, 1992.
998 F.2d 53 (1993)
UNITED STATES of America, Appellee-Cross-Appellant, v.
Felix FRIEDMAN, Lawrence Tinnirello, Paul Tinnirello, Lorenzo Gregory, a/k/a "Fat Larry," Frank Mucchiello, a/k/a "Frankie Mooch," Joseph DiSomma, a/k/a "Joe Diamonds," Francis Tinnirello, Michael Pugliese, and Charles Lachterman, a/k/a "Charlie Lucky," Defendants,

Charles Lachterman, Defendant-Appellant, and Joseph DiSomma, Defendant-Appellant-Cross-Appellee. Nos. 617, 446, 467, Dockets 92-1373, 92-1274, 92-1306. United States Court of Appeals, Second Circuit. Argued November 30, 1992. Decided June 10, 1993.

James B. Comey, Asst. U.S. Atty., New York City (Otto G. Obermaier, U.S. Atty. for the S.D.N.Y., Andrew C. McCarthy, Asst. U.S. Atty., New York City, of counsel), for appellee-cross-appellant.

Linda Imes, Richards Spears Kibbe & Orbe, New York City (Michele R.M. Campbell, Debevoise & Plimpton, New York City, of counsel), for defendant-appellant Charles Lachterman.

Joann Harris, New York City, for defendant-appellant-cross-appellee Joseph DiSomma.

Before: OAKES and WINTER, Circuit Judges, and CONBOY,* District Judge.

WINTER, Circuit Judge:
This appeal by Charles Lachterman and Joseph DiSomma involves questions regarding the applicability of U.S.S.G. § 2X1.1 to Hobbs Act convictions, a sentencing court's degree of discretion in applying an obstruction of justice enhancement when the jury has necessarily concluded that the defendant lied at trial, and the proof sufficient

to establish that predicate acts are related to a criminal RICO enterprise.
[998 F.2d 55]
We affirm in part, vacate in part, and remand for resentencing.
DISCUSSION

These appeals arise from convictions following a government investigation into the criminal activities of the "Friedman/Tinnirello Organization." Viewing the evidence in the light most favorable to the government, the following facts were established at trial. Since 1983, the Friedman/Tinnirello group, operating from a variety of retail stores and jewelry booths in Manhattan's 47th Street jewelry district, fenced hundreds of thousands of dollars worth of stolen personal property and jewelry. Members of the group also maintained a steady supply of jewelry through a wide variety of robberies, burglaries, and fraudulent schemes. The nucleus of the group consisted of three brothers, Lawrence, Paul, and Francis Tinnirello, as well as Felix Friedman, Joseph DiSomma, and Lorenzo Gregory. This opinion concerns only the activities of Joseph DiSomma (Tinnirello's cousin) and Charles Lachterman, see Note 1 supra, who were convicted for their roles in the organization.

A. Joseph DiSomma

In the fall of 1989, Lawrence Tinnirello, Lawrence Taylor, and Richard Skowronski conspired to rob the Telco Jewelry store where Skowronski worked. United States v. Skowronski, 968 F.2d 242 (2d Cir.1992). The government alleges that Joseph DiSomma, Skowronski's closest friend, was part of this conspiracy and was instrumental in its planning. The store carried between $200,000 and $300,000 in inventory and was equipped with a safe and a metal roll-down gate which covered the storefront at closing. Between Thanksgiving and Christmas, the period of the conspiracy, the store also employed security guards during the evening hours of business. The plan called for the robbers to enter the Telco store after the exterior window gates had been closed for the day and "clean ... the whole ... place out."

Government wire-taps revealed that on November 18, Tinnirello and Taylor discussed the proposed robbery. Tinnirello indicated that he would "check ... out" the Telco store, pretending to be an ordinary customer, and that they would "move" if the store contained at least $200,000 in jewelry. Two days later, Tinnirello left a message on DiSomma's answering machine saying that he wanted "to meet Richie [Skowronski] this week and take a look at that thing." DiSomma returned the call, saying that he had spoken with Skowronski about the plan. The two agreed that they should meet with Skowronski after Thanksgiving. On November 27, Tinnirello informed DiSomma that he and Taylor would check out the Telco store the following day, but would warn Skowronski of their planned visit. DiSomma added that Skowronski should not greet them, thereby revealing that he knew them, but should just "be cool" when they arrived at the store.

On Thanksgiving morning, Tinnirello recruited Charles Lachterman, a professional thief, for the robbery, saying:

I got an inside guy that works somewhere. The same thing that me and you are into.... Its just him and two girls, and he wants to take the whole ... place.... I already, right, have two guys.... Now my friend works in there. You understand? So it's a setup. Ya put the ... gate down, ya take the showcases, the ... vault, and leave.

On December 13, attempting to prevent the robbery, FBI agents visited Skowronski, accused him of planning to rob the Telco store, and implied that one of his associates had informed on him. Skowronski asserted his innocence, denied knowledge of any wrongdoing, and the agents left. Skowronski drove to a phone booth, made three phone calls, and returned home. Shortly thereafter, DiSomma arrived at Skowronski's residence. The two drove to a pay phone booth and called Tinnirello. DiSomma told Tinnirello that "[w]e got trouble" and urged him to "go out to a pay phone and call me back." Tinnirello protested that he had no car available and asked what was wrong. DiSomma answered that there was trouble for them and Skowronski, but told Tinnirello to keep quiet. When Tinnirello insisted his phone was not tapped and pressed DiSomma for details, DiSomma refused to disclose more, saying only that the situation was serious [998 F.2d 56] and that Tinnirello must get to a pay phone. Later that day, DiSomma and Tinnirello spoke of the FBI's visit to Skowronski and the possibility that Skowronski would cooperate with the government. DiSomma argued that Skowronski would not cooperate because he is a "stand-up kid." DiSomma later advised Tinnirello that he had taken care of Skowronski's nervousness. Two days later, DiSomma told Tinnirello in a coded conversation that Skowronski's co-worker at the Telco Jewelry store had been contacted by the FBI but that "everything is good." *Tinnirello conveyed that DiSomma should dispose of his firearm,* and DiSomma replied that both he and Skowronski already had.

DiSomma was later arrested and charged with RICO conspiracy and substantive offenses, a Hobbs Act violation, and mail fraud. A jury convicted him only on the Hobbs Act charge. He attacks this conviction as unsupported by the evidence, violative of his due process rights, and improper because the lower court should have dismissed the charge for lack of venue. He also challenges the sentencing court's three-point addition for possession of a firearm in connection with the robbery conspiracy. We affirm.

The government cross-appeals DiSomma's sentence, arguing that the district court improperly applied U.S.S.G. § 2X1.1 and improperly considered the obstruction of justice enhancement as discretionary. We agree and remand for resentencing.

DiSomma argues that the evidence does not support his conviction under the Hobbs Act. First, he claims that there is insufficient evidence of any conspiracy at all. The wiretaps, in his view, record only Tinnirello's rambling, incoherent monologues and not a conspiracy joined by others. He next argues that, even if Tinnirello and others were planning a robbery, there is insufficient evidence that he was involved. DiSomma characterizes his phone calls to Tinnirello as part of his effort to help his cousin through a difficult time. As for the references to "the thing" involving Telco Jewelry, DiSomma claims that it is just as likely that he was simply directing Tinnirello and Taylor to Telco in order to facilitate a legitimate jewelry purchase. He claims Taylor was looking for a diamond engagement ring and that he referred him to Skowronski for the purchase. He also argues that his incriminating phone calls to Tinnirello following the FBI visit may be equally well understood as reflecting his concern over unrelated schemes.

DiSomma mistakes our task on appeal. DiSomma's testimony was submitted to the jury who weighed it and found it wanting. It is not for us to weigh, as DiSomma would have us, "competing inferences and explanations" about which explanation is more likely. United States v.

Stanley,928 F.2d 575, 577 (2d Cir.), cert. denied, ___ U.S. ___, 112 S.Ct. 141, 116 L.Ed.2d 108 (1991). We cannot reverse a conviction merely because the defendant's exculpatory account is plausible. Rather, we must affirm so long as, drawing all inferences in the government's favor, a reasonable jury might fairly have found DiSomma guilty beyond a reasonable doubt. See United States v. Buck,804 F.2d 239, 242 (2d Cir.1986). The evidence here was sufficient.

First, we have already rejected Skowronski's challenge as to the sufficiency of the evidence as to the Telco conspiracy. Skowronski,

968 F.2d at 247-48. We therefore obviously reject DiSomma's first contention that the evidence will not support the finding of conspiracy; at the very least, Skowronski and Tinnirello could be found to have actively conspired to rob the store.

Second, DiSomma's challenge to the evidence of his involvement is similarly unsuccessful. After establishing the existence of the Telco scheme, the government presented evidence that DiSomma: set up a meeting with Skowronski and Tinnirello to talk about the plan, warned Tinnirello not to visit the store without first warning Skowronski, and made incriminating phone calls to Tinnirello upon learning of the FBI's visit to Skowronski. This evidence was more than sufficient to allow the jury to conclude that DiSomma was one of the "two [other] guys" with whom Tinnirello and Skowronski were conspiring to rob the store...

In addition to this affirmative evidence of guilt, the jury was entitled to draw negative inferences from DiSomma's testimony at trial.

United States v. Eisen, 974 F.2d 246, 259 (2d Cir.1992), cert. denied, --- U.S. ----, 113 S.Ct. 1840, 123 L.Ed.2d 467 (1993).
"By taking the stand and offering his own version of events, [DiSomma] ' "waive[s] any claim as to the sufficiency of the Government's case considered alone. " ' " United States v. Roldan-Zapata, 916 F.2d 795, 803 (2d Cir.1990), cert. denied , --- U.S. ----, 111 S.Ct. 1397, 113 L.Ed.2d 453 (1991) (quoting United States v. Tyler, 758 F.2d 66, 69 (2d Cir.1985)) (citations omitted). DiSomma's testimony was, as Judge Cedarbaum found, "entirely incredible." In light of the government's evidence, the jury was entitled to conclude that DiSomma's version of the events was false and thereby infer his guilt.
United States v. Marchand, 564 F.2d 983, 985-86 (2d Cir.1977), cert. denied, 434 U.S. 1015, 98 S.Ct. 732, 54 L.Ed.2d 760 (1978). In short, there is substantial evidence that DiSomma was part of a conspiracy to rob the Telco Jewelry store...

I would like to point out that in the above decision the sentencing court added three points to DiSomma's conviction for possession of a firearm. This man is around children every day at St. Francis Prep, and handling millions of dollars in tuition money and donations. Does this make any sense to you?

As for McLaughlin, yes, his former wife had left him for another woman. McLaughlin's first wife married her new love once gay marriage became legal in New York State. I think this is absolutely poetic, because the circumstances of McLaughlin's divorce injected an interesting twist in what was to be a colossal wrongful termination lawsuit to hit the school in 2012.

As for the history between Robyn Armon and McLaughlin, several teachers and staff members confirmed what Brother Mark had told me. Years later, I would meet a young lady who had very in-depth knowledge about all this, and who would give me additional insight into how the affair between McLaughlin and Armon unfolded, and how Armon's promotion had demoralized so many.

For now, let's discuss Brother Mark's points four and five, which really, truly represent the foundation of all the problems at the school. In my mind, all problems manifest at St. Francis Prep because of the precedent established by these core policies.

St. Francis Prep's grading system is rigged to inflate student grades. This is a fact. They kept this secret hidden from the public for decades, until I exposed it in a blog I wrote on New Year's Eve, 2012. Basically, St. Francis Prep tells you in its public literature that the minimum grade for passing a course is 75. They like to tell everyone that because it makes them seem like their standards are higher than other schools, where the minimum grade for passing is 70, or sometimes even as low as 65. But in actuality, the effective passing grade at St. Francis Prep is lower than 75; it is 71.

I repeat, you will not find any of this information in any publication given to students or parents. And that's a shame, because for $9,000 a year in tuition, they deserve better. This information is distributed to faculty only, like in the email below, which can be found as an update in that 2012 New Year's Eve blog:

....

Sunday, June 16, 2013 9:42 AM

TO: All Faculty Members
FROM: Br. Lawrence Boyle

RE: FAILURE VERIFICATION SHEET

Failure Verification Sheets were placed in your mailboxes on Sunday Morning. They reflect all grades entered into **Grade-Book** by Saturday Night at 8:30. Any grades placed after that time would affect what is on your list.

The grades reflect Final Marks submitted for all Courses that are completed.

If you had no failures then there is no sheet for you.

Teachers whose grades are not due until the Regents is over should ignore the mark shown as they are incomplete. But check the marks for any courses now completed. Return them with failing grades after you graded your Regents.

Ignore the ID number it is an internal computer program number.

Please check the marks to see if there are any errors. If you have some please provide the new grade on the sheet and see Mr. McLaughlin about filling out the Correction Form. It is important that you do this so we have a record showing changes to prevent confusion about wrong grades being recorded and that the Failure Notice is correct.

No student is to fail a course with a grade of 71% - 74%.

Please sign the list with changes or no changes and return it to my mailbox in the General Office ASAP.

Senior notices were sent out two weeks ago and there are several updated notices going out today as courses either ended or we are waiting on a completed Regents.

It is my hope to see the Freshmen Notices sent out on Tuesday Morning so it is imperative for every one who is finished with grades to return the sheet today.

Sophomore and Junior Notices will go out as soon as the Regents Grades and Final Grades are entered.

I urge all teachers to complete their grades as soon as possible with out making any errors.

....

In addition to the above grade curve, the minimum grade any student can receive for the fourth quarter at St. Francis Prep is 55. That means, even if little Sally or Johnny really earned, through their own effort (or lack thereof) a 40 in Chemistry, they will still get a 55 on their report card. In addition, final exam grade failures "below 55 must be recorded as 55."

Here is an actual excerpt from the 2012 faculty handbook which states this:

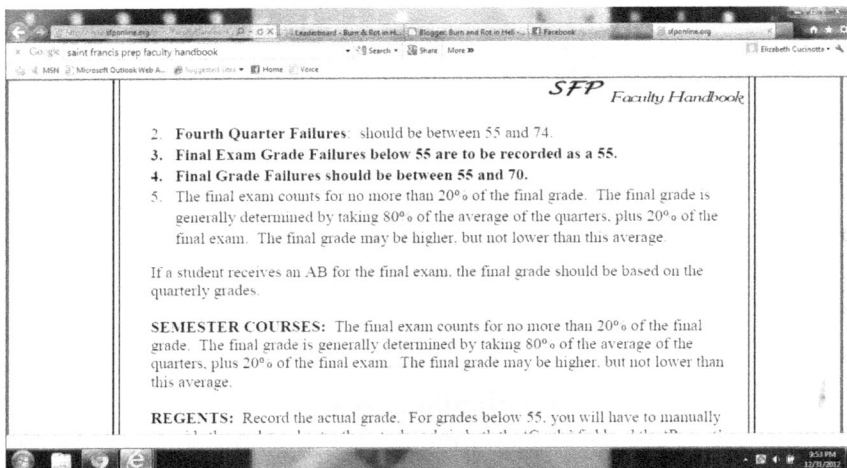

What is amusing to me is that in the above excerpt it states for Regents Exams, teachers are to "record the actual grade." Isn't that a novel idea?

So how does this play out? Let's say that at the end of the school year, after all the quarters are averaged with her final exam, Sally's final grade is 73, which should be failing because passing is stated to be 75 in the school calendar. However, a teacher is prohibited from giving a final grade for a course in the range of 71-74. If the teacher fails Sally with a 70, her mom or dad comes in and says, "But her average is 73, so why did you give her a 70?" What would you say as a teacher? How would you explain giving a grade lower than the actual average? You would never actually lower a kid's real average purposely, right? To do so would mean you are an obvious liar and horrible person. So you bump the 73 up to 75 so that Sally passes the course. No parents would complain about you adding a couple of points through the goodness of your heart. Even if a teacher insisted on giving the lower failing grade, it is prohibited. If a student's real grade for a course is 71, they are REQUIRED to be bumped up to a passing grade of 75. Look above where it says "the final grade may be higher, but not lower than this average."

The required minimum grade of 55 for the 4th quarter also bolstered the averages, as I had mentioned earlier. Some teachers were pissed about this, having to give a phony minimum grade of 55 instead of the lower, real grade. So what they would do is give 55 on the report card, but then for the year end average, use the real quarterly grade that was lower than 55 instead of the falsely inflated one. This, however, was not really "supported" by the powers that be. They wanted to keep the averages as high as possible so it could look like students at Prep earned better grades than they actually did.

At the end of every school year, I and many other teachers had ethical concerns with the 71-74 thing. The faculty would frequently talk about that situation - why not just make passing 70, like at most other schools, and give kids their real grade?

The implications were clear – we were indirectly teaching children to cheat. The children were aware of what their real averages were. They knew when they were bumped up to a higher grade for no reason. A few, I have learned, even were aware of the actual inflated grading policy. Is this what we want to teach them so the school can maintain some sort of elite status in the eyes of the community?

And what about all the student college applications that reflected these phony grades? If Applicant X sent his real average of 87 to College Y, and St. Francis Prep Grad sent his fake grade of 87 to College Y, how is that fair to Applicant X?

What is just as egregious as the phony grading system is the teacher evaluation system. It is very simple, yet very flawed.

Year one, you are evaluated by the Assistant Principal of Faculty and Instruction, who, my first year teaching, was Patrick McLaughlin (who is now Principal). The second year, you are evaluated by the Assistant Principal of Curriculum, who is Joseph Castellano, and the third year you are evaluated by the Principal, who back when I was teaching, was Brother Leonard Conway (who is now President).

You are evaluated via classroom observation. However, these are not spontaneous classroom observations, like many schools have. The observations at St. Francis Prep are scheduled. In other words, you are given a note in your teacher mailbox, stating that you are due to be observed by one of these three administrators. The note goes on to say that if you would like them to observe a particular lesson, to please let the respective administrator know the date and time of the lesson you would like him to attend.

Do you see the inherent flaw?

Spontaneous observations allow an administrator to observe a teacher in true form. Planned observations do not. In fact, planned observations help conceal the type of teacher one really is, and allow child predators to go undetected.

Logically, if I know you, as Assistant Principal, are coming to my classroom on Wednesday at 10:30, I am fully prepared to have an awesome lesson ready and to be on best behavior. But do I act that way every day? This is the perfect opportunity for me to fake who I really am.

It is my opinion that this is the actual point of St. Francis Prep's observation evaluation system. These men in charge are not stupid. Everything they do is designed to protect the school. They are very aware that you will be on best behavior when they come to observe your class. Then they sit there for a while, take notes about how great your lesson was, and write up a report saying you're wonderful.

Then, should anything ever happen the rest of the year, like for example, you molest a child, they can say, "Well, we had no knowledge of any inappropriate tendencies by teacher Jones. His classroom observation was very good." In other words, the observation is a way to deflect liability. It is St. Francis Prep's way of showing they did their due diligence. It is a way to purposely turn a blind eye to the reality of who is working there, so that later on, they can say they had no reason to question a specific teacher's behavior.

It took me a while to get this and really understand the insidiousness of what happens in that building. I would imagine it is almost like being a Scientologist. They pound into you that they are above it all, and that they are right, and that they are accountable to no one, and you almost start to believe it.

I remember several occasions when I came home from work upset and told my mother that I felt like I was working for the Catholic mafia. It was an "if you protect us, we protect you" atmosphere. I could clearly see it was easy to get away with many bad things just because of the flawed teacher observation system, and it upset me greatly.

After a few years of going on like this, I couldn't take it anymore. I knew there was no way I would put in twenty years at that place so I could collect a pension from the Brooklyn Diocese. I started to slowly consider other options.

This is where it gets really interesting.

CHAPTER FIVE

CAROL

I met the woman who was to become my future wife right around my son, Andrew's, second birthday. We met through Match.com, started dated, fell in love, and the rest is history.

Everyone who knows Jo will tell you that she is an extremely good, caring, and honest person, tolerant and generous as well.

Given that, let me say one thing: she hated Carol from Day One. That should have been a clue for me.

Carol refers to Carolyn Szostek, the former Dean of Women and Assistant Vice Principal of St. Francis Prep, whom I became friends with during my second year teaching at the school. Carol was my sophomore year Spanish II teacher in 1984-1985, and she had always been very nice to me. The winter of 1984 had been an especially harsh one, and many times Carol had offered to give me a ride to Woodside, where we both were headed after school. I lived there, and Carol's husband operated his law practice out of a building on Roosevelt Avenue that her family owned.

I never accepted Carol's offers. I'm not sure why. It would have been a lot easier to get home in thirty minutes in a nice, warm car rather than take a bus from first to last stop and a train from first to last stop in inclement weather. It made me uncomfortable on some level, and at age fifteen I already knew that if something made me uncomfortable inside, I shouldn't do it.

In any event, when I began teaching at St. Francis Prep, I naturally gravitated toward her, as the familiar. She was outwardly still the same pleasant person, and she had a good sense of humor.

In 2009, Carol's husband, Fred, was suddenly diagnosed with cancer and given only three months to live. I felt so bad for her that when she discussed it with me, I cried right in front of her. I had just gone through this with my own mother two years earlier.

Fred died during the summer break in 2009, right when the doctors said he would. I went to the wake, and it was just so sad. Wakes are always awful for me, no matter whether I am related to the deceased or not. I have a hard time with the whole idea of them. When I go someday, I don't want a wake. I don't want anyone, especially my son, staring at my dead body in a box. Take my body, cremate it right away, and spread my ashes over whatever is the most meaningful spot in my life at that point. Release the shell that held my spirit into the air, and smile, knowing I moved on to a better place.

It was from that point on that Carol and I became very good friends. She relied on me more and more, and I didn't mind. Her daughter, who is an only child, wasn't around much, and so I think I filled the gap for her. I was worried about her, as she was drinking heavily, and on more than one occasion she had memory lapses, including forgetting where she had put her teeth. This prompted a phone call or two to help her find them, and once I had located them under an armchair in her living room.

Carol had revealed to me that her husband was an alcoholic, and she had spent many years in Alanon to cope with his addiction. My dad was an alcoholic, so I had easily recognized that Carol, too, had addict tendencies. I think this is also part of the reason I wanted to help her, because I did not want her to lose more after having just lost so much.

The more I got to know Carol, the more I recognized she had some very serious personality flaws. One was that she was just about the cheapest person I had ever met. Carol counted every dime, and she didn't need to. Fred had left her with a million dollar insurance policy, and an expensive house that was almost paid for. She had a nice pension coming to her, since she had been at the school for forty years. I could not understand all the concern she had over money, because it was so extreme that it was annoying. Like, for example, at my son's fifth birthday party, she handed me his gift and explained that the books she had purchased for him were buy one get one free, so she had gotten a great deal on them. It was strange, and I could only attribute it to someone who had gotten through some lean years and couldn't let that experience go.

Carol, as Dean of Women, was also responsible for disciplining the female students for infractions. A common infraction was smoking. Students were not allowed to smoke within a three block radius of the school. It was perceived by the administration, of which Carol was a part, that students smoking on or near school grounds would give a bad impression to the community about the quality of a St. Francis Prep education. Part of the school's graduate profile states that students are to "to accept and nurture our bodies as gifts of the Creator." Smoking does not exactly fit that description, and it is understandable why the administration wanted to limit it. However, what bothered me was that Carol herself smoked like a chimney. What bothered me even more was that she had told me that the former head of the foreign language department used to grow pot at his house, and doled it out to teachers (including her) who enjoyed a good toke now and then. Carol was obviously a big hypocrite.

What I failed to absorb, though, was that hypocrites can't be trusted, even if they say they are your friend. That's a lesson I would learn the hard way.

In early 2010, Carol and I were serving on the school's internal Middle States Association Accreditation Committee. The Middle States Association as an institution accredits pre K-12 public, private, parochial, and charter schools, and many other educational institutions. To receive and maintain accreditation, a school must show, among other things, that it:

- Uses its mission, beliefs, and goals as the basis for daily decision-making;
- Operates in the public interest and in accordance with ethical practice;
- Accepts responsibility for the level of performance of its students;
- Remains committed to continuous improvement in student learning and to its capacity to produce the levels of learning desired and expected by its community;

When I was on the internal committee with Carol, it was the second go-round with Middle States for St. Francis Prep, so re-accreditation for the school. The task was to examine the school's policies and procedures, and find two big goals for the school to set and work on over the next few years.

I heard from other teachers that during the initial accreditation period in 2002, a homeless man had broken into the school and set the cafeteria on fire. Here is the press release issued by the Queens District Attorney:

Friday, October 25, 2002
HOMELESS MAN CHARGED IN ST. FRANCIS PREP SCHOOL ARSON AND THOMAS EDISON HIGH SCHOOL BREAK-IN

Queens District Attorney Richard A. Brown today announced that a homeless man has been charged with having set last week's fire at St. Francis Preparatory School in Fresh Meadows, Queens and this morning's break-in of Thomas Edison High School in Jamaica, Queens.

District Attorney Brown said, "The defendant is alleged to have started a fire last week in a kitchen-area office of St. Francis Prep which was occupied by more than a dozen clergy whose lives were endangered by his reckless conduct and to have unlawfully entered this morning Thomas Edison High School by breaking a window and climbing inside the premises. Fortunately, an alert 107th Precinct police officer, sent in response to a burglar alarm, apprehended the defendant as he was climbing out of a broken window in the rear of the high school building."

District Attorney Brown identified the defendant as James Parks, 33, no address, who said he is homeless. He has been charged with Arson in the Second Degree, Burglary in the Third Degree, Reckless Endangerment in the First Degree, Possession of Burglar's Tools and Criminal Mischief in the Second Degree and faces up to 25 years in prison if convicted.

The criminal charges allege that the defendant, on October 20, 2002, unlawfully entered St. Francis Preparatory School at 6100 Francis Lewis Boulevard in Fresh Meadows, and, while inside, set a fire in an office in a ground-level kitchen area thereby placing at grave risk the lives of clergy asleep on an upper floor of the building. It is additionally alleged that the defendant, on October 25, 2002, unlawfully entered Thomas Edison High School at 165-65 84th Avenue in Jamaica, Queens after breaking a window in the rear of the building and that a screwdriver and a pair of goggles were recovered from the defendant's back pack.

The investigation has disclosed that the defendant also had in his possession keys to a prep school vending machine, on which his fingerprints were also found, and that his presence inside and outside the prep school was recorded by a security camera.

The prep school was shut by last Sunday's fire, which caused damage to the cafeteria kitchen area of between $500,000 and $750,000. Classes resumed earlier today.

The defendant was arrested earlier today by New York City Police Department Police Officer Kenneth Clausey of the 107th Precinct which is under the command of Captain Patrick Heaney. The arson investigation was conducted by New York City Fire Marshal David Winter under the supervision of Supervising Fire Marshal Thomas Williams and the overall supervision of Chief Fire Marshal Louis Garcia.

Assistant District Attorney Diane Peress, Deputy Chief, of the District Attorney's Economic and Environmental Crimes Bureau,

is prosecuting the case under the supervision of Assistant District Attorney Brian J. Mich, Chief, and the overall supervision of Executive Assistant District Attorney for Investigations Peter A. Crusco and Assistant District Attorney Linda Cantoni, Investigations Division Counsel.
It should be noted that criminal charges are merely an accusation and that a defendant is presumed innocent until proven guilty.

Believe it or not, this incident had occurred during the first actual physical visit by the official external Middle States Association evaluation committee. The school was mortified, because one of the things the official evaluation committee assesses is student safety.

What I want to point out is this. Carol told me herself that not even one of the school security guards had been on duty the day the school was set on fire. In fact, she said they were not on duty on the weekends ever because the only school activities were teams practicing and the coaches were always around. My personal feeling is that it's probably not a good decision to leave the school unlocked so that anyone can walk in and out and not have at least one guard on duty.

It's also my feeling that the students should not be used as security guards.

That's right. St. Francis Prep hires untrained students not affiliated with a security company as part-time security guards. One of my own students, who was a senior at the time, was employed as a security guard for the school. *Isn't a school supposed to protect the children, and not the other way around?* Is it worth compromising a student's safety because he is cheap labor? What I learned loud and clear in the years that followed my leaving St. Francis Prep, is that Prep's priorities always come down to dollars and cents, and that they are penny wise and pound foolish.

Carol told me that for this second Middle States go-round, the administration did not want any mishaps or any questions by the official external committee of basically anything. So, I took the opportunity to test the waters and see exactly how honest St. Francis Prep would be in this process.

My former very good friend, Andrea, who is the Programming Director at the school, had been butting heads with the convicted felon financial controller Joseph DiSomma over a number of things, including her salary. In 2009, their disagreements had come to a head, and she was heard discussing "Joey Diamonds" in the faculty room.

She was promptly called into McLaughlin's office, where Joey was also there waiting for her. She told me that McLaughlin said in no uncertain terms that she was affecting Joey's livelihood by talking about his past, and she should never discuss it again.

Andrea left McLaughlin's office that day nervous and afraid, and told me what had happened as soon as she got back to her desk. The next day, she told me her husband had reached out to a few old contacts, and they had told him not to mess with Joe Diamonds.

I thought the Middle States re-accreditation was a good time to probe the waters where Joe Diamonds was concerned.

As part of the school's internal Middle States process, surveys were distributed to stakeholders to see how they felt about certain issues at the school. Consistent with this, surveys were distributed to teachers, and they could be submitted anonymously.

On my anonymous survey, under the comments section, I stated that I thought it was necessary to have the background of the financial controller investigated, his credentials re-evaluated, and a full audit made of all the school's financial records.

One afternoon, Carol sat me down in a conference room to go through the survey results. One of the secretaries had compiled all the comments from all the surveys in one big report, and Carol and I were reading them one by one. When we got to my comment about DiSomma, she crossed it out. Her exact words to me were "There's no reason for anyone to see this one."

Seriously? There's no reason for anyone to know that the man who is in charge of the school's money was convicted of conspiracy to commit robbery?

I did not tell her it was me who made that comment, as in that moment I saw where her loyalties lied. Her loyalties lied to the school, and certainly not to the parents who were paying tuition. But for some reason, I still thought she would be loyal to me.

I made it my mission that day to expose Joey Diamonds. I did not know how I would do it, or when I would do it, but I knew I would eventually do it. I decided this despite obvious concerns for the safety of my family. If you Google the Tinnirello Crime Family, whom Joey is affiliated with in his court cases, you will see why I was so worried.

Over the coming months, Carol and I spent a lot of time together. She was lonely, she needed help, and I was willing to give it. Carol complained so much about being lonely that I was very worried for her. She was still drinking heavily, and it was obvious to our co-workers that something was very wrong. One of the music teachers who was Co-Chair of the Middle States Committee with Carol, Robert Johnston, approached me one day to tell me Carol had gone off the rails. He said she had basically abandoned her duties on the committee, and he was flying solo. He was more annoyed than sympathetic, and it did not play well with me. He asked me to do an intervention of sorts, and I agreed, because I did not want the situation to spiral out of control.

My intention was to get Carol focused on something else besides booze. So, I set up a profile for her on Match.com.

At first, Carol was reluctant. However, within a few weeks she was having fun with it, and went on a date. The man's name was Gerry, and he was a retired cop who for the vast majority of his career, hunted mobsters. How ironic.

Well, Carol's whole personality changed once she started getting laid again. Now, instead of our conversations being about how lonely she was, they were about how many orgasms she'd had.

It was also around this time that I had what I considered a big win in my teaching career. My accounting students had won the New York City Stock Market Game sponsored by SIFMA (Securities Industry and Financial Markets Association). My blue collar kids had beaten 1,446 teams, including teams from some of the best and most expensive high schools in NY, including the High School of Finance and Economics in Manhattan. It was my third time playing the game, and it was unheard of for a teacher to win it with so few years of teaching experience behind her. In fact, the Economics teacher at Prep had been playing the game for years, and she never even came close to winning. I was very proud of my kids, and the New York Daily News did a feature story on us titled "Whiz Kids Stock It To Competition: Teens Beat Market and Rivals."

That was such a great way to end that school year. I still keep in touch with a few of those kids, and I will never forget them. Geniuses, all of them.

Over that summer, I did some soul searching. Despite my big win, I was very upset about many things, all related to St. Francis Prep. Here's the short list:

1. Joey Diamonds;
2. Rampant hypocrisy;
3. The administration's lack of enforcing appropriate boundaries between teachers and students.

I have spoken a lot about numbers one and two, but number three I need to address. Number three is a biggie. Number three laid out the framework for the next several years of my life, and is the reason I am writing this book.

After Sue Vivona told me on my very first day teaching about the art teacher who had been fired for having an inappropriate relationship with a freshman, I had been on the lookout for such behavior. I never noticed anything inappropriate until 2009. In the very late spring of 2009, one of my co-workers in the Business Department, James May, told me that if I should hear about a senior dating a social studies teacher, that rumor is true, and that this social studies teacher had been given permission by the administration to do so. He told me that the girl was 18, and so nothing illegal was going on. It was highly inappropriate, but not illegal. He also said that the teacher and the girl had been spotted by other seniors during Senior Week at Splish Splash water park on Long Island kissing, and so word was spreading quickly amongst the students that those two were a couple.

I did not ask the student's name, and I did not ask the teacher's name. I didn't want to know I guess, because they had been given permission, and so that was that. If there is one thing you learn as a teacher at St. Francis Prep, it is that you are never right if you disagree, no matter how right you are. In fact, if you do disagree with the administration, from that point you are marked. You are marked, your career prospects are marked, and your family is marked. You are marked by the administration, and you are marked by Joey. You are marked.

I did, however, march in to Carol's office and bring it up with her. I told her quite emphatically I didn't think it was a good idea to have let this happen. Her answer to me was that it hadn't been her decision, and that she had nothing to do with it. I believed her on that point, because when the good old boys lock the doors, the ladies are always on the outside.

I would learn years later the name of the teacher, and the name of the student, from the same young woman who would tell me many details about the teacher who had been fired for being involved with a freshman. As you will see, this one particular young woman had much information about many things, and together we forged a path for change.

The second time I was made aware of "current" inappropriate activity between a teacher and a student was in 2010. One of my accounting students had approached me about a teacher having hugged her much too closely. I was not surprised, because the man she was complaining about was my boss, Joseph Sciame.

Brother Mark had left Prep at the end of my first year teaching. He just couldn't take it anymore. Dealing with that trio of idiots – Brother Leonard Conway, Patrick McLaughlin, and Joseph DiSomma, had taken its toll on him. On his last day, he apologized to me. He said "I'm sorry I won't be here to protect you anymore." He was always good to me.

His replacement was a man named Joseph Sciame, a portly, unkempt veteran teacher who had left the Science Department and was looking for a new home. Make no mistake, I had assertively thrown my hat into the ring for that position as head of the Business Department, but I was told that even though I was doing very well, I had been teaching at the school less than a year so they didn't feel I was qualified. In retrospect maybe I should have sucked off McLaughlin. Then I would have been a shoo-in for the promotion.

By March, 2009, less than two semesters after Sciame had taken over the Business Department, I had reported him for speaking inappropriately to me. It wasn't sexual in nature, but it was an overall demeaning, misogynistic way of speaking to me that had a threatening tone. I had reported him to McLaughlin, and was told by him "I thought Joe was over doing those things." That is a direct quote, and it clued me in that the man who was my direct superior had a history.

So in 2010, when my student came to me upset about being hugged inappropriately by Sciame, I went straight to Carol and told her to do something immediately. Technically, I should have reported it to McLaughlin. However, if he knew Sciame had a history of this type of behavior, which McLaughlin indicated he did, and Sciame was promoted to Chairperson of the Business Department despite this, I could not logically expect him to do a damn thing.

To my surprise, Joe Sciame's strange history with women was corroborated by a graduate of the class of 1993, in an email to me dated July 11, 2015:

> I had Sciame for sophomore honors science. In class, I was witness to Sciame's schoolboy crushes & inappropriate comments. He particularly liked a tall, leggy girl who was also in my Cor. She would get embarrassed by his attention & subsequent ribbing from classmates who referred to Sciame as her "boyfriend". That school year, I was known for my shrine to John F. Kennedy Jr. Every inch of my locker was covered w/JFK jr pix (yes, I was obsessed!). Teachers (like Peggy Bergin) would stop by to check out pix & share their admiration for JFK Jr - all in appropriate, good fun. I remember Sciame walking by & seeing my open locker. He came over to check it out. His reaction was interesting. He said it was no fair that JFK Jr got that kind of attention. He said that he & JFK Jr were the same age & he (Sciame) is not dead b/c he's a teacher! It was like a childish, jealous rant!

Carol saw how pissed I was – I was breathing fire. She called Robyn Armon in to her office, they both spoke to my student, and they handled it with Sciame. Exactly three years later, I would find out that he took that warning with a grain of salt and had inappropriate interactions with another girl almost immediately.

Thus, at this point, my soul searching began. I clearly would not make it to twenty years at the school, nor did I want to. I was done, and I needed an exit plan.

So, I planned.

CHAPTER SIX

BRH BOUND

2010 was pretty much a horrible year for Americans. We were in the thick of the recession, and everyone was miserable. The job market sucked, and even if you had a job, there was very little probability of getting a raise.

Online forums were full of people complaining about the government, the economy, health care reform, and everything else in 'Murica.

In this general dismay I found opportunity.

By the end of the 2009 – 2010 school year, I already knew I would never become an old-timer at Prep. I had spoken frequently with my friend, Andrea, the Director of Programming, several times about packing up and moving to San Diego. Nice weather year round, no shoveling snow, and more space seemed like a good option at this particular juncture in my life.

In August, 2010, my wife and I began to talk about our options. I thought perhaps we could start a web-based business that would give us more personal freedom. I was new to social media, only having joined Facebook exactly a year earlier, but I was aware of a few sites that I found interesting. One, obviously, was Facebook, another was FML, and Wikileaks, and Rate My Teacher.

I thought how interesting it would be to combine all of these into one site, where people could discuss anything that annoyed or upset them, and possibly divulge information that the public might find important. This would be a site where people could post anonymously, without fear of speaking their mind, consistent with the First Amendment.

This would not be a happy-go-lucky site, although there was the potential for humor. It would be a sort of Facebook for angry people, with the ability to post, comment, and private message. Everyone I discussed it with thought it was a good idea, so I knew I was on to something. However, I was having a lot of trouble coming up with a name. Every domain name I came up with was already taken. I learned quickly that domain names are like real estate, in that the good properties are scooped up and their resale value is off the charts. I wanted a name that was tongue-in-cheek, that people would remember. Those were my only criteria, and yet, the name was eluding me.

Then my wife made a suggestion. This suggestion would have an impact on our lives that we never could have imagined. She said to me, "You know, when I'm pissed about someone or something, I usually say it can burn and rot in hell. How about that?" Well, that sounded fine to me! Why not? You can't get more tongue in cheek than a little devil winking at you and smiling. That day, we purchased Burnandrotinhell.com.

It was not that farfetched a name. The domain name Rotinhell.com was taken, and Burninhell.com was taken. Burnandrot.com was also taken. We snapped up Burnandrotinhell.com just in time. What I didn't know at that moment was that it would become the absolute most appropriate name for our website we ever could have wanted.

I was not sure how developing this type of website with this particular name would impact me at work, and I did want to stay employed until we eventually moved out of New York. I decided it would be a good idea to meet Carol for dinner and run it all by her.

When I told Carol our idea she thought it was hilarious. She did not see any problem with the name, nor the proposed content so far as my continued employment by the school was concerned. I gave her full disclosure, and told her there would be many sections for venting, including Exes, Co-Workers, Rude People, Bad Teachers, Bad Students, Celebrities and Politics. She gave me the all clear to start developing it.

Over the next several months, Carol would play an integral role in the development of the website. She reviewed and modified my terms of use, made suggestions for additional categories, and even served as a moderator on my Facebook fan page for the site. Her daughter, who had a position in publishing, advised me regarding trademarks and copyrights. I had approval for everything I did every step of the way, and was assured none of it would be a problem. When I had a segment on Sirius XM booked to promote the launch of the site, I had asked Carol if I should let Brother Leonard know, and she told me it was fine, and that she would handle it.

What a lying sack of crap she was, but I just didn't know it yet.

Carol spoke freely about my website to faculty and staff members, including the school Chaplain, Reverend William Sweeney. I still have his "Sounds great!!!! Can't wait to see it!" message in my Facebook inbox, referring to his enthusiasm for the project. Carol monitored my fan page closely, and warned me about certain imbalanced students who had "liked" it, and what they might say. She had told me time and time again how much she hated her job, and considered it pointless giving children detentions for wearing the wrong shoes, and how she welcomed this opportunity to be involved in something fun and new. We worked closely all the way through, from Day One.

In March, 2011, we launched. Hundreds of posts went up almost instantly. However, within a day, students from the school were posting about sexual harassment and inappropriate teacher and staff behavior in the Bad Teachers section of the website. It became obvious where this was headed.

The third morning after the launch, Patrick McLaughlin appeared in my classroom door, and told me he needed to speak to me. It just so happens that this particular morning, I was lecturing about sexual harassment in the workplace. Another teacher took over for me, and I followed him to his office.

It was always a laughable experience for me speaking with Pat. He probably has the most undeveloped intellect of any man I have ever met. Up to this point, I had never been able to have anything that even resembled an intelligent conversation with him. As we walked down the hall, I recalled my last conversation with him, which was in the school cafeteria, and revolved around his marveling at the speed with which one of the seniors had grown his facial hair into a beard. This was not going to be a talk with the Dalai Lama or Stephen Hawking. This was going to be a discussion with a man who had demonstrated to me little beyond a basic grasp of the English language, and who was good-looking and knew all the right Brooklyn boys, and who had, in my opinion, built his career on that.

We arrived at his office, and Pat closed the door. I sat down, and he was stone-faced. I tried very hard not to laugh. He began by telling me that he had done nothing for the previous two days except deal with my website. He found many of the posts in the Bad Teachers and Bad Students sections upsetting, and he wanted those two sections – and only those two – taken down. He brought up one specific post, about a teacher whom a student complained had been "whispering in her ear."

I had of course seen that post, and I knew that teacher, and I had also been warned by Carol many times that he is a pervert. I asked Pat point blank "Don't you want to know these things so you can do something about it?" He didn't answer. That was all I needed to know. So much more is said in silence than with words sometimes.

I told him I would not be taking down any sections of my website. He commented "Why? Because it isn't good for business?" I had learned very clearly over the past four years that Prep would do just about anything to protect its "business." That was clearly the pot calling the kettle black, and it pissed me off. He went on to tell me that he was advised some of the posts could be considered defamatory, and he was having an attorney look into it.

I wish I could have taken a picture of my face so I could show it to you now. As a response to the defamatory comment, I purposely made a face like "Seriously? You must be joking." With his tail between his legs Pat replied, "Umm, maybe not then."

I hate when people use big words they don't understand. Defamation is a very specific thing. In a blog I would write years later, I would say the following about this topic:

"Defamation means a false statement. It does not mean a statement you don't like, or a statement that makes someone look bad. True statements are not defamation. They are called "the truth", and that is what has been written in these blogs. In order to sue for defamation, someone would have to prove a statement is false, and that the person making the statement was negligent in making them. Then, they would have to prove damages attributable specifically to the alleged defamatory statements."

The student posts that were going up were clearly not defamation. They were detailed accounts of experiences, or matters of opinion. If I say you are an asshole, that's my opinion, and I can proclaim it freely. If you whispered in my ear and it creeped me out, that's the truth and I can also proclaim that freely.

Well, Pat didn't have much to say to me after I gave him that look. He sent me back to class, and when the end of period bell rang, he was in my doorway again. "I need you to come with me to Brother Leonard's office," he said.

I followed him down the hallway again, and into Br. Leonard's office we went. Br. Leonard was sitting there, and so was Reverend Bill Sweeney, who had sent me that "Sounds great!!!!" message about my website on Facebook. Pat sat down and they all put little notepads in their laps, and I just about wet my pants and had to dig my nails into the palm of my hand so I wouldn't laugh.

Here's a big shocker: Carol was nowhere to be found.

The conversation was short and sweet. Leonard wanted those two sections of my website down, I told him to forget it, and that it wasn't happening. So, he sent me home, suspended, with pay.

When I got back to my car, I called my wife and told her I was suspended. She was upset, but I wasn't. I also called my website consultant. I told him what happened, and within five minutes he called me back and told me Fox 5 New York was on their way to my house to interview me. All this happened and I hadn't even pulled out of the Prep parking lot yet.

About an hour after I arrived home, reporter Andrea Day, now at CNBC, showed up at my door. We did a short interview, and I mentioned how I had gotten approval for my site, even from the school Chaplain. I mentioned that my kids had won the Stock Market Game, and I held up the Daily News article, which I had gotten framed.

At the end of the interview, Andrea asked me this simple question: "Is there anything else you want to say to the people who suspended you?"

I looked right into the camera, sighed and answered "Burn and rot in hell!"

That was thunder heard around the world. The Huffington Post picked up on the story, as did The Daily Mail in the UK, and The Young Turks did an analysis of me and my website. Ana Kasparian gave BRH (as people started to call it at that point) a big thumbs up. Cenk Uygur did an impression of me that was just hilarious. The website exploded, and there was no turning back.

The next morning, I got a call from Brother Leonard's secretary, Camille. She told me I was to report to school by 2:37 (the end of the school day) to meet with the administration or I would be fired. I asked if I could come in Monday to speak with them instead. I was actually laughing in my head, because I told them to burn and rot in hell on national tv and they still wanted to meet with me to discuss options. I am guessing they knew even then the writing was on the wall for them, that this little powerful website was a Pandora's Box of truth and they wanted to buy me out. Br. Leonard relayed to Camille that he would not give me until Monday. I said in that case, please terminate me, and they did.

In the meantime, thousands of users were signing up on BRH every day. Little memes of me with devil horns on my head started popping up on the internet. Bloggers were blogging about me, some saying I am a crazy lady.

Maybe I am, but I like me this way.

The following week, the mother of a senior that I was friendly with called me. Her son had brought home a letter that Pat and Leonard were circulating about me, basically insinuating I was a rogue teacher who did all of this without anyone's knowledge, and that my website is offensive and wrong.

I was very, very angry. I called Andrea Day. I told her about the letter, and while she was sympathetic, she stated that she would need something more to run the story. So, I gave it to her.

The previous year, there had been a scandal at the school, when it was discovered that the gay, closeted Science Teacher/Director of Student Activities, David Ganci, had been videotaped marching in the NYC Gay Pride Parade in his underwear. I learned about the video like most other teachers at the school, by word of mouth. If you go to YouTube and search "2010 New York City Gay Pride Parade Hot Sexy Muscular Studs in White" that video will pop up to this day, and David Ganci, the overly muscular Tom of Finland wannabe, is in the center of the thumbnail, waving a giant flag. I felt this was the fodder for a really good story and it would be well-received.

Andrea Day played the video in the segment, and I ended the story with saying how awful it was that the school had disseminated that letter about me.

However, I was wrong about how the Prep audience would take it. I was blasted by the alumni base for outing a beloved teacher. The alumni are very strange. It was of no consequence that Ganci outed himself by marching in the parade, and that the video was already watched by virtually everyone at 6100 Francis Lewis Boulevard. Many are blindly loyal to the school, and sometimes can't see clearly the information being presented to them. It was my opinion, and still is, that it is not acceptable for a teacher to march in a parade in his underwear (or Speedo, or diaper, or whatever the fuck it was). In addition, Ganci was the only one dressed that way in the video. All the other guys were wearing shorts or pants. Get a grip, Dave. You work out. We get it.

Let me make this clear right now. Up until a year ago, I regretted that I had put David Ganci on blast. I felt guilty about it. However, knowing what I now know now, I consider it to be a good decision. Why? Because in 2014, one of his former biology class students contacted me. She said that she was in his class the day after the video aired on Fox 5 and David Ganci had this exchange with them:

"How many of you go to parades?
(The majority of students raised their hand.)

"How many of you go to the St. Patrick's Day Parade?
(Several students raised their hand.)

"How many of you go even though you are not Irish?"
(A few students raised their hand.)

"Well, class, I was marching in the Gay Pride Parade as a favor to a friend because one of the color guards had gone missing."

Now, that's the biggest load of hypocritical horseshit I have ever heard. Yes, Dave, you were marching only as a favor. Was it a favor to your ex-lover, Scott, who was the moderator for the St. Francis Prep color guard? David Ganci is so proud of his gayness that he marched in the PRIDE parade, yet he misled his class about it, knowing damn well the odds were there were at least a couple of gay kids sitting right in front of him. Disgusting.

Over the next few weeks, my website traffic declined. One reason for this was students were threatened by the administration about posting on BRH, and students at other schools had also been warned. Some Prep seniors had actually been suspended and I called the ACLU to see if they could step in. However, private institutions, especially religious ones, constitutionally march to their own tune, so the ACLU couldn't do a damn thing. I would spend the next several years of my life exploring this idea of separation of church and state, to see if exceptions could be created when the safety of children are at stake.

Everything got very quiet, very fast. The silence in my world was deafening. And then Angel Amore sent me a message.

CHAPTER SEVEN

HOW DO YOU TALK TO AN ANGEL?

The morning of April 6, 2011 started like any other day. I got out of bed, had some coffee, and got my son off to school. When I arrived back home, I sat down with my computer to, among other things, check Facebook and see what was going on in my circles, just as I did every day.

That particular morning was the first morning I was contacted by the anonymous, kinky, highly sexually active Angel Amore, who would serve over the next several months as an informant regarding decades of corruption and cover-ups at St. Francis Prep. My contact with him would affect my life for years to come, in ways I never could have imagined.

Let me tell you right now I still don't have any idea who Angel really is. All I know about him is what I am telling you in this chapter. I've included several of his messages at the end of the book, just so you can get your own idea of what he was like. Enjoy, and try not to blush.

Angel, in his very first message, told me "Joe DiSomma is a jewel thief," and "Carolyn Szostek is on Match.com." With these two brief statements, I immediately knew two things about Angel: he was a Prep insider or closely connected to one, and, if he was an employee, he was not someone who knew me very well. The reason I say the latter is, everyone at Prep I was friendly with knew I was the one who had put Carol on Match. So, if Angel and I knew each other well at Prep, he would have known that fact, too, and would have no reason to share it with me.

Initially I found Angel's contact with me somewhat disconcerting. He friend requested me soon after our conversations began, and his profile picture was a pretty, young woman whom he said was his primary sexual partner at the time. On his timeline, there were many pictures he had taken of her at porno shoots, working. Angel loved porn, loved sex, and was a self-described swinger. He had lots of sex with lots of women lots of times (including some members of the Prep staff), and he said he had their pictures posted on his "conquest wall". I would later find this last statement to be true, when I was invited to an exclusive peek into his world on AOL Instant Messenger. By the way, his AIM username is EatinMuf, so look him up if you dare. I did not know Angel's world from Adam, and I didn't want to know it. I never asked him personal questions, but he chose to tell me lots of personal things about himself, and his aspirations. One of these was to bang Carol:

What is CS's phone number and address? I think I am going to try to get some action from her so I can put her pics on my "conquest" wall. I'll bet I can even get her to do some serious kink shit too: then I can mail you action shots of her getting rammed. I'll show that widow who's "Dean of Discipline!"

What does one say to something like that? Is it funny or is it just gross? Is it both? Could I laugh and still be a good person? These were my daily dilemmas when communicating with Angel.

I also want to say right now I don't like surprises. This includes messaging directly with someone who won't give me their real name. It is an uncomfortable position in which to be, because you can be held accountable for everything you say, but they can't be held accountable for a damn thing. I never would have guessed that being contacted this way would happen to me over and over again for the next four years, by hundreds of people who didn't want to be "marked" by Prep. I understand, but all these years later, I still don't like it, and I am extremely cautious when communicating this way.

After my appreciative response to his first message, Angel ramped up his intel game. His next clue was "look into the Brothers Dominic and Ben situations." Suddenly I felt like Agent Starling in Silence of the Lambs – "Look deep into YOURSELF, Clarice." What was happening was surreal. I apparently had a real mole who wanted to give me leads. But to what end?

I had heard these two names before in passing while I was teaching at the school, but had never heard anything negative mentioned about either of these Brothers. I didn't know what "situation" I should look into, and had no one else to ask about said "situations."

I asked for more information, and Angel willingly gave it. He told me that

Brother Dominic had been accused of kissing a boy some years earlier, and that I had a friend on my BRH fan page, who Brother Ben had "said things to."

Now I understood, loud and clear. Angel wanted me to go full force in exposing the hypocrisy of the school.

With a little more pressing, Angel gave me the name of the young woman I should contact about Brother Ben. Her name is Felicia Mooradian, and she would become a hero for thousands.

CHAPTER EIGHT

MS. MOORADIAN

It is very difficult for me when I contact someone out of the blue who I have reason to believe has been the victim of sexual harassment or sexual abuse. The last thing I would ever want to do is upset someone or make them feel uncomfortable or ashamed by bringing up an unpleasant and harmful experience from their past. A choice of words can make all the difference in how someone reacts. It is a tender spot for both the sender and the receiver of the message and it is not a moment to be taken lightly.

Therefore, caution was my overriding concern as I typed my first Facebook message to Felicia Mooradian on April 12, 2011. Here it is:

> *Hi, Felicia. Thanks for your support on the fan page. I appreciate it so much, how much I don't even think I can express. I want you to know people are contacting me from all over about Prep, and one person in particular, whom I have never met, insisted I contact you about Br. Ben. I had something similar happen to me in 1987, when I was a senior. Anyway, if you would like to tell me your story, you can email me on facebook or call me at 917 000 0000 if you are more comfortable with that.*

And here is what she answered, later that same day:

Hi there! I am more than happy to give whatever support I can, as I feel you suffered an unbelievable injustice. And I can't stand the immaturity of the students attacking you- that one ringleader and his friends chiming in because they have nothing better to do.

Regarding Br. Ben, talk about a blast from the past. I'd be glad to discuss that story with you, along with a few others in the same vein, but I do have concerns about my name being published if you chose to go public about that matter. I'd like to know who insisted that you contact me- but I respect anonymity. The Br. Ben story does fit right in with the Prep hypocrisy news.

I'll be in touch- I just found out my aunt is terminally ill with cancer, so I'm very hectic in dealing with doctors etc., but you have my support 100%.

After reading this, I knew many things. Felicia was a good writer, intelligent, caring, and equally cautious. All of these qualities would be confirmed in the years that followed. I can say now that she is one of the brightest, bravest, most caring and wittiest people I have ever met.

I was upset I had disturbed Felicia at this particular point in her life when she was caring for her aunt. There is a right time and a right place for everything, and perhaps this was not the time for me to pursue any sort of inquiry with her. When I am not sure about things, I often turn it over to the universe. I am a firm believer that if something is meant to be, it will. So I answered Felicia with this:

Oh my God, I am so sorry about your aunt...illness is rough, I hope she doesn't suffer and I will keep her in my prayers (I DO pray, contrary to what some people think).

I would never publish your name, absolutely never, unless you told me I could. I am trying to get the school on the Bishop's radar so that he steps in and does something to save the school. That is my intention at this point, because the school will not make it unless a new administration is appointed. By the way, I don't know this guy who told me to contact you! It's freaky! As best as I can tell, it is a fake Facebook profile. He is on the fan page, he made a comment.

By the way, I was harassed, hunted actually, by a teacher at the school in 1987 and he went on to be a grifter across the U.S. I will tell you the full story when we speak. Call anytime, my phone is always on, but if it is after 9pm I probably won't answer because my son is sleeping and he wakes up easily. Thanks so much for your help, hope to speak with you soon.

I told Felicia this because I wanted her to know I understood and she was not alone, if her experience at Prep had been anything like mine my senior year. I think she appreciated what I said, and she responded:

> *Thanks for the prayers, I'm a big believer in prayer myself. I will call you asap with as much information as I can provide. Prep really does need a new administration. I could go on for ages about how ridiculous they are.*
>
> *That teacher from 1987 sounds SO scary. I am glad you have the courage and the wisdom to speak out, FINALLY somebody with a spine!!*
>
> *By the way, I saw your pics, and your son is adorable x 10. I have a four year old brother, my heart melts for kids. He obviously has a very good mommy!*

Being a mother is the best job I have ever had. I would not trade it for anything, ever. Kids are the future of the world, and they are a precious gift we must cherish. This is why I was hoping someday to speak with Felicia, so perhaps we could join forces and see if together we could push for change at St. Francis Prep.

Again, there is a right time and a right place for everything. Other things needed to happen before we would connect.

I did not hear from her again until almost two years later.

CHAPTER NINE

DAVID INVESTIGATES GOLIATH

For the next several months, Angel Amore kept the information flowing. There were so many disturbing incidents he told me about, that I could hardly keep track. I wanted to investigate everything, including things Carolyn Szostek told me about that Angel never mentioned.

It was during this time that my family also made a big decision. We were moving to San Diego. We were tired of New York winters, tired of brutally hot summers, tired of not having enough living space, and overall tired. Our son was in parochial school, and we were paying a lot for what I considered a mediocre education. Public schools were not an option, because they were worse. There was just no reason for us to stay.

We picked the best public school district in San Diego, then selected a house near the school we wanted Andrew to attend. We were excited and feeling good.

Moving is not easy, especially clear across country. We coordinated this move for the three of us, our two mothers who were moving with us, and our six pets – a dog and five cats, all rescue animals. In addition, we had two homes to sell, one in Sunnyside, Queens and one in Williamsburg, Brooklyn. We bit off a lot, hoping we could chew it all before August, 2012, when Andrew would be starting second grade.

Even in the middle of this personal chaos, continuing to investigate Prep was on my mind, playing like a screensaver, popping up whenever some mental space was free.

I made a punch list of things I wanted to look into, and it went something like this:

1. What had happened to Brother Ben?
2. What happened to Brother Dom when the boy accused him of sexual misconduct?
3. What can I confirm about Joe DiSomma's criminal history?
4. Carol had said the previous principal had been taken out of the school in handcuffs for child molestation. This was circa 1980. Angel Amore also said he had been dragged out in handcuffs. What happened to him? Did he go to jail or was he still out there roaming free?
5. Carol had told me deceased social studies teacher and football moderator, Robert Stenger, "liked to touch the boys" – was he a child molester?
6. What exactly happened regarding the social studies teacher who was given permission to date a student in 2009?
7. What happened with the art teacher who Sue Vivona said had a relationship with a freshman girl?
8. Angel told me there had been a freshman blowjob ring - did this actually happen? Specifically, he said: *"There were a group of freshmen giving blowjobs for $20 a BJ in the bathroom on east top. That caused the school administration to hire a crisis pregnancy expert to come to school: Pam Stensel I think her name was. I don't think any of the ladies were kicked out of the school either."*

I really didn't know where to start. Many of these issues would involve speaking with graduates and former teachers, or even current teachers. I just did not have that kind of access anymore.

What I did have, though, was the internet, and some friends. This would be enough to get me going.

I decided to start with what was most easily provable. That was the criminal history of Joe DiSomma/Joe Diamonds. I had a friend named Sarah Armaghan who was a reporter for Newsday, and I asked her to find out what she could about him. She verified more information about him in a few days than I ever thought she would.

Sarah wanted to run the story, but her editors told her that she would need one person at the school to verify Joe Diamonds' identity and comment about him. She called several people at the school, but not one of them would say a word – not even people I knew hated his guts.

I could not blame them. The idea of Joey was scary - a conviction for conspiracy to commit robbery, five years in federal prison, points added for gun possession, and an affiliation with mobsters. No wonder my friend Andrea never spoke about him again after that meeting in Patrick McLaughlin's office.

I would eventually make sure that not only the Bishop knew about this man's history, but alumni, donors, and tuition-paying parents as well. Contrary to whatever Prep might have been thinking, people do have a right to know who is handling their money.

If everything I had heard about Joe Diamonds over the years was true, then I knew in my gut that most everything else on my list would be true. I would find out what I could, and I would go to the Bishop with it. That was my plan.

Over the next year, I would gather many random facts that together would paint a grim picture of the school, and what had happened over the past thirty years since Brother Leonard Conway came into office as principal.

One thing that I found very interesting was information given to me by my dentist. I didn't know it when I started going to her for exams, but my dentist is a Prep alum. Not only that, but she keeps in touch with several people she graduated with, some of whom work at the school. She confirmed for me Brother Ben's long history of sexually harassing girls. Specifically she mentioned that for decades, he would ask girls to do splits in their skirts for extra credit points. Once she told me this, I was anxious to speak with Felicia. Months had gone by and I hadn't heard from her. I was tempted to message her, but I didn't want to bother her while she was caring for her terminally ill aunt. I focused on my belief that what was meant to happen, would, and I left it at that.

Next, I started looking into Brother Dom. I found some articles online that said he went to Rome for a two year period starting in 2004. I also saw that when he returned from Italy in 2006, he went to teach at Bishop Ford High School in Park Slope, Brooklyn. This was odd to me. He spent over thirty years at Prep, but he went to teach at another school? Why? His whole life had been about Prep. Why not return to the place he called home for so long? There was something to that story Angel had told me, I just knew it. However, despite my best efforts, I could not locate the young man whom Angel said reported Dom for sexual misconduct. This story was obviously not meant to be – yet.

Next I started looking into the freshman blow job ring. I googled Pam Stensel, the name Angel had given me. The correct spelling is Pam Stenzel, and she is actually what I consider a crazy lady. Have you seen this stuff she says?

Here is an excerpt from an article that ran in the Huffington Post on April 12, 2013, by Emma Gray:

Pam Stenzel, Abstinence-Only Sex Ed Speaker, Reportedly Tells

Students 'If You Take Birth Control, Your Mother Probably Hates You'
"Pam Stenzel, an abstinence-only speaker, sparked controversy after giving a talk to an assembly of West Virginia high school students this week. Stenzel, whose website describes her as someone who "talks about the consequences — both physical and emotional — of sex outside of marriage," reportedly made extreme (and false) comments such as, "If you take birth control, your mother probably hates you," and, "I could look at any one of you in the eyes right now and tell if you're going to be promiscuous," reported the Charleston Gazette."

Do you think this is the right message to give teenagers? I don't. I think attempting to slut-shame impressionable teenage girls is clearly not the way to go.

I wanted confirmation that Pam Stenzel spoke at Prep, and why. I would get that information, and much more in the years that followed, from both graduates and former teachers. What I would discover is that yes, what Angel told me about the freshman blow job ring, and Pam Stenzel being brought in as damage control, was true. In fact, it was so true that when religion teacher Sue Vivona was informed about the twenty dollar price for the blowjobs, her response was "Only twenty dollars? Mine are worth a thousand."

Good for you, Sue. You and Robyn must have a lot in common.

In any event, at this point I felt I had enough concrete information to bypass the Bishop and start a dialogue with Cardinal Dolan, the Archbishop of the Archdiocese of New York, and tell him what I found. Prep's employment of Joey Diamonds alone would be enough, I thought. Surely, he would find the employment of a convicted felon with a history of firearm possession as Controller of the largest private, Catholic high school in America problematic.

Then again, maybe not.

CHAPTER TEN

ONE MARGARITA, MANY BLOGS

By the autumn of 2012, the changes my family had been planning manifested. We moved to a beautiful family and pet friendly neighborhood in northern San Diego, and Andrew started school on time, just as we had hoped. I found a new job, and we were loving the consistent seventy degree weather and sunshine.

All the ducks were in a row except one very big duck. I had gathered a significant amount of disturbing information about St. Francis Prep and I needed to decide what to do with it. After a lot of thought, I concluded that perhaps the best course of action would be to bypass the Bishop of the Brooklyn Diocese entirely and go straight to Cardinal Dolan with what I had learned.

Do you know anything about Cardinal Dolan, the current Archbishop of the Archdiocese of New York? I didn't really know much about him when I first wrote to him regarding corruption and student sexual harassment and abuse at St. Francis Prep in late 2012.

Since then, however, I've learned quite a bit. My first eye-opener came when watching the HBO Documentary "Mea Maxima Culpa: Silence in the House of God". In the film, Cardinal Dolan is said to have purposely shielded millions of church dollars from clergy sexual abuse lawsuits when he was Archbishop of the Archdiocese of Milwaukee. The New York Times published a huge article on this topic in July, 2013, stating that:

"Files released by the Roman Catholic Archdiocese of Milwaukee on Monday reveal that in 2007, Cardinal Timothy F. Dolan, then the archbishop there, requested permission from the Vatican to move nearly $57 million into a cemetery trust fund to protect the assets from victims of clergy sexual abuse who were demanding compensation... The Vatican approved the request in five weeks, the files show".

What a piece of crap Dolan is, seriously. It is my personal feeling that his leanings toward protecting the church at all costs explains what happened in my life after I wrote to him.

At that time, the Cardinal did not have a public email address. There was not even a way to contact him directly on his website. There was, however, an email address for media inquiries. How convenient. I decided to use it. I sent a very long message to Cardinal Dolan's attention with great detail about what I discovered had happened at St. Francis Prep over the last thirty years. Days went by after I reached out to him, and I didn't hear back, not one word even acknowledging that I existed.

However, coincidentally, this post suddenly showed up on my website:

Liz C (or Liz S now) The Administration…Faculty…and staff wish you a Blessed Christmas and health and happiness in the New Year. May you find peace in your heart so you can no longer wish others to……. Burn and rot in hell!

That post was made on December 19, 2012 in the category "Other Stuff", from a non-traceable email and IP address.

I found the timing of this post to be uncanny. I hadn't heard anything from the school in well over a year, and a few days after I emailed very damning information to Cardinal Dolan, a post turns up on my website from the administration wishing me peace in my heart.

I was furious. What hypocrites, all of them!

I stewed about this insulting post non-stop. (I'm a Scorpio; we do that kind of stuff.) My anger was clearly affecting my enjoyment of the holiday season, because I couldn't think about much else. Finally, on Christmas Day, my wife handed me a margarita and said "I know how upset you are. Maybe you should blog about this." Well, that was all the encouragement I needed. What a fantastic idea.

There was a blog linked to my website that I hardly used. It can be found at blog.burnandrotinhell.com. I have always been a writer at heart, and when

I created this website, I wanted a blog attached so that should I have musings I wanted to make public, the vehicle would be in place. Well, here was that moment.

I spent much of the rest of Christmas Day writing, and I clicked the "publish" button on December 26th. I posted the blog to my timeline on Facebook, and sat back and released it to the universe. I didn't check to see how many people had read it for about three days. Then, I saw it had sixty thousand views. Sixty thousand, and all I had done was post it once. Apparently, a lot of sharing was taking place.

Here is an excerpt from that very first SFP scandal blog, affectionately titled "I am EC, and Saint Francis Prep Has Mistaken Me For Someone Who Gives a Shit - And Who Is the Mole?"

I hope you like it:

It's been too long. It's time to tell the whole story of this website, how it came about, and all the things that happened after it launched. I am an owner of the company that owns this website. On various posts on my website you will see users calling me EC. I attended Saint Francis Preparatory School in Fresh Meadows, NY, from 1983 - 1987. I was an honor student. I had a pretty good experience there up until 1986. In 1986, the head of the Phys. Ed department, Thomas Nuzzi, was my driver's ed teacher. He was a disgusting pig. He tried to get me alone in the driver's ed car or back at his house on several occasions. He often asked me to come over and help feed his dogs and told me he would drive me home. He constantly said things like, "my wife is dying of a brain tumor and I am lonely." He said things like "you are special." He made passes at me in the driver's education car. He made passes at me in front of my friends. When I did not show interest, he got angry. He said he would fail me for driver's ed. Somehow he had "never received" my project that I handed to him directly two weeks earlier. I didn't tell anyone. I was afraid if I told that my father would kill him and go to jail - that's how Italian men feel about their daughters. Later in the semester, Tom Nuzzi and two of his friends were fired for fraud- they were telling parents student ski trips they organized cost more money than they did, and they were pocketing the difference.

Years later, in 2007, I taught business at Saint Francis Prep. I had been a lawyer for several years, but wanted a change. I believed what had happened 20 years earlier was an isolated incident of madness. I was mistaken. My very first day teaching, a religion teacher told me about a freshman girl who had slept with a teacher. I was told that the administration did nothing until a little girl gave graphic details.

The longer I worked there, the more people came to "the lawyer" with their concerns. A few months into working there, I was told by my then department head, Brother Mark, that the man in charge of the school's finances, Joseph DiSomma, is a convicted jewel thief who was tied to the mafia, and whose mob name is Joey Diamonds. He said everyone in the building knows, but they all overlook it. I googled it. You can google him yourself and see what you think. Brother Mark promised to protect me as much as he could from all the sordid characters at Saint Francis Prep. Those were his exact words, "I will protect you." Brother Mark quit at the end of my first year there. It was unheard of for a Franciscan Monk to quit working at a Franciscan school and he had to get permission from the powers above him in the Franciscan hierarchy. I was very sad to see him go. He was a good man. He stood up for what he believed in. He gave me three reasons why he was quitting - Br. Leonard (the Principal), Pat McLaughlin (the Assistant Principal) and Joe DiSomma (the Controller).

Time went on. Story after story after story was told to me by others. Like, for example, how a couple of years before I started working there, a homeless man walked into the school cafeteria and set it on fire. The doors weren't locked and there was no security that day. The reason it wasn't in the news is because the school has graduates working at most of the major networks and they covered it up.

I witnessed horrible injustices myself. At the end of 2008 the school was going to be featured as Cosmopolitan Magazine's Ultimate Prom. The head of the guidance department, Robyn Armon, pretty much hand-picked who would win prom queen, because her niece was involved in running the contest for Cosmo. She picked the cheerleader daughter of the the football coach/Italian teacher. I was advocating for a student in my accounting class who had cancer, and who came to class weak, bald head and all, so she could graduate with her friends. Robyn told me she wasn't "the face of SFP." Really? I would like to think that type of person is exactly who we would want to be the face of SFP. But I guess I was mistaken. (By the way, the head of Campus Ministries was present for that conversation, so please Prep don't try to lie about it, it would be really pathetic.) And Suzy R., I am sorry I let you down. I tried.

In 2009, my best friend at the school, Andrea, was overheard talking about "Joey Diamonds" with her coworkers. She was called into McLaughlin's office for a meeting. Joe DiSomma was there. She was warned and told never to speak of it again. So she didn't. Later, when all the shit went down with this website, and tons of posts were going up about shady situations at the school, Andrea was accused of being the mole. This information was leaked to me by the real mole, who didn't work at the school at all. But more about the mole later.

During my third year teaching, there was a kid in my accounting class named Brad. Brad was obviously high in class on more than one occasion. I kept sending him to the Dean until he was drug tested. His drug test came back inconclusive because the school nurse had left Mr. Clean on the counter in the bathroom where he had to pee in the cup. So he poured the Mr. Clean into his urine sample. Bingo, he was let off the hook! They let him out of the nurse's office high and he threatened to beat the shit out of me. The next day they sent him back to my class. A few days later, in my communications class (yes, I was blessed to have him as a student in two classes!) he came in asking if anyone had change for a $100 bill. Then he asked to go to the restroom and took his backpack with him. With the help of another student, I put two and two together and I had called security to come to my classroom when he came back from the restroom. They found drugs and cash in his backpack. He had confessed to dealing drugs to hundreds of kids at the school. My question was, why did I have to keep pushing this issue to have some action taken? Oh, because his dad was President of a corporation on Long Island...I see, I see.

It was around this time that the former Dean of Women, Carolyn Szostek told me about a teacher whose name was Stenger. I remembered his name vaguely from when I went to Prep in the 80's. She had said that the administration knew he "touched the boys" and was a "pervert." The administration never did anything about it, and Stenger taught there pretty much until he died. By the way, she said he left almost his entire estate to the school, and made one of the teachers his executor. She had reviewed the accounting for the estate and made sure the teacher had received his executor's commission. A nice, happy ending, except for the decades of boys who had been touched inappropriately by this man. Carol told me about another teacher who was generally considered a pervert. It was someone in the religion department. When my site went live, a student posted about this man repeatedly whispering in students' ears...coincidence? When Patrick McLaughlin saw that post, he asked me "How could you let such a thing go up on that site about _____?" This is how I could let it go up, Pat, BECAUSE HE IS a pervert, and somebody f*cking needs to do something about it...

At the end of my 3rd year teaching at the school, my accounting students won the NYC Stock Market Game sponsored by SIFMA. This is no small feat. We beat 1450 teams and were featured in the Daily News, and on the radio news shows in NY. I was temporarily a superstar among the administration. Later, when all the shit went down with my website, teachers were instructed to spread a rumor that I had paid off SIFMA to win. Wow, you guys are loooooowwwww... attack me all you want, but to diminish the efforts of brilliant graduates at your school, that's beyond shitty.

At the beginning of my 4th year working there, I had an idea for a website. I wanted a venting site that people could go to and let off steam. With the recession in the U.S., people were angry. I was going to call it Burnandrotinhell.com, like tell all your troubles to Burn and rot in hell! It was actually my wife's idea to call it that, because that's what she says about things that piss her off. I thought it was a great idea. I asked the Dean of Women, Carolyn Szostek, if I could do such a thing. I asked her because we were friends and she was also the principal's right hand person. She was all in - 150%. She was made an administrator on my facebook fan page. I have her handwriting on my terms of use, which she reviewed and made suggestions about. Her daughter researched copyright issues for me. When I found out I was going to be interviewed about it on the radio, I asked if I should let the principal know. She said "No, it's not necessary."

She knew I had told some graduates and current students about the site and she didn't have a problem with it. I was not hiding anything. I talked about it openly with faculty and staff (right Ms. V?). I asked the school priest if it was ok to use that name for the site since I worked in a Catholic school. He said it was fine.

Months later, when the website was up and running, kids started posting about their experiences at the school. I was also inundated with Facebook messages from students, past and present, asking for help. Atrocious, egregious, and inexplicable situations at the school were coming to light.

The Assistant Principal Patrick McLaughlin called me in to his office. He said he didn't care about the website but wanted the Bad Teachers and Bad Students sections taken down. The rest could stay. I said I wouldn't do it. He said "Why, because it's good for business?" This man should really be the last one talking about business ethics.

The Principal, Br. Leonard, met with me. Let me rephrase that - he didn't actually "meet" with me. Patrick McLaughlin called me into an office with the school priest and Principal and they sort of ambushed me. They had their little notepads on their laps. So scary! And gee, Carolyn was nowhere to be found! Why wasn't she there? Br. Leonard said he wanted those two sections of my website down. I said no. I had asked him why it was ok for one of his teachers to be in a YouTube video marching in the gay pride parade in his underwear but it was not ok for me to have my website. Everyone knew about this video, which was a year old, and which teachers made fun of and gossiped about constantly (which is how I found out about it). Brother Leonard Conway lied to me and said that the video had been taken down. He lied right to my face and I knew it! Then I said I wasn't taking down those sections of my site, and he suspended me. Funny, that Dean Carolyn Szostek was not suspended also. They sent me home.

That night, I told most of the world what had happened on Fox News. The next day, the principal's secretary called me and told me that if I did not come in by 2:37 pm to meet with the principal I would be terminated. I knew they were going to ask me to take down my site. I didn't go. I said "terminate me" instead...

I continued to see disturbing posts and receive messages about things going on at the school. Some of this information was posted or sent to me by "the mole." There was someone on the inside who wanted the truth to come out! However, the mole was not someone who worked at the school. The mole was someone who had f*cked someone in the religion department. The mole was a "swinger". Someone who has lots of sex with lots of people. In fact, the mole had sex with about 1/2 of Prep's female population, both married and unmarried. These swingers meet at a specific bar in Queens and "hook up." (I know which one, I have checked it out, but I won't tell you which one it is. Let them have their fun.)The mole went by the name Angel Amore. Every bit of information he sent me checked out. He told me how to contact graduates who had been sexually harassed by their teachers, and boys who had been grabbed and kissed by the Franciscan Brothers. He gave me info about teachers who had done some naughty things, like loaded porn on school computers. I never asked Angel Amore's real name, and I didn't care. As proof of his swinging with the women of Prep, he gave me access to pictures of him having sex with these women who worked there, and a list of names of his conquests. I don't know if these women know they were photographed, so if they didn't before now, surprise from me to you! You're on Amore cam, parked on AIM. You may call Angel a pervert, but I won't. I'm a lesbian and I'm sure a good portion of the country, even in the year 2012, would call me a perve. What Angel and these women do is consensual and private. I won't judge it.

So, there were two accounts of Brothers kissing male students. There were several stories of sexual harassment of female students by teachers. There weres stories of extreme nepotism that were purposely being hidden from the faculty by McLaughlin so as to not create a stir (like the head of the religion department hiring her niece and niece's fiance to teach in her department), and there is much more.

There was one post on my website made by a student who had written an article for the school paper about why students should not be forced to wear leather shoes. The premise of the article was that St. Francis was an animal advocate and he wouldn't approve. This student's story was quashed by the administration - too controversial. I am an animal advocate and this, combined with everything else, just about sent me over the edge. Teachers apparently can do basically anything they want at Prep but a student there can't question in a newspaper article whether it is a good policy for students to only wear leather shoes? Does that seem a little unfair to you?

Threats came on the phone and in the mail telling me to take the posts down. A friend of Joey Diamonds' posted on my site about taking the posts about his true identity down. In the process "Michelle DeRosalito" confirmed (accidentally?) his identity. The posts stayed up. Time went by. I received more threats. Ones I got in the mail were more scary because they always have that "I know where you live" overtone. I got nervous about my family's safety, and the posts came down.

Ironically, just a few days ago a post went up on my website from the administration, faculty and staff wishing me a Merry Christmas and peace in my heart. Really? I find this amusing. I wonder what precipitated that, almost two years after I "was terminated." Be assured, I do have peace in my heart. You can have peace when you know you are pursuing justice. I now know all the things you've covered up, Administration, and I know I provide a vehicle to bring these issues to light. Hopefully someone in a position of authority will see this - the Pope maybe? - and do something about it.

I have been asked by those closest to me what result I am hoping for from all this now. I only want what will keep children safe. So I guess I want the administration replaced. All of them, every single one. Nothing will change until that happens. I like change, change is good.

I am still so very proud of this blog. I am proud because it was the first time, ever, that someone stood up publicly to the incompetent administration running St. Francis Prep and exposed their bullshit in print.

This was the first of dozens of blogs I would write over the next two and a half years. I released the Kraken, and it was a very good thing.

CHAPTER ELEVEN
MS. MOORADIAN, AGAIN

Just keep blogging, just keep blogging, just keep blogging…

That was the thought running through my head after my first St. Francis Prep scandal blog went viral. There was a lot of truth to be told, and I was going to tell it. I released a new blog every few days from that point for about a month. There was no way I was stopping.

I had committed to this despite the fact it had become apparent to me and many others that I had haters. Huge haters, who wanted to say disgusting things to me and try to humiliate me. Here are some examples of comments made on the "I am EC" blog:

> tony cucionota December 27, 2012 at 1:46 AM
> Dayummm…sfpalum SFP speaks the truth. RESPECT mah niggah.
> Shut your mouth you lesbian slut

That's a great one, isn't it? Someone thought creating a Google Plus profile with a variation of my maiden surname and posting something like this was clever. It's a little scary what schools turn out these days…

Another hater:

> SFP Defenders December 27, 2012 at 2:01 AM
> I am digusted by reading these complete lies that you are making up
> about this wonderful institution. The fact that people came to you and

told you this information is total bullshit. You were a nobody at that school and a shitty communications teacher. Thats just a joke class that no one cares about. You think they care about letting you go? Any idiot could teach that subject. I find it unbelievable that a nobody like you at that school could come across such info like this when no one else in the school had ever even mentioned anything like this. I dont care what the hell happened to you in the 80s, those are probably lies as well. The principals at prep have no problem approaching people who are harmful to the school environment because thats why they fired your ass. I find it amusing how you are coming out with all of this wonderful info now. It probably took u two years to make all of this shit up. SFP should sue u for all this garbage that u are putting on this site.

There's just no words for disputing something as stupid as this. Did this person really think the administration would walk around the building telling the student body how many pedophiles they were aware of?

It was hard to take sometimes. But, I am happy to say, for every jerk like the ones above, there was someone who knew the truth and wanted to keep it coming:

Brit MetalQueen December 27, 2012 at 4:20 PM
I'm an SFP Alumnus as well, but I'm not going to hold onto the school like it's precious and as if its staff could do no wrong. I got a great education there, and I made a few friends, but many students and staff there are bad people. I can only be thankful that I didn't buy into religion and was already an agnostic, because this school's example of corruption and politics within religion would have confused the hell out of me. We all knew about at least SOME of the shit that was going on. You're either a liar or an idiot if you act like SFP is a paradise of no wrong actions. I'm tired of the naivety and I'm tired of the wrongdoings going on - financially, sexually, morally, ethically, etc. Good for you for getting this info out there at some point. Late is better than never, and of course SFP would want to make it look as if you made this all up because of your termination. Of course the Ultimate Prom thing was fixed. I remember when Graziella won when Suzy won the votes, but it was said that she was too weak to go and that it would be too much of a shock for her. REALLY, SFP, REALLY? And I can attest to Brother Ben asking cheerleaders to do splits for extra credit. If I can attest to that, I can only imagine that at least some of this other stuff is true. I'm not saying this post is full of lies, but I'm not saying it has to be all 100% true. We don't really know, do we?

If you are an alumnus or current student of SFP, the least you can do is be realistic and keep an open mind to this stuff. You can't be that stupid and think everyone who ever stepped foot in SFP is a damn saint. Just because it's a Catholic school, that doesn't mean they practice what they preach. Stop being naïve or burn and rot in hell.

And someone like this:

Jezebel Valenzano January 4, 2013 at 3:41 PM
Seriously? really?
I graduated 1986.. Stenger smacked a student in front of me and threw a chair because he was after third bell. Buddha threw numerous chairs across the room in cor to get to a kid and pin him against a wall. I was told to wear a short skirt and a low cut blouse to drivers ed to pass. I was bullied beyond belief in Prep: my locker being broken into and pants having the crotch cut out, my diary being stolen and read by the football team, thrown into garbage bins, I could go on and on. My mother was called in and told that if I was more normal, I wouldn't have trouble and the culprits of everything were never even asked about it. Football players who cheated (three copied the same paper, two were given C's so they could play, and one an A because he changed one sentence). It was 4 years of hell.

What I was discovering was that the alumni defending St. Francis Prep seemed a lot like Scientologists – people with blinders on who drank the Kool-Aid because someone told them it would be good for them. They were loyal to this school and calling me a liar despite the fact other people were sharing their own horrific experiences. I recently heard from someone who went to Penn State that many Penn alumni still don't believe that Jerry Sandusky is a child molester and that Joe Paterno knew what was happening and stood by and watched it happen. But I know this: Sandusky is in prison and the deceased Paterno's statue is down. All revelations of this magnitude take time. In January, 2013, I was just at the beginning of a journey that would change the course of history in Catholic education.

By January 4th, 2013, I had written five blogs, all exposing different examples of what I considered corruption and extraordinarily poor judgment by the Prep administration, including the phony grading system and using students as security guards. On that day I received a special Facebook message. This message was from a friend of mine from St. Sebastian (Elementary) School in Woodside, New York who had attended St. Francis Prep with me in the 80's. He sent me a letter being distributed by Brother Leonard Conway.

Here it is:

As we begin 2013, we have much to be thankful for in our St. Francis Prep community. At the core of our community, we are blessed by a dedicated faculty and administration. Year-after-after, our teachers and administrators make it possible for SFP to maintain the highest standards of Franciscan Catholic secondary education. We are most grateful for our students, who work so hard to fulfill their personal potential, as well as our spiritual and academic mission. They do so with passion, regardless of whether they are in chapel, in the class room, in our surrounding community, or on the athletic field. We also remain indebted to and thankful for our supportive parents. Without their sacrifice and trust, we would not be able to succeed in spreading St. Francis' message of peace.

It is also important for us to remember that while we will always be accepting of those who respectfully choose not to support our mission, we will not stand still when someone or something seeks to unjustly harm our community. Nearly two years ago, SFP dismissed a teacher when she refused to discontinue her involvement in a public web site that encouraged bullying, and that contained content that is wholly contrary to and in conflict with the SFP mission. Over the Christmas vacation, I received several disturbing emails from members of our community stating that the content of numerous recent "blog" postings on that internet site are defamatory and have crossed over the line of free speech.

We are investigating those postings and evaluating all available responsive action with the assistance of legal counsel. Please know that SFP will pursue all appropriate remedial action in order to protect our mission and the members of our SFP community. I ask that you also remain mindful that, just as the First Amendment protects freedom of speech, it also ensures the free exercise of religion.

In the interim, I kindly request that anyone with further information about this matter to contact me or Pat McLaughlin without delay. We will investigate this matter fully, fairly and in conformity with our established policies and practices. As always, our policy and operational decisions will be made to ensure that SFP will remain a trusted institution for the education of the soul, as well as the mind and the body.

SFP's mission will always be rooted in the good news of the Gospels and St. Francis' message of love, dignity, respect and forgiveness. Speech is not "free" when its purpose is to bully, to convey hatred, or to spread malicious lies and unsubstantiated rumors. Please remember that, as a member of our community, you must resist participating in or assisting the spread of invective speech. There is no place at SFP for actions or communications that detract from that mission, that prevent the liberation of the soul, or that create an impression, real or perceived, that SFP's mission is disingenuous or may be compromised in any way.

I wish you all the best in 2013 and may the Blessings of St. Francis always be with you.

Sincerely,

Bro. Leonard

Principal, St. Francis Prep

This letter was sent out to Prep's fifteen to thirty thousand living alumni, and also posted on their Facebook fan page, which, at that time, had five thousand fans. This part of the letter was especially interesting to me: "Speech is not "free" when its purpose is to bully, to convey hatred, or to spread malicious lies and unsubstantiated rumors... There is no place at SFP for actions or communications that detract from that mission, that prevent the liberation of the soul, or that create an impression, real or perceived, that SFP's mission is disingenuous or may be compromised in any way."

They insinuated that I am a liar, and I was angry. I was angry because they knew I was telling the truth and this was obviously an attempt to scare me by making me think they would sue me for defamation.

Well, I didn't buy it. I didn't buy it because truth is an absolute defense to a defamation claim. I told myself they could go screw themselves. Now, I committed to the universe that I would make sure everyone knew every ounce of the unfettered truth about the school.

I called them out about that letter they posted about me in a blog I titled "Defamation for Dummies". I also intimated that I could sue them. The next day, Prep removed that letter from their Facebook page. A bully always backs down when you stand up to them.

On January 7, 2013, all hell broke loose again. However, it had nothing to do with me. On that day, it went public in national news that a religion teacher fired by St. Francis Prep had filed a wrongful termination suit against the school. This teacher was Mark Krolikowski. When I say "was," I really mean "was," because Mark became Marla Krolikowski. After thirty-two years of teaching at St. Francis Prep, Mark was fired for being transgender.

The alumni were in an uproar over this, and rightfully so. The newspaper article in the New York Post said that an administrator allegedly called Mark "worse than gay." When I read that, I could not help but think it was Patrick McLaughlin who said it. As I mentioned previously, his wife had left him for a woman, and I could see bitterness over that having easily been redirected toward Mark.

I knew Mark not just from working with him, but from my student days. Mark had been a very popular teacher when I was attending SFP, young and hip with a haircut like 80's Bono from U2. A lot of my friends thought he was hot. In 2011, Mark was just as popular among the students, trusted and a good, supportive ear when they needed one. I was just as disgusted as everyone else that he, now a she, had been terminated.

I decided to check out the St. Francis Prep Alumni Facebook page to see what graduates were saying there about Mark/Marla. Let me clarify something for you: The school moderates and operates its official Facebook page, but a graduate of the class of 2009 moderates and operates the alumni Facebook page. This would, over the coming months, be a major thorn in the school's side, because the alumni page was not a forum the school could control. In fact, I would learn shortly that they had zero control over it. This was a school that was used to controlling everything and everyone, and now they had lost control on all fronts. It could only get worse for them, and I knew it, and on some level, they knew it.

As I expected, alumni were posting their outrage about the Marla Krolikowski firing. I decided to chime in. This was my first time posting on the school's alumni page ever, and it was an almost unbelievable feeling to have that kind of direct access to this particular audience. The power of social media was fully present, and welcomed by me.

It occurred to me – if the alumni page moderator permitted, I could talk to alumni directly through this forum and get my message of corruption and child sexual harassment and abuse out even more. That same day, I wrote a blog discussing my disgust at the firing of Marla Krolikowski, but also conveying the fact that I was not the least bit surprised by the administration's decision. I also included some damning comments directed toward the school made on my website and blog. I posted the blog on the alumni page, and waited for it to be taken down. But it wasn't. The moderator left it there. That simple fact let me know he knew I was telling the truth, or at least believed in exploring it. From that day forward, I would use the alumni page so much to post my blogs and express my viewpoint on various Prep matters that the faculty and staff began calling it Liz's website. It was just too funny.

Within a few days, my Facebook posts were the source of major controversy among the alumni. Some people hated me, and some people loved me. But it was clearly either/or, with no one in between. Some alumni threatened me, and called me all sorts of horrible things, including "noisy cow." I began receiving many hang up calls from blocked phone numbers on both my unlisted home number and cell phone, and several attempts were made to hack my personal email accounts. Someone even looked up my place of employment on the internet, and emailed my boss stating that I am a "hate blogger" and should be fired. I became concerned for my safety. These SFP Zealots, as I would come to call them, were truly crazy.

I felt that first and foremost, I needed to protect the information I had gathered. The guaranteed survival of the information protected my family from lawsuits, and likewise I thought that if the right people had it, it would protect us from bodily harm.

But whom should I give it to? The police were out of the question. I am not bashing cops, but I do know that the force in New York, at least, has a large group of Prep alumni who love their school. I felt I couldn't trust them. I decided to take another route. I uploaded all the information I had gathered to the secret servers hosted by the vigilante group Anonymous. I uploaded it with a note asking that they please hold on to this information because I felt that my family's safety was possibly in jeopardy, and that there had been several attempts to hack my email accounts to obtain it. I felt better almost immediately, like I had taken power from the evil villain.

Then, something else happened, right out of the blue, and frankly, it was the last thing I expected.

Felicia Mooradian sent me a Facebook message.

I hadn't heard from her in twenty-one months. For twenty-one months I had wondered how she was, how she was coping with her aunt's illness, and what exactly happened with Brother Ben.

This is what she said:

> "Hi there- just wanted to say you are AMAZING and I love the burn site and the blogs and you deserve credit. That A--- kid is such an ass, pardon my French. He did a good thing and now it's all about the ego. You rule and I hope the information keeps coming. I hated my 4 years at Prep. My hat goes off to you."

I answered:

> "Oh my god, I am so happy to hear from you Felicia! I often think about what you're thinking about all this. I am so appreciative of your support. I am doing everything I can to get the administration to resign. I am hopeful we're getting closer to that...
>
> I am not going to stop, until something happens, whatever it is. My family and good people like you support me and that's all I need.
>
> Thanks again! Please feel free to friend request me if you want. No pressure, just if you want.
>
> I will keep you posted though, no matter what. I am getting a lot of threats, it is really getting on my nerves..."

Felicia and I traded phone numbers and began talking, and talking, and talking some more.

Prep was not going to be happy. Felicia's aunt had died, and she was now forward-thinking. She realized her negative experiences with Brother Ben and other teachers at Prep actually gave her the power to try and change things for the better.

Try she would.

CHAPTER TWELVE

FELICIA'S FRESHMAN YEAR: BROTHER BEN

Felicia never wanted to go to St. Francis Prep until the day she received her acceptance letter in the mail. For some reason the school had always rubbed her the wrong way. She grew up regaled with anecdotes from her uncle, an accomplished man and someone she deeply respected, who credited St. Francis Prep with his success. He had told her many times he walked into the school a scrawny, academically floundering, socially-awkward kid, and that all the right teachers had taken him under their wings, shown him some kindness, and shaped him into a well-educated, charismatic man by the time he graduated in 1984. So goes the story of many a graduate of St. Francis Prep, but Felicia never bought it. She always had the impression that the school was creepy in an incestuous cult-like way, and until the acceptance letter came, she had wanted no part of it. She says now that she should have gone with her instincts, but as frequently happens, God had other plans for her.

Felicia attended public school in Queens from kindergarten through eighth grade. She was a star student, having made it into the Magnet program for gifted children in middle school. As junior high came to an end and chatter of high schools started, Felicia was fully intent on going with her friends to Francis Lewis, a local public high school down the road from St. Francis Prep.

It was Felicia's mother, seeing the potential she had and wanting the best for her, who had convinced Felicia to apply to St. Francis Prep. Consequently, Felicia took the Catholic high school entrance exam and listed St. Francis Prep as her first choice.

A few months later, an envelope from St. Francis Prep came in the mail. Felicia and her mother tore into it together. She remembers reading the letter out loud, her eyes drawn to the bold, italicized lettering in the middle of the page: "You have been awarded a full, four-year scholarship…" Felicia and her mother were ecstatic. Validation from a prestigious school will do that to a child. At that moment, despite Felicia's gut feelings, the decision to accept was made.

Felicia says that as of that moment, everything about St. Francis Prep was suddenly appealing to her. Gaining entrance had earned her the respect of her family, and it was to be a fresh start after all those years of public education. She daydreamed about having a locker and making friends and meeting inspirational teachers. Nine Septembers later, she would be referring to the institution as "St. Francis Predatory School" in the New York Post. It breaks my heart.

Her uncle was there the day Felicia started at Prep, passing the proverbial torch to his niece, hopeful that she would emerge another lifelong loyalist of the school. When she arrived home after that very first day, she called her uncle, and listed her teachers for him. Felicia says he didn't know most of them, but her Spanish teacher, Brother Ben O'Reilly, struck a nerve. "Watch out for that Brother Ben," he had said, "he likes the pretty girls." 2005 was a long way from 1984, she had thought, and so she didn't give much credence to her uncle's comment. She would learn the hard way.

Brother Ben took an immediate liking to Felicia. I have seen Felicia's pictures from her freshman year. Although she was a child, you could already see the beautiful woman she would become. She was a naive freshman in an advanced, rowdy sophomore class, and she was fluent in Spanish, which made her the prime candidate for teacher's pet. And she says that's all it was, for a while. Brother Ben called on her a lot, he complimented her frequently, and her grades were wonderful. Brother Ben, funny, witty, and charming, had long gained her trust by the time she began to notice his behavior transitioning from innocuous to inappropriate. It happened gradually, as is often the case with men who prey on girls. The pats on the shoulder became squeezes, the occasional eye-contact became long, lascivious gazes, the compliments shifted from academic praise to outright flirtation. Still, Felicia tried to dismiss this behavior with all the denial her fourteen year-old self could conjure until the truth was indisputable. She realized that Brother Ben was a lech sometime in March, 2006. While his students were watching a video, Brother Ben remarked that a woman in the film was attractive. His quip drew the usual "ooooh," of the adolescent class. Without missing a beat, Brother Ben smirked, turned to Felicia's desk and said quite loudly, "You can be on a diet, but you can still look at the menu." That was a defining moment for Felicia - she knew what was happening, but not what she should do.

Unfortunately, Felicia was no stranger to predators when she started at St. Francis Prep. She had been sexually abused by a friend of the family (unbeknownst to her parents) from the time she was eleven. It was still going on when she was a freshman at Prep. By the time she was fourteen, she knew very well the game child predators played. She was no teacher's pet; she perceived herself as a prospective victim being groomed. This sweet, young girl had walked into St. Francis Prep with a target on her back.

High school should have been an escape from the secret Felicia was carrying in silence. It should have been fun and free of worry. She should have been thinking about her hair and what to do on the weekend with her friends, and not some creepy old horny Franciscan Brother. I wish I could turn back the clock for her.

A few weeks after the "menu" remark, the last straw came for Felicia. It was lunchtime in Brother Ben's class. At Prep, the different grades ate at separate times. If you were a freshman in a sophomore class, you were stuck with the sophomores, which meant sitting alone. Brother Ben seized the opportunity to invite Felicia to his classroom, alone, while the rest of the class went away to lunch. She reluctantly obliged. Brother Ben asked her to take a seat next to him at his desk in the empty classroom. He had invited her, he said, to listen to a few love songs in Spanish. Brother Ben liked to use music to help with language acquisition, and he said that he wanted Felicia's opinion as to which song would work best for the class. Yeah, right. Ok.

Felicia says that before Brother Ben played his CD, he grasped her hands in his. He looked into her eyes and, coming quite close to her face, said, "You know, Felicia," (as he passed a thumb over her knuckle), "my goal in life is to give you pleasure." Stunned, nauseous, and confused, Felicia left his classroom and resolved that she would report Brother Ben to the administration of St. Francis Prep.

And she did.

CHAPTER THIRTEEN

FELICIA'S FRESHMAN YEAR, PART TWO: THE ART TEACHER

Felicia had become close friends with another freshman (let's call her Ann), in Brother Ben's class. Felicia confided in Ann, via in-class note-passing (as teenagers do), that she was preparing to report Brother Ben to the St. Francis Prep administration for sexually harassing her. After some back and forth, Ann revealed to Felicia that she, too, was experiencing inappropriate conduct from a younger art teacher. According to Ann, this twenty-eight year old man had begun sending her sexually explicit online messages. Ann told Felicia these messages included asking her whether she liked to masturbate, informing her that he was masturbating during their conversations, and sharing his experiences with the drug known as ecstasy. Ann insisted to Felicia that she did not want to report him, but Felicia felt obligated to protect her friend.

I want to say right now, this is Felicia's nature. She is a protector of those more vulnerable. She protects people, she protects animals, and if you, reader, called her today and told her you needed help with some awful situation that was thrust upon you through no fault of your own, she would help you, too. It was for this reason Ann told Felicia about this man, and it is for this reason the universe picked her to assist me in exposing decades of corruption at St. Francis Prep. The universe is wise, and it always knows the fastest way to solve any problem, if you trust it and does what it suggests.

74

After hearing Ann's story, Felicia turned to the teacher she trusted most: her cool, down-to-earth, funny religion teacher, Sue Vivona. At the end of class, Felicia approached Sue and asked her "Do you know Ann?" Sue nodded yes. "She's being sexually harassed, if not worse, by _____," Felicia informed her. Felicia told me Sue's eyes filled with tears. She was obviously gravely concerned. Sue told Felicia that she would report the situation to Patrick McLaughlin, who was then the assistant principal. Felicia also blurted out that Brother Ben was a problem, too, but Sue, who was consumed with the situation regarding the art teacher, dismissed it. "A Brother would never do that," Sue told her.

Later that day, Felicia found herself sitting next to Sue in McLaughlin's office. Felicia's heart was pounding and she was sick to her stomach as she told him the whole sordid story. It is Felicia's perception that McLaughlin did not seem surprised, or even the least bit fazed, by what Felicia was saying. In all fairness, though, perhaps it was just the blank stare McLaughlin usually carried on his face. I'm going out on a limb her to say that probably was the case, because Felicia says throughout the session he simply punctuated Felicia's statements with, "Oh, boy" and no other commentary. This meeting concluded with McLaughlin assuring Felicia that while he had an obligation to protect his employees and it would be difficult to take any action based on Felicia's word, the matter would be investigated.

Let me stop here for a moment. Do you think that's the way it should be? Do you think that administrators whose reputation may be ruined if they uncover rampant abuse and sexual harassment by their faculty should be the ones conducting these sorts of investigations? What is their motivation for uncovering the truth, if it can irreversibly damage their careers and the school?

The answer is that on a practical level, they have zero motivation to uncover abuse and sexual harassment. This is why the Catholic Church is in big trouble this past decade. The motivation is to always cover it up. Cover it up, because if it gets out, you will lose credibility, lose followers, and lose tuition money.

It's obvious to me that these investigations must be conducted by neutral third parties if we are going to protect children. It's a necessary cost of doing business for private schools. They have no problem taking your tuition money to pay your children's teachers – likewise, they should have no problem using that money to protect them from the bad ones.

Felicia left McLaughlin's office that day and headed straight for the school chapel, where she prayed for a while. She wrote down her name and Ann's name in the prayer intention book and braced herself for the ensuing fallout she knew was inevitable. It was inevitable because she would never back down, no matter what. She accepted it as something she must do. Ben and the art teacher would be dismissed from the school.

Fast forward a few days, and both the art teacher and Brother Ben are still roaming the halls of St. Francis Prep. Brother Ben has begun to act distant and rude towards Felicia. The change isn't subtle; Brother Ben's disdain for Felicia is salient. Imagine that. What do you think caused that shift? Do you think maybe McLaughlin had told Ben about Felicia's complaint against him?

Furious at what seemed like retaliation, Felicia rounded up as many girls who had unsavory experiences with Brother Ben as she could. Felicia instructed the girls to write down everything Brother Ben had done and/or said to them. The large group of girls marched to McLaughlin's office and inundated him, one by one, with disturbing tales of Brother Ben's twisted behavior.

Felicia's parting words to McLaughlin that day were, "Is this enough for you?" She was tough for a 14 year old, and she is tougher now.

It wasn't enough. Brother Ben and the art teacher remained. Ann had begun to grow frantic; the art teacher knew he had been reported and was under investigation, and Ann blamed herself. Instead of staying away from Ann, though, this man was deepening their friendship. Ann told Felicia that they were seeing each other outside of school, which sent Felicia over the edge. Felicia ran back to Sue Vivona to let her know of this development. What she found, though, was a woman whose entire demeanor had changed. Gone was the affable teacher Felicia had grown to trust so much- in her place was a cold, detached woman. Felicia begged her to do something more but was met with, "The wheels are in motion. Let the adults handle it."

The adults who handled it best turned out to be Felicia's parents, who rightfully became fed up with the school's seeming lack of action.

Felicia's father called to speak with McLaughlin regarding Brother Ben. Felicia says that instead of attempting to assuage her father's anger, McLaughlin hung up on him. There was no explanation, no apologies, no formalities- he just hung up the phone. Felicia's mother called back, pleading with McLaughlin to think of his own son in Felicia's situation. McLaughlin relented and agreed to a meeting with Felicia's parents. It was this meeting with McLaughlin and then principal, Brother Leonard Conway, that made all the difference. McLaughlin did not say much, but Brother Leonard was profusely apologetic and even admitted to Felicia's parents that he had repeatedly chastised Brother Ben for his sexually inappropriate conduct, such as asking girls to do splits in their skirts for him. After admitting Brother Ben had a history (bear in mind that McLaughlin's initial response to Felicia's complaint was that her word was not enough), Brother Leonard elected to remove Brother Ben from his classroom pending investigation, and had arranged for Brother Ben to be evaluated by a psychologist in Boston.

Though Brother Ben was removed, Felicia still had Ann's situation to contend with. Another art teacher overheard Ann talking to Felicia about him, and reported what she heard. In addition to what she overheard, this art teacher knew that another member of the department had reported him for being alone with a female student in a dark, closed classroom. In 2014, Felicia found out that yet another teacher had already reported him, long before she had, for bragging that he had his "pick of the litter," among the female students.

After the reporting art teacher corroborated Felicia's report, the alleged predator was finally terminated. As far as Felicia knows, the police were never called. It is important to note that all teachers at St. Francis Prep are mandated reporters, meaning they are mandated by law to report even a suspicion of child abuse. Nobody reported anything, and to this day, this man is free.

The psychologist in Boston eventually determined that Brother Ben O'Reilly was unfit to work with children. Brother Ben never denied the charges against him. Instead, he spun them: his flirtation was his way of, "connecting with the girls." Brother Ben was formally fired, but was permitted to remain living in the monastery on the third floor of St. Francis Prep.

Though Felicia managed to get both Brother Ben and the art teacher out of their teaching positions, she would soon learn her war with the administration was far from over.

CHAPTER FOURTEEN

FELICIA'S FRESHMAN YEAR, PART THREE: MEN ARE FROM MARS, WOMEN ARE FROM VENUS

It didn't take long after the announcement was made that Brother Ben would not be returning to teach that the student body realized it was Felicia who had gotten him fired. While a handful of students were supportive of Felicia, the vast majority were not. Brother Ben had a niece who was, at the time, a senior at St. Francis Prep. Brother Ben's niece was livid that her uncle had been fired, and routinely sent other students to harass and threaten Felicia. The bullying was exacerbated when Brother Ben felt it would be wise to visit his former classroom, where he spoke to his former students and maligned Felicia, calling her "crazy," and accusing her of having, "a vendetta against men." Brother Ben conveniently left out his decades-long reputation and notoriety for sexually harassing girls. In fact, in 2013, a classmate of mine named Lynne Vaccaro O'Leary came out publicly on the St. Francis Prep Facebook alumni page to support Felicia. When she read Felicia's story, she said it was almost exactly, word-for-word, what Brother Ben had done to her in the 80's, twenty years earlier.

As Brother Ben was charming and well-liked by students who didn't know any better, he managed to turn more of Felicia's peers against her. Felicia's mother called the school again, and Brother Leonard made sure that Brother

Ben O'Reilly made no more visits to his old classroom. The bullying, however, did not cease, and McLaughlin suggested that Felicia talk to Robyn Armon, the Director of Guidance, for support.

Upon meeting Robyn, Felicia thought she was fantastic. Robyn was on a first-name basis with the students and appeared to be genuinely concerned with their well-being. Felicia spent some time with Robyn, discussing what had transpired with Brother Ben and the young art teacher. After Robyn had earned her trust, Felicia decided it was time to put a stop to what was happening to her outside of school. Felicia blurted out the truth to Robyn - that a family friend had been abusing her since she was eleven years old. It was the hardest thing Felicia ever had to do in her life. Robyn, instead of comforting Felicia, seemingly turned frigid, as though irritated by Felicia's disclosure. Robyn asked, "Are you going to tell your mother, or am I going to tell her?" Felicia recalls that her tone was matter-of-fact, business as usual, about the worst thing that had ever happened to this little girl. Felicia said nothing. Robyn dialed Felicia's mother and told her, "There is a situation involving your daughter that you need to talk to her about." The end. There was the bomb. Felicia's family would be forever changed. One poorly handled ten-second phone call is all it took. Robyn then sent Felicia back to class, so she could sit there sick to her stomach, knowing that when she got home, she would have to explain an awful situation to her mother with no support network in place. How sensitive.

Robyn, as Director of Guidance, was mandated to report the abuse to New York State. She never did. Felicia was on her own, left to shoulder the bullying over getting Brother Ben removed, with a fractured family to carry. Felicia's parents eventually met with Robyn and they were appalled by Robyn's behavior. Robyn, it seemed to them, couldn't care less about what happened to Felicia. In fact, rather than assisting Felicia's family with pursuing charges against her abuser, Robyn advised Felicia's mother not to bother with the police. Felicia's father was especially disturbed, unable to comprehend that his little girl had been sexually abused. When Felicia came to Robyn asking for advice on how to help her father handle the situation, Robyn pulled out a book: "Men Are from Mars, Women Are from Venus". This was the best the Director of Guidance at America's largest private Catholic high school could offer.

Following the chaos of the end of her freshman year, Felicia fell into a deep depression. As time passed, she developed an eating disorder and dependence on alcohol to cope. Despite this, Felicia was determined not to leave St. Francis Prep. She was on a full scholarship, she had made close friends, and she had done nothing wrong: the adults around her had. Felicia resolved to stick it out. She struggled through her sophomore year and finally began to improve when junior year rolled around. What Felicia didn't know was that her junior year would make her regret ever having met two more teachers: Christopher Mendolia and Fernando Sicilia.

CHAPTER FIFTEEN

DRIVER'S ED

Flash forward and the nightmare of freshman year was two years behind Felicia. Her junior year, she was doing great and looking forward to a bright future. As most juniors do, Felicia signed up for driver's ed with one of her best friends. Felicia and her friend were assigned to Christopher Mendolia, the current Assistant Principal of the school and then Chairperson of the Social Studies Department, for instruction. Christopher Mendolia is one of the few teachers who Felicia says singled her out and embarrassed her for being depressed during her sophomore year. He had been her social studies teacher then and in Felicia's opinion, showed little sympathy for her. As a result, Felicia had disliked him immensely. Connor King, Felicia's best friend and grandson of legendary St. Francis Prep football coach Vince O'Connor, remembers clearly how poorly Mendolia treated Felicia in social studies class to this day. This is how much of an impression it made on him. By junior year, however, Felicia put the past behind her, and assumed that having Mendolia as her driver's ed teacher would be fine.

Felicia says at first, Mendolia was very different from the way he had been in the classroom. He was friendly and eager to chat with the driver's ed students. Felicia and her friend truly enjoyed driver's ed until Mendolia's convivial banter started to stray into more personal topics. It started with questions about which teachers Felicia liked and disliked the most. Then, it was about family. Felicia had a little brother around the same age as Mendolia's daughter and he

81

used this common ground to broaden the scope of their conversations. Felicia says that soon, Mendolia was drawing comparisons between Felicia and his wife.

A few weeks into driver's ed, Felicia's friend convinced her to run for student government. When Mendolia found out that Felicia was running for student government, he told her she should watch a film called "Election", which was, as he put it, "about a girl running for student president who's fooling around with her teacher." That day, Felicia went home and watched "Election". Within ten minutes, there is a scene with a teacher talking about how wet a student's pussy is. In fact, the entire movie is filled with grossly inappropriate content. The plot revolves around a girl, Tracy, running for student president who had an affair with her teacher (who was subsequently fired.) After that teacher is fired, his best friend, a social studies teacher named Mr. M, becomes obsessed with Tracy: he both hates her and fantasizes about having sex with her. The film even includes a scene in which Mr. M is having sex with his wife and fantasizes that his wife is Tracy. Tracy's superimposed head starts telling him, "Fuck me, Mr. M!" Can you imagine Felicia's shock upon watching this film? To Felicia, the parallels between the film's antagonist and Mendolia were more than striking. "Election" is a funny, satirical film – but in my opinion not one that a high school teacher should recommend to a high school student, particularly when the high school student is running for student president and the teacher recommending the film is a social studies teacher named Mr. M.

Felicia told her friends about the movie; they were all appalled. They watched the film several times, in disbelief that a teacher would have the audacity to tell a student to watch it. After what happened to Felicia her freshman year, she was afraid to confront "Mr. M" about the film. She never mentioned it again. Mr. M's behavior, however, allegedly became more overt. Later on that Spring, Felicia's friend had photographed her for an art class. Felicia and her friend were sitting in the back seat, discussing the photographs, which her friend had just developed and was showing to Felicia. Mr. M turned around, asking to see the pictures. (By the way, this transpired while a student was operating the driver's ed vehicle.) Felicia's friend told Mr. M that she didn't think it was a good idea for him to look at the pictures, as they featured Felicia in provocative clothing and poses. Mr. M reached around and snatched the photographs from Felicia's friend's hand. As he was perusing them, (again, with a student driving the car,) Mr. M commented that the photos were, "a little risqué." On another day of driving, Felicia was behind the wheel. She was having trouble accelerating, so she asked Mr. M if she was hitting the gas pedal properly. Allegedly, Mr. M demonstrated how Felicia should hit the gas by grasping her thigh with his hand. On another occasion, as Felicia was driving,

Felicia alleges Mr. M leaned over, brushed back her hair, and commented that she had, "very interesting ears," as he touched one.

Felicia was thrilled when driver's ed was over. However, Felicia never formally reported Mr. M's misconduct to an administrator. She did, however, decide to sue over it years later. Why the wait? Because Felicia was told that long before she ever attended St. Francis Prep, Mendolia had been reported for misconduct. Marla Krolikowski told both Felicia and me that she reported Mendolia multiple times: both for inappropriate behavior in the driver's ed car, and for comments he made to girls in class.

The reason I use the word "allegedly" in the description of events above concerning Christopher Mendolia is that as of January, 2016, these events are still unproven. They are detailed in Felicia's lawsuit complaint, but this case has not gone to trial. I will discuss the specifics of this in coming chapters.

While Mendolia was Felicia's driver's ed teacher, she did confide in another teacher, Fernando Sicilia, about these incidents. Little did she know that Sicilia would turn out to be a bigger jerk than any others she had encountered at St. Francis Prep.

CHAPTER SIXTEEN
WE'D LOVE TO HAVE YOU

Fernando Sicilia was Felicia's music teacher her freshman year. Fernando was a Jack Black kind of guy with long hair, hilarious, and very popular with the students. He was the cool teacher, and many students considered him more of a peer than an authority figure. Felicia enjoyed his class and thought he was a good person. She and Fernando both came from Cuban families, and they shared funny family stories with each other. When Felicia found out at the end of her junior year that Fernando was leaving St. Francis Prep, she was shocked. Fernando told her it was by choice. However, as I recall, there were a lot of rumors surrounding his sudden departure.

Fernando was one of the few men Felicia felt safe with after so many negative experiences with men in the past. She routinely visited him on her free periods to chat. When Felicia heard he was leaving at the end of June that year, she made it a point to stop by his classroom and wish him well.

Prior to Felicia going to visit Fernando this one last time, one of Felicia's savvy male friends had warned her against it. From his own general observations, Felicia's friend suspected insidious motives on Fernando's part. Despite her friend's concerns, Felicia went to visit Fernando anyway. Felicia says that almost immediately she noticed something different about Fernando's demeanor. She says it was like he had gotten the "all clear."

After a brief chat, Fernando was not shy that day in asking for a goodbye hug. Felicia gave it. I believe he was already manipulating the situation, knowing Felicia would feel compelled to please him as he would not be returning. Felicia told me this was no ordinary hug, though. It was a lingering, overpowering hug that Felicia says made her feel uncomfortable. In the moment, Fernando actually said to her, "You smell really good."

What a charmer he was.

Felicia says that's when things took a turn. Fernando sat down in front of Felicia and allegedly told her, "I go to a place where people are really....open.... with their bodies. There's no age requirement, and you're so beautiful. We'd love to have you." Felicia says she was flabbergasted. Did this asshole just invite her to a sex club? Yes, it seems that's exactly what he did. Just to drive the point home to her, Felicia says Fernando continued to intimate that he couldn't stop cheating on his wife.

I hope Fernando is reading this now, and I hope his wife smartened up over the years and left him. He's not fit to lick the dirt from the bottom of Felicia's shoes.

Felicia ran right after this incident to the one man she knew, without a doubt, she could absolutely trust: her English teacher, Nick Paccione, whom Felicia knew well, and whose son she was dating. She told him what happened, and he was enraged. He told her, "I'd like to swing that asshole by his ponytail." I wish he would have. But Felicia begged him not to say anything, because she was terrified of a repeat of her freshman year. To her knowledge, Nick never reported Fernando.

I just want to point out that even though Felicia asked Nick not to say anything, if he did comply with her request, it was the wrong thing for him to do. When a sixteen year-old girl comes to an adult, who is a mandated reporter, telling this adult that a teacher has just invited her to a "place where people are really open with their bodies", the adult has the responsibility to report it. All teachers in New York, whether at public or private schools, are mandated reporters. M-A-N-D-A-T-E-D. It does not matter what the sixteen year-old girl wants you to do; you do what you have to do. Nick should have told her, "I have to report this. I know you're scared, and I will protect you, but it is my job to report this."

Fernando is still a teacher and of course able to live his life in whichever way he chooses.

So much for mandated reporting.

CHAPTER SEVENTEEN

ENTER KEVIN MULHEARN, ATTORNEY AT LAW

I t is so strange how events unfolded through this journey, that I could not help but think the universe was guiding me along the way. I felt very strongly soon after I published the "I am EC" blog that I was protected by a higher power. This feeling only got stronger over time, as stranger and stranger things kept happening. I never believed in coincidences, and I still don't. The collective unconscious wants what it wants, and sometimes the only thing you can and should do is go with the flow.

The popularity of my Prep scandal blogs had spread, and by the end of January, 2013, old friends my family had not heard from for a while had contacted us to give us their support. One of these friends was one of my wife's former coworkers. She suggested I take some kind of legal action against the school for all the harm they caused children over the years. She told Jo that there was an attorney who handled a very big win against Poly Prep Country Day School in Brooklyn, and perhaps I should contact him.

This attorney is Kevin Mulhearn, and he is a very good man.

Twelve men had hired Kevin to represent them in a lawsuit against Poly Prep stemming from sexual abuse they suffered decades ago when they were molested and raped by now deceased star football coach Phil Foglietta. I read the background of the cases online, and what Kevin accomplished in court was a miracle. The statute of limitations for school sexual abuse cases in New York expires when the victim turns twenty-three. This is the harshest statute of limitations in the country, and it is absolutely disgusting. The reason I am so vehement about this is because I have come to learn that many abuse victims cannot even accept that they were abused until decades after the abuse occurred. Many block it out, and only experiences they have later in life begin to trigger their repressed memories. This obviously is a defense mechanism to the emotional pain they experienced when they were abused. Age twenty-three is still a baby in my eyes. When I was twenty-three I was mature in some ways and not in others, and I had not yet begun to deal with my own emotional baggage from my childhood. I cannot even imagine the amount of courage it takes to confront child sexual abuse head on and actively choose to pursue one's legal rights in one's early twenties.

Why is the statute of limitations so strict in New York? This is a very simple answer: the Catholic lobby groups. The lobbyists will do anything to stop the Church from going bankrupt because of clergy abuse, and so they pour millions of dollars into political campaigns to prevent this.

I am of the mindset that the Church and Catholic schools should be held accountable for years of purposely neglecting the safety of children by moving child molesters around from place to place, over and over again. WWJD? Seriously, what would Jesus do? Would he tell the Catholic hierarchy it's acceptable to hide from the consequences their actions caused, or would he flip over the altar in St. Patrick's Cathedral and tell Cardinal Dolan he's an asshole?

Kevin Mulhearn's genius found a way around this statute of limitations. That was the miracle I refer to above. He carved his own exception to the statute by applying principles of equity, or fairness. He made a plea to the court that the statute of limitations for child sexual abuse should not apply when a school actively covered up the abuse.

I took my wife's friend's advice and called Kevin. I explained who I am, and what I discovered about Prep. He asked me a few questions to verify that I wasn't a crank, like "What famous people graduated from St. Francis Prep?" I listed a handful for him, and he seemed satisfied with that. He also told me his father had graduated from Prep, and that he was very interested in what I had to say. I directed him to the "I am EC" blog, and he told me he would read it and call me back.

He called me the next day. He started our conversation by saying he was somewhat in shock. Apparently, six months earlier, he had received an email regarding the deceased St. Francis Prep social studies teacher/football moderator Robert Stenger. If you recall, Carolyn Szostek had told me years earlier that Stenger "liked to touch the boys." The email Kevin received detailed how Stenger would lure boys down to the gym in his basement and make them dress in women's underwear or Speedos, and molest them.

That confirmed for Kevin that I was telling the truth. He said he would help me any way he could.

I told him about Felicia, and what had happened with Brother Ben. Initially we were thinking her case could fit under the sexual abuse statute of limitations, which was age 23. Felicia had just turned 21 the previous November, so she would have plenty of time to file. The difficulty we encountered, however, was that Brother Ben never actually touched her anywhere except her hands. He came close to touching his nose to her face, but he never actually did it. So the abuse angle was not going to work, even though so many of the things he said to Felicia were revolting.

I suggested to Kevin that we pursue a sexual harassment angle instead. This was going to be more complicated. Felicia couldn't actually sue the school for sexual harassment – she would have to sue them for being negligent for keeping Brother Ben as a teacher when they knew he had a history of sexually harassing girls. This cause of action is called negligent retention. The statute of limitations for that is three years from the end of the harassment. This brought the statute of limitations to the late Spring of 2009. However, here we were in February, 2013 – how could we get around this?

In New York, a minor can toll the statute of limitations until they reach the state age of majority. So we were clear until November, 2012, when Felicia turned twenty-one. That left us three months past the deadline.

Kevin's initial reaction was that filing for Felicia was a lost cause. However, Felicia and I had spoken so often about all she had been through emotionally in the years that followed her experiences with Brother Ben, I thought perhaps I could find a loophole. I began to research statute of limitations tolling for temporary insanity. In New York, the relevant statute provides "that where a person is under a disability of "insanity" at the time his cause of action accrues, the limitations period in a personal injury action will be extended to three years after the disability ceases." Could this buy us an extra few months?

Kevin thought it could work, and he took her case. This was just the beginning of St. Francis Prep's long legal battle with what Kevin called "The Three-Headed Monster."

CHAPTER EIGHTEEN
THREE-HEADED MONSTER

Things were moving very quickly. I kept blogging, and graduates and teachers were sending me more and more information every day. I was working with Felicia on a daily basis to get her lawsuit in order, and Kevin had suggested to me that I file a defamation claim against St. Francis Prep for that letter they had published about me insinuating that I am a purposeful, malicious liar.

I want to reiterate this particular point, because a lot of the Kool-Aid drinkers who think they know what they are talking about have called me a money-hungry so-and-so because I decided to sue the school: It was not my idea. It was Kevin's idea. It had not even occurred to me to sue the school. My only concern at this point was helping Felicia. However, Kevin told me from an objective eye, what the school had done to me by publishing that letter to their alumni base was awful and I should pursue my rights.

I gave it a lot of thought, and decided he was right about that. Sending that letter out, knowing that I was telling the truth wasn't exactly "Franciscan." It was, truly awful. The people running that place are loathsome creatures and hypocrites. I decided I would file, and show them clearly that they can't just say whatever they want about someone, and not suffer consequences for it.

This is exactly why St. Francis Prep had gotten away with so much over the years. They had never suffered consequences for their actions. Felicia and I had made up our minds to stop that pattern. The era of non-accountability and insulation from public scrutiny would end with us. We would push for change until it happened. Guaranteed.

The more I came to know Felicia, the more I was amazed at the similarities in our personalities. We often say we are the same person. I cannot possibly convey how true this actually is. We have the same thought process, the same Scorpio intuitive nature. We both go with our gut instincts even when our head says otherwise. We both value the same qualities in people. We both are too trusting, and we give the benefit of the doubt when we shouldn't. We both learned lessons the hard way and believe that what doesn't kill you makes you stronger.

Felicia is the 23 year old version of me, that's for sure. However, I personally think Felicia will be a much better person than I am, stronger, and much wiser when she is my age. She will be much kinder, much more patient, and a bigger force to be reckoned with than I ever will be. You can put your money on that.

While both Felicia and I were getting on board with Kevin as clients, I decided to blog about him, just to make the school employees and alumni base aware of his existence, and let them know he was another pair of eyes watching. This is what I said:

> This has been a long road, and it has taught me many things about myself. One very important thing I have learned is, that I want to be a woman who finishes what she starts, and sees things through to the end. So in this regard, let me introduce you to attorney Kevin Mulhearn.
>
> Kevin is a smart man, a dedicated man, and a good man. Most importantly, he believes in putting the welfare of children first, and seeking justice, even when the odds are stacked against him. Last year, after a three year battle, he won settlements for a dozen men, who when they were boys, were molested by a coach at Kevin's alma mater, Poly Prep in Brooklyn. Kevin recently filed an abuse lawsuit on behalf of a former student of Yeshiva University's High School for Boys in Manhattan as well.
>
> Kevin is now officially examining a large amount of issues related to alleged misconduct at St. Francis Prep. When I sent Kevin some of the documentation I carefully amassed over the past two years, he could not say no. Ironically, someone had contacted Kevin about the former St. Francis Prep teacher and child predator Robert Stenger, months before I even knew Kevin's name. So when I sent Kevin the information I had about Stenger, he was not surprised at all.
>
> Kevin was recently sent an email by a former student at St. Francis Prep who had been horribly sexually harassed by a teacher. I was

cc'd on this email. It is the kind of stuff you see in movies, but you don't think would actually happen. It is the kind of stuff you don't want to believe could happen because it is so disturbing. It is sad, and upsetting, but it is reality. Now something has to be done about it...

As for me, I am taking a bit of a break from blogging. I am dedicating my attention to helping Kevin work through all the information I have for him. There is a lot and it is going to take some time. However, if something irritates me enough that I feel I have to say something, you should know by now that I will.

That break from blogging lasted three days. It only lasted that long because in preparing my and Felicia's documentation for Kevin, I came across the school's child sexual abuse and harassment reporting policy in their faculty handbook, and I felt I needed to share it. Here's what I said:

I know I said I was taking a break from blogging, and I will. I just had to publish this though because it is actually a perfect example of the hypocrisy I have been blogging about. There will be more very public examples of this hypocrisy soon, but for now just read this.

This is Section E-12 from St. Francis Prep's Faculty Handbook, and it discusses Child Abuse. The link is: http://www.sfponline.org/docs/FacultyHandbook.pdf

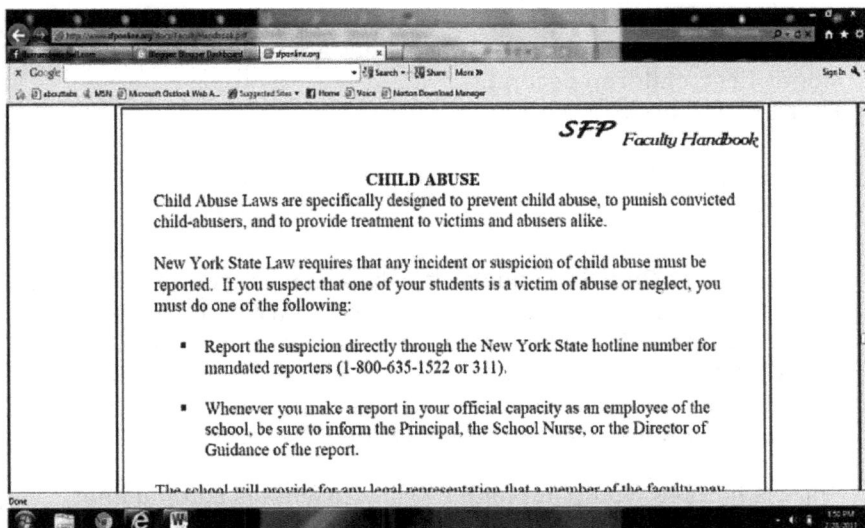

SFP Faculty Handbook

CHILD ABUSE

Child Abuse Laws are specifically designed to prevent child abuse, to punish convicted child-abusers, and to provide treatment to victims and abusers alike.

New York State Law requires that any incident or suspicion of child abuse must be reported. If you suspect that one of your students is a victim of abuse or neglect, you must do one of the following:

- Report the suspicion directly through the New York State hotline number for mandated reporters (1-800-635-1522 or 311).

- Whenever you make a report in your official capacity as an employee of the school, be sure to inform the Principal, the School Nurse, or the Director of Guidance of the report.

The school will provide for any legal representation that a member of the faculty may

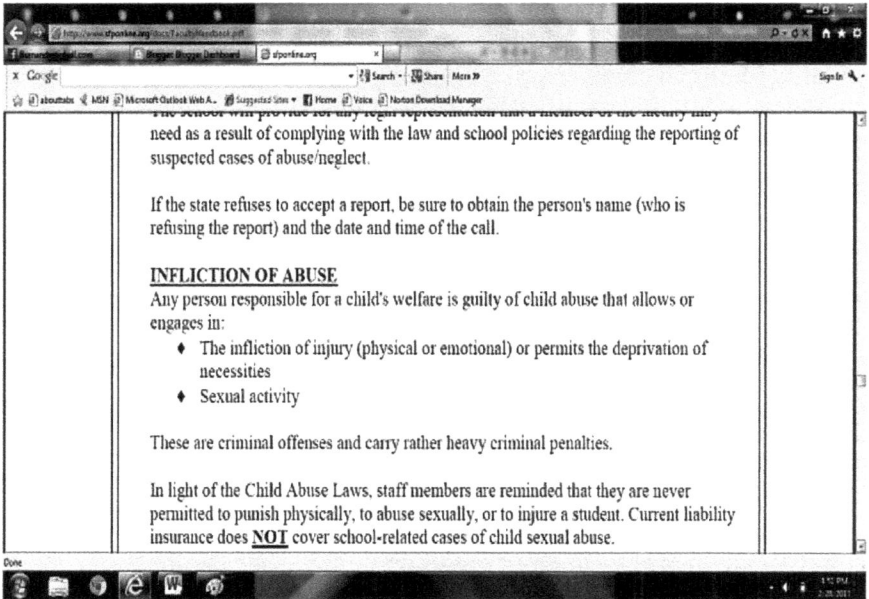

All staff members are REMINDED that they may never sexually abuse a child? And wait, here's the important reason why...because their INSURANCE doesn't cover it? Are you fucking kidding me?
Prep, really, you could not be more clear about your priorities - Money first, children second.
That's disgusting.

I published this blog on February 28, 2013. On March 2nd, I added this to it:

Note on March 2nd: St. Francis Prep has now password protected access to its Faculty Handbook, obviously as a result of this blog. So I apologize, but the link I mention below no longer works. I am glad though, that I took these screen shots. I also printed the entire copy of the Faculty Handbook. If anyone wants one, please let us know and I will be happy to send it to you. The Administration at SFP are cowards, liars, and idiots and they are running scared. Even St. Francis himself would not help them with what is coming next.

I did this a lot, fuck with heads of the SFP Scientologists and the administration. Many of my blogs were directed just toward them. It doesn't matter how many people read a blog. What matters is who is reading it. Writing is about knowing your audience, and I knew they were reading every word I said, and every word that was posted on my website. They were all obsessed with what I would do next. I had a captive audience of the right people.

Soon after these back-to-back blogs, Kevin called me and told me someone who was physically abused by deceased pedophile Robert Stenger in 1985 had contacted him and wanted to sue. This man, Mark Evangelista, had seen Stenger's name in the blog about Kevin, and he felt he needed to do something for this cause.

Kevin's thought process was to use the same strategy he had used in the Poly Prep case - allege that St. Francis Prep had known Stenger was an abuser before 1985, and continued to employ him anyway. The only difference between this case and the Poly Prep case, however, was that Robert Stenger did not molest this graduate. He punched young Mark in the face while he was sitting in his seat before class began, right out of the blue. The former Dean of Men, Gaspar Abruzzo, had said to Brother Leonard Conway right after the assault that "Stenger has gone too far," and "this has got to stop."

I had already received accounts from alumni that Stenger was reported for sexually inappropriate activity with boys in the mid 70's, so Kevin and I knew the school was already definitely aware of his pedophilic propensities in 1985. We had a shot at a successful lawsuit for this man.

That made three lawsuits that would be filed against St. Francis Prep, each with a different plaintiff and for a different reason. Kevin called it his Three-Headed Monster.

While Kevin was preparing the massive complaint, Felicia and I were involved in serious discussions about whether he should file for her as "Jane Doe." Felicia's part of complaint would contain the most personal facts out of all three lawsuits. A lot of the allegations would involve her past abuse and addiction to alcohol and we were concerned about her name being attached to a public document with this information in it. To be on the safe side, she chose to remain anonymous. It was a good, solid decision, and easily understandable under the circumstances.

One other thing we were all grappling with at the time was where to file the complaint. There were two choices: Federal District Court or Queens County Court. Each has its advantages, but overall Kevin thought the best bet for all three plaintiffs was to file in federal court. My case could definitely be filed there, because I had diversity of citizenship with the school. In other words, I was living in California, and the school is in New York, so the parties were "citizens" of two different states and federal court had jurisdiction. As for Felicia and Mark, it was a tougher call. Both were residing in New York and didn't have diversity of citizenship with Prep. The only way we could file their lawsuits in federal court was if we could show the school received federal funding, and Title IX applied.

Title IX is a federal statute which states "No person in the United States shall, on the basis of sex, be excluded from participation in, be denied the benefits of, or be subjected to discrimination under any education program or activity receiving federal financial assistance." Both Felicia's and Mark's lawsuits were a form of gender discrimination under this statute. Stenger targeted boys, and Br. Ben targeted girls.

Kevin asked me about whether Prep receives federal funding, and I honestly had no idea. I knew they applied for state funding occasionally, but had no clue about federal. I did some digging, however, and saw in one of their old annual reports that they once had received some donor money through a federal program. Kevin said that could be enough to get Felicia and Mark by.

Once the cases were filed, the New York Daily News picked up on the story immediately. It was not front page news, but news nonetheless. The article was on page seventy-two, covered by award winning journalist Michael O'Keeffe, who had reported about Poly Prep. We were glad to have the publicity and very thankful to Mr. O'Keeffe for the article. We already knew from settlement negotiations with St. Francis Prep that the school was counting on the three of us and the cause just fading away at some point. Media coverage would prevent that. It would overcome their loyal alumni base, and give validity and credibility to what we were saying. We knew early on that this war could only be won in full view of the public and it was my plan to get the word out as much as possible, by using my blog, social media, and mass media. It would be a continual and relentless media blitz.

Six more victims contacted Kevin Mulhearn as a result of that Daily News article. Two of them said they were assaulted by a Franciscan Brother still teaching and coaching at the school. However, none of these people who had reached out wanted to sue. They just all wanted to be heard. We understood. Coming forward about this is not an easy thing.

One of the victims was very adamant about his story being told. He asked me to blog a statement he had written. Here it is:

TESTIMONIAL:
I am a sexual abuse survivor.
For personal reasons, I will remain anonymous for now. I graduated Saint Francis Prep in 1985, one year prior to Mark Evangelista. I along with several other boys were taken on dozens of weekend trips (in a school van) by a Franciscan brother, Brother Joseph Mussa. These trips were to see professional hockey games in places like Boston, Philadelphia and Hartford. It was this brother and

4 of us boys. Common sense would have the hotel rooms having two double beds for us boys and a rollaway cot for him. He never allowed that, it was one of the boys on the floor and one of the boys in a bed with him. Wrestling in underwear led to nighttime genital fondling until after about a year I was able to find the strength to break away from the group. I told St. Francis Prep's Principal, Brother Richard McCann, and Brother Joe was transferred to a school in Brooklyn where I believe he taught for a number of years.

I buried these horrific memories for over 15 years. Like so many victims I drank excessively and made poor decisions that led to a 3 year prison term in 2001. It was in prison where a therapist confronted me and stated that it was her opinion I had been sexually abused, it was like a weight had been lifted off my shoulders as I was not ashamed for the first time in my life and was able to finally talk about it. Upon my release I felt empowered and immediately scheduled a meeting with the Superior General of the Franciscan Brothers at their headquarters in Brooklyn, NY. I thought I would be met with doubt and skepticism. I told the Superior General that I would take a lie detector test and would demand this brother take one as well. I guaranteed I would pass and he would fail and that if that was not the case I would leave his office and he would never hear from me again. I could only imagine he knew my claims were legitimate because he said a lie detector test would not be necessary and that he wanted to help me. He encouraged me not to go public due to public scrutiny to my family but that I should continue my therapy. He gave me thousands of dollars on two different occasions, checks in which I have copies of. Brother Joe also gave me thousands of dollars.

I am interested in finding out if anyone else was abused by Brother Joe, either before or after I reported him to St. Francis Prep. It concerns me a great deal that by not responding to my allegations appropriately, St. Francis Prep may have permitted this man to go free and sexually assault other innocent children. I also wonder whether any persons reported Brother Joe to St. Francis Prep administrators before I was assaulted by him. I wonder whether all the pain I have suffered from could have been avoided if St. Francis Prep officials had been more caring and compassionate to the needs of children like myself.

To all victims of sexual abuse out there, let me say "hang in there, it will get better." So stay strong.

After this man contacted me, I did a little research on Brother Joe. This man was correct. He was transferred directly to Xaverian High School from St. Francis Prep, even though he was a child molester. This made me very,

very angry - more angry than you could ever imagine. So, I called Xaverian, and asked to speak with Brother Joe. I said I was a parent of a graduate and I wanted to thank him for being such a good influence on my son years ago when Brother Joe was his hockey coach.

I was told by the operator that he had retired from teaching and that he was living in the friary on Remsen Street in Brooklyn. She offered to give me his cell number so I could contact him.

Well, that was the day after my blog was published, and Brother Joe wasn't picking up that phone for anyone. I still dial it once and a while, hoping I can get him. I will keep trying. I have a lot to say, especially since last year, another victim of Brother Joe's came forward and asked me to tell his story. It is one of the most disturbing stories of child sexual abuse I have ever heard. I will have more about that, and the way it was handled by the Franciscans, in a bit.

Kevin also received an email from someone who had been tracking Brother Michael Moran, the St. Francis Prep principal who was removed from the school in handcuffs for child molestation in 1980. (If you recall, both Carolyn Szostek and Angel Amore told me about this incident.) What this person had to say was so disturbing, that I almost couldn't breathe when Kevin read me the email.

Over the coming months, I was receiving my own emails regarding Michael Moran. Apparently, there were still a lot of graduates who were angry about what happened. I put a lot of time into researching Michael Moran, and eventually published this, in early 2014:

> Three people have contacted us so far about Br. Michael Moran, the principal who was arrested for child molestation in 1980 and taken out of St. Francis Prep in handcuffs.
> The first person who contacted us is an alumna, and was a neighbor and friend of the boy who pressed charges. She recounted for us what he said Br. Michael did with him in his office.
> The second was someone who had tracked Br. Michael for 20 years since he left St. Francis Prep. This person shared information about what supposedly had happened when Br. Michael left Hofstra in 1983 and his alleged crimes while running a soup kitchen on Long Island after that. He lost track of Br. Michael about 12 years ago and asked if we could try and find him. It wasn't asking really, it was a plea for help. This person is extremely concerned that Br. Michael is still molesting little boys somewhere.
> The third person graduated from St. Francis Prep in 1980 and contacted us this past week. She sent us this:
> I saw in one of your blogs, a request for information about the

former principal of St. Francis Prep, Brother Michael Moran. What type of information are you looking for and what do you plan to do with it?

We answered with this:

We received a plea from a graduate asking us to please help find him and do what we could to make sure he is not hurting children. This person tracked him for 20 years, then lost track of him when he left the food bank he was operating on Long Island. We received very detailed information from this person from which one could easily conclude that he did not stop his questionable activities when he left SFP. We received another letter from a close friend of someone he hurt. If you have any information about him, it would be appreciated.

And then, she sent this last night:

In the spring of 1980, a relative of mine worked in the 107 Precinct, the same precinct where the school is located. My relative saw the police report detailing the sexual abuse that took place between the principal, Bro. Michael Moran and a student. I was told by my relative, Bro. Michael Moran had sodomized a male freshmen student in his office on several occasions. There were several students, like myself who had relatives in the police department and we all heard the same thing from our cop relatives. The police investigated the charges and believed them to be true. It was a fact not a rumor.

Bro. Michael Moran was immediately removed from his position at the school. No explanation was ever given to the students. No criminal charges were ever filed against Bro. Mike because the student's parents agreed not to press charges when the Franciscan Brothers said they would relocate the principal to a place where he would not have contact with children again.

At the time, it seemed like a win-win. Lock the pedophile up in a monastery somewhere and save a victim from having to testify. Little did we know back then, the Catholic Church didn't always follow through on their part of the bargain and pedophile priests would often end up in locations where they could continue their abusive behavior. I have often wondered if the same was true with Bro. Michael Moran.

A Law and Order show made think about Bro. Mike again. I tried googling his name and came across your blog. I have no idea of his current location. Your response leads me to believe he was never "put away". It makes me sick to think the Catholic Church has once again failed to protect innocent children.

No, Bro. Michael Moran wasn't "locked away" in a monastery. He went from Prep directly to Hofstra University to serve as Chaplain. In 1983, he started a food bank on Long Island now named Interfaith Nutrition Network. The person who wrote us asking for help also alleges that in 1983, he was reported at Hofstra for having sex with an 18 year old freshman boy and that is what actually prompted his departure from the school. This person also alleges that Michael Moran used the soup kitchen as a way to have access to the homeless boys whose families came there for help. This is the same MO of Father Bruce Ritter at Covenant House.

Here is a New York Times article discussing Br. Michael and the history of the food pantry:

http://query.nytimes.com/gst/fullpage.html?res=9901E2DD1531F937 A35751C1A9639C8B63

Michael Moran is out there because St. Francis Prep did not help put him away. I have an 8 year old son, and this disgusts me to no end. It makes me physically sick. Do you care about children at all SFP? It is a legitimate question, because many of you, including some people in the administration, like Ted Jahn (joined SFP administration in 1978), were there in 1980 when Br. Michael was quietly "removed." How do you sleep at night? Do you wake up and look in the mirror and think you are spectacular people doing God's work?

If anyone reading this has any information about Michael Moran's whereabouts, we would appreciate it. The greatest concern with pedophiles is that they DO NOT STOP. They keep doing it until they are caught and put in prison.

The more I learned about the history of St. Francis Prep, the character of the administration, and the lasting effects on the alumni, the more sick to my stomach I got. And things only got worse. Much, much, much, much worse.

CHAPTER NINETEEN

ANONYMOUS SHADOWY MONIKERS AND THE NON-PROTEST PROTEST

Once floodgates open, they are open and there is no turning back. That summer of 2013 proved this one thousand times over.

People were contacting me on a daily basis about their own horrific experiences at Prep, and their friends' experiences that were equally disturbing. Posts were going up on burnandrotinhell.com that were outrageous. Some of these posts involved very intimate details of faculty members' lives, especially the head of guidance, Robyn Armon. I was accused publicly on my website of being the one making these posts, but it wasn't me. I didn't know who it was, but it was definitely someone who knew Robyn very well, and disliked her immensely.

Several other posts on the website referred to "DC", meaning David Correira, the social studies teacher/swim coach who was given permission by the administration to date a senior in 2009. David was the young lady's coach. They started dating mid-way through her senior year, after she had turned eighteen.

My understanding is, there had been a long period of flirtation between the two, and once David had realized their relationship was going in a more serious direction, he asked the administration if he could date her. And of course, their answer was yes.

What do you think about that, given the fact these very same administrators were aware of how many inappropriate relationships had occurred between teachers and students (some resulting in pregnancies) in the past? My answer would have been this to Mr. Correira: "David, you may date her after she graduates. If you date her now, you will be fired."

Is it me, or are these people bat shit crazy in how they handle these matters?

For the record, I never knew Robyn well, but I knew enough to dislike her very much. After she pulled that stunt regarding the Ultimate Prom contest ousting my cancer-surviving student from the competition, I had no respect for her. And after what Felicia told me about Robyn's handling of her abuse situation, I considered her to be a vile human being.

Anyway, my point is, that these types of posts unleashed a litany of attacks against me and my family. My haters were consistently trying to paint my site as "cyberbullying". Was it? Is it bullying, or is it swift retribution for causing others immeasurable pain? I couldn't help but think Joe Diamonds was involved somehow, although I had no way to prove it. I don't know of many others at the school who would be capable of posting something like this:

> "Liz, do me a favor and stick your finger in Josephine's ass and then stick it in your twat. I saw your mother the other day at Macy's working. She is a fucking lowlife cunt like you. You will get what is coming to you.... you seaman sucking bitch...you and Josephine are 2 pussies....I am telling everyone the truth that Tom N. got you pregnant and then dumped you. Could he be the father of that bastard child....I bet ANDREW fell out of your ass instead of your cunt. Do you have a cunt...I bet you have a big dick and I bet Josephine sucks it every night...Your greaseball father hated you...despised you... wish he shot his load out the window the night he got your mother pregnant. I know the cash is running out. You are almost out of time... and moves..you world is caving in. Suck my asshole Liz.....you are a low life cunt.... I hope you get fucked in the ass when this is all done... EAT ME !!! then burn and rot in hell!"

Very Franciscan, isn't it? It's lovely calling my then 8 year old son a bastard child because I conceived him through artificial insemination. On the upside, one would only write something this disgusting if the situation at the school had clearly gone bonkers. They were clearly suffering and on the ropes. I took comfort in that.

During this time I also kept the blogs coming fast and furious. One particular blog that caused a huge stir was about the art teacher Felicia reported in 2006 for having an inappropriate relationship with a freshman. As I said before, this is the same teacher that Sue Vivona told me about my very first day teaching back in 2007. When I posted this blog, Prep graduates were in an uproar about my boldness in calling this man out publicly for his behavior.

However, I had the corroboration, and so I did it without hesitation and without fear. The truth always wins.

The alumni attacked me for this blog, and called me all sorts of awful things, including liar, and accusing me of fabricating the whole thing. This pissed Felicia off to no end, and despite my warning to stay out of it, she chose to comment and discuss what she knew to have happened with this art teacher back in 2006.

That resulted in a legal maneuver by the school that neither of us had anticipated. The school had already filed a motion to dismiss all our lawsuits, and we were waiting for a decision on that. However, they also decided to file a motion to reveal Felicia's identity, making the argument that since she was commenting publicly about the case, Jane Doe couldn't have her cake and eat it, too.

I never anticipated this move by the school because it would be such a disgusting thing to do, and it would only hurt Prep's public image even more. In my opinion it was clearly a means of scaring and intimidating Felicia. We had to take some time and think about how to address this, because our counter-move could be a game-changer if we were smart about it.

It was clear from everything that was going on that the mood had shifted to a "no holds barred" situation. Everybody's gloves were off! It was obvious that in light of very specific information being continuously released on my website and blog the school was trying desperately to maintain an ounce of credibility with their faculty, staff, and constituents.

This led to the now infamous anonymous shadowy moniker email, sent "with High Importance" by President Brother Leonard Conway to all faculty and staff. This email was leaked to me anonymously via email about five minutes after it was sent:

LEONARD CONWAY

TO: FacultyandStaff

Monday, October 7, 2013 8:11 AM

This message was sent with High Importance

Dear Faculty & Staff,
You may be aware that lawsuits were recently filed against the school involving former students and former teachers. We are taking this opportunity to assure you that the school denies the false allegations that have been made against it, and is working with its attorney in defending these lawsuits.

Controlled Burn:

Unfortunately, in the midst of the publicity surrounding the lawsuits, there are a few individuals, hiding behind anonymous shadowy monikers, who have sought to express negativity via the internet that are directed towards members of our school community. We are hopeful that you would not give credibility to the hateful absurdity voiced by these anonymous people. And, we take this time to ask you to join us in praying for them and hoping that they will find the right path in life.

It is a shame that our students, teachers, and administrators have been the subject of hate voiced by these anonymous individuals. To those who have worked here for many years, you know that we have a distinguished faculty, here for the growth and development of the young people before us. For our new teachers and staff, please trust that we have and will continue to serve the Mission of the school in spite of the venomous allegations that are attempting to diminish us as a school and as individuals. Know that the allegations in the lawsuits in question were addressed in a very comprehensive and professional manner at the time of their occurrence and not all the information you hear from the individuals spewing hate is truth. Nothing is being "swept under the rug." We must stand together, united to this Mission, and support each other in good times and bad. Gossip, hearsay, rumor, negative talk and discussion on "hate" websites have no just place in society, let alone our classrooms or department offices, and we must remain professional regarding these matters. In this regard, we are proud that so many of our alumni, who truly know the school, continue to offer their support during this time. We assure you that the administration, which is committed to building the faith and character of our children, will stand tall and not sway in the face of unjustifiable hate.

We ask that you please focus on your personal mission as faculty and staff members in a religious school that has always stood for the respect of the individual. And, to the extent that family, friends, and students inquire about the lawsuits or internet postings, we ask that you share with them that the school denies the false allegations that have been made against it, and is working with its attorneys in defending the lawsuits as well as investigating the conduct and identity of the aforesaid anonymous individuals.

We hope that you appreciate that given the status of the pending litigation that we are unable to discuss with you specific details regarding the matter. And, in the interim we ask that you continue to lend your prayers and support to the school in its continued mission to provide its students with academic success, respect, integrity, and joy.

Thank you for your support during this time.
Sincerely,
Bro. Leonard

This letter can be viewed on imgur: http://imgur.com/8ltkGAO#sthash. WIDSBadQ.dpuf.

I would like to point out a few things. For example, notice the wordsmithing here, most likely vetted by the school's attorney, Phil Semprevivo – "we deny the false allegations." Notice the school is not giving a blanket denial of all allegations. Can you imagine why? Could it be because they knew damn well that both Felicia's case regarding Brother Ben and Mark Evangelista's case regarding Robert Stenger were well documented? They knew that this information, if the cases went to trial, would come out in discovery. Hence, they would look like even bigger liars if they had denied these incidents had ever happened.

Secondly, yes, the school did investigate who was posting on my website. In fact, they spent thousands and thousands of donor dollars trying to figure it out, to no avail. It was reported back to me that the school was in a virtual lockdown as a result. The administration thought I had planted spies inside the building to get me information – hence, they started requiring that all faculty and staff wear ID badges. If you did not have a badge on, you were stopped and questioned, even if you had been teaching there 25 years. Desperate times were calling for desperate measures, and yes, they were very desperate.

My final remark concerning this letter is actually a question to you. Do you see how out of touch the people running the school really are? Who, in 2013, would even think of using the term "anonymous shadowy monikers?" Aren't those what most people call usernames?

When a good friend of mine read this letter, the first thing he picked up on was Brother Leonard's request that recipients continue to pray for the school, and not for the victims whom they know exist. Hypocrisy at its best, it seems. Again, I was not surprised. It was my opinion that this school would deny all wrongdoing until the bitter end. I saved this letter for that glorious day when they would have their tail between their legs, which I knew inevitably would come.

This letter was sent out just a few days before the school's Fall Open House, obviously as a means of damage control and a way to improve morale amongst the employees. The Open House is a critical day for the school in that it's their main showcase opportunity for 8th graders who are contemplating attending. The enrollment numbers for the succeeding school year depend to a significant degree upon the success of the Open House.

It was brought to my attention in September that some victim supporters were planning on protesting outside the Open House. They posted this information on BRH, and emailed me as well. Even Felicia received some emails regarding the protest plans.

A successful protest could possibly destroy the school. Like for all Catholic schools, success is a numbers game - keep enrollment up, increase tuition slightly, hope that veteran teachers retire so you can hire young ones for cheap. Everything about Catholic schools is number driven, and bad numbers would be bad news all around.

On the day of the Open House, former students of mine contacted me to tell me they drove by the school, and it was like 6100 Francis Lewis Boulevard was a war zone. Police and extra security lined the perimeter of the school.

What did the administration think would happen exactly? Protesters would show up with pipe bombs? Well, needless to say, no one was going to put themselves at personal risk by protesting outside the building. So what people did was bring hundreds of photocopies of articles about the lawsuits against the school and leave them all over inside the building - in the bathrooms, in the auditorium, in the hallways, and in some classrooms.

How humiliating for Prep. They spent thousands of dollars providing extra security, they called the police and had SWAT teams outside, and a bunch of people walked right in and littered the building with newspaper articles about sex abuse at the school.

You know what struck me most of all about all this? In a heartbeat the Prep administration summoned law enforcement to dissuade a peaceful protest, but for decades, they never once by their own volition called the police about a single child abuser at the school. No police, not once, not ever.

Prep's karma was clearly coming for them, and they would not be happy.

CHAPTER TWENTY
MARLA WINS BIG

Courts are slow. It doesn't matter if it's federal court or state court - litigation is a painfully slow process. Marla Krolikowski filed her discrimination suit back in January, 2013, and mid-summer, there was still no news.

As they would do for every lawsuit brought against them, St. Francis Prep filed a motion to dismiss Marla's lawsuit once they were served with the summons and complaint. Here it was, months later, and this motion had still not been decided.

Everyone, especially Felicia and I, were anxious to see if Marla would make it to trial. The school's lawyer, Phil Semprevivo, had made what we considered asinine arguments in the motion to dismiss, including that Marla was not just a religion teacher, but was essentially a minister. If the court determined that Marla was, in fact, a minister, then the school would have the absolute right to fire her for being transgender because of the constitutional separation of church and state. But there was no way Marla was a minister. Marla was a religion teacher, and she taught about abortion in her classes. If she had in any way, shape or form been a minister, they would have altered her curriculum ages ago.

If I were Mr. Semprevivo, I would have just stuck with the sane argument that as a religious institution, St. Francis Prep could legally discriminate against a transgender teacher based upon the tenets of Catholic teaching. This is a right unequivocally afforded religious institutions under the First Amendment.

Taking a solid freedom of religion stance to the next level and arguing that "Marla is a minister" is just one of many stupid things in my opinion Mr. Semprevivo would do in the coming years. I actually detest Mr. Semprevivo for several reasons, including that in the past, he represented Dominican College in a lawsuit filed by the mother of a girl named Megan Wright who had been raped on campus and who subsequently committed suicide.

According to a news story run by WABC NY back in July, 2008, the lawsuit stated that "Dominican College never conducted its own investigation. It directed Megan to pursue the investigation with a detective in the Orangetown police department who, unbeknownst to Megan at the time, was employed by Dominican College as an instructor."

So, the investigating detective was on Dominican College's payroll. How convenient for the school.

What kind of a man would take a case like this? There is an old adage in the law called res ipsa loquitur. It means the thing speaks for itself. Defending Dominican College is probably the clearest indicator of Phil Semprevivo's character that I could ever find.

We found out at the end of August that the court hearing regarding the school's motion to dismiss Marla's complaint was scheduled for September 9th. Former students of Marla's were posting the information on the Facebook alumni page, asking supporters to attend.

Felicia, who was still Jane Doe at the time, wanted to go. Initially, I wasn't sure whether this was a good idea or not in that it might antagonize the school against Felicia even more. But then, after speaking with Felicia, we both reached the conclusion that Prep could go fuck itself. They had tried to bully her by filing a motion to make her name public, and the worst thing we could do would be to show that it had scared her. This was a strong, strong young woman, and they would have to suffer the consequences of messing with her.

On September 9th, 2013, Felicia showed up at the Queens County courthouse to support Marla. She was one of three alumni there.

Felicia was texting me the play by play from the courtroom, and from what she was saying, it appeared that a miracle was taking place - the judge was ruling firmly against Prep on every point in their motion to dismiss. They were in deep shit, and this case was going to trial.

It was a huge victory for Marla, and a huge victory for LGBT rights. From now on in New York, Catholic schools could no longer fire teachers for being transgender. I, personally, was crying when I saw former WABC reporter Sarah Wallace's report about this historical legal decision on the news. The administration's bullshit and arrogance had done them in.

After the hearing, Felicia and Marla talked a lot. Marla was very thankful that a graduate she did not know had taken the time to come out and support her. Felicia did not reveal herself to Marla as Jane Doe, as there was no need. This day was about Marla, and nothing else.

There would be plenty of time for Felicia to discuss her case with Marla later. This would be an interesting development, and take Felicia's and my quest for justice down a new path.

The "Trilogy of Terror," a term the school's administration would come to use to refer to Marla, Felicia and me, was born.

CHAPTER TWENTY-ONE

OVER A BARREL

As I mentioned, when Felicia first filed her lawsuit against St. Francis Prep, she elected to do so under the name, "Jane Doe." This was mainly due to the fact that Felicia did not want public attention given the sensitive nature of her claims. St. Francis Prep was given Felicia's name and some of her highly personal medical records in exchange for their compliance with keeping her anonymous. That was the deal. However, as the lawsuits heated up, and public attention grew, St. Francis Prep took a continuously more and more aggressive position with Felicia.

Instead of negotiating a fair settlement with Felicia, St. Francis Prep's tactics became a game of trying to wear her down. That's what one resorts to when the truth is not on their side.

Because of Felicia's public comments about the school, St. Francis Prep's attorney was able to file a motion forcing Felicia to proceed under her true name. Felicia had a choice: settle for peanuts, or have the world know she was the Jane Doe plaintiff. Felicia was unsure of what to do until she received an important message from an ally inside St. Francis Prep.

There are several moles within St. Francis Prep who use, as Brother Leonard so eloquently put it in his letter, "anonymous shadowy monikers" to communicate information either by e-mail with me or on BurnandRotinHell.com.

One such mole is a diehard supporter of me and has been very sympathetic to Felicia, as well. Much is owed to this particular mole, whose identity is unknown to both Felicia and me. Felicia would like to thank him or her, and hopes he or she knows who he or she is upon reading this.

It was the aforementioned mole who reached out to Felicia with an interesting quote. He or she had overheard McLaughlin bragging to Christopher Mendolia that the school had, "Jane Doe over a barrel." Over a barrel. This was the alleged choice of words used by a key administrator of St. Francis Prep to describe Felicia, knowing full well that she had been victimized at St. Francis Prep. It was clear now that the administration had no sympathy for Felicia. They had no remorse for what had happened to her at their school. Instead, they looked at her as a weakling they held an advantage over.

They were very wrong.

Felicia was apoplectic. Upon receiving that message from the mole, Felicia immediately called Kevin Mulhearn and told him she would take St. Francis Prep's chip away and out herself before they could do it. Kevin arranged for Felicia to speak to the New York Post, and on September 23rd, 2013, Felicia's photograph appeared in the paper, beneath the headline, "A Brave Face." She was quoted as saying, "It should be called St. Francis Predatory School." I laughed so hard when I read that I thought I had given myself a hernia.

The tide was turning. St. Francis Prep lost their upper hand, hoist by their own petard. In an attempt to silence Felicia, the school had instead galvanized her to broadcast her message far and loud. Felicia had nothing to lose.

Who was over a barrel now?

CHAPTER TWENTY-TWO

NOISY COW AND OBNOXIOUS LOUDMOUTH

Once Felicia came out as Jane Doe in that New York Post article just two weeks after Marla's victory, everything went crazy. CNN called Felicia for an interview, Katie Couric called her for an interview, and many of the local television stations in NY called her as well.

Felicia decided to do the interview with a local television station only - WPIX. The reporter was very nice and sincere, and she had mentioned that her producer had a child attending Prep and was very interested in the story. I thought the interview was fantastic. Felicia hit all her points home, and her story was so detailed that anyone with half a brain could see she was telling the truth. I posted the link to that interview everywhere I could think of, including the Facebook alumni page, my website fan page, and my personal Facebook timeline. The result was a flurry of emails and direct messages to both Felicia and me, showing support, asking us for help, and giving us information about various predators who had worked at Prep.

It was during this time of big publicity that Marla Krolikowski reached out to Felicia to show her support. Marla could not believe she was talking to Jane Doe at her hearing and didn't know it. She told Felicia it was obvious that Brother Leonard Conway, Patrick McLaughlin, and Phil Semprevivo were irritated and disarmed by Felicia' presence, but Marla had no idea why at the time. Well, this explained it! I think they all pretty much hated Felicia's guts. How dare she stand up for herself and expose the school to such ridicule!

Felicia and Marla became fast friends that autumn, trading war stories from the halls of Prep, and discussing many of the teachers who had left them both with less than a savory feeling. One teacher that came up in conversation was Mr. Driver's Ed, the man who was now Assistant Principal of Faculty and Instruction, Christopher Mendolia.

Marla told Felicia that she had reported Mendolia many times over the years for both bullying students and for inappropriate conduct with girls. What Marla said jived with Felicia's own experiences, and so they believed each other.

Then Marla dropped a bomb of Hiroshima magnitude. She told Felicia she made a documentary in the 90's about the rampant sexual harassment at the school. She went on to say this documentary was played for faculty and staff at an assembly to help stop the inappropriate behavior. She said there were about a dozen girls on the tape, all discussing their horrible experiences with teachers.

This was the precise moment that Felicia decided she would sue the school regarding the sexual harassment she alleged to have experienced with Christopher Mendolia. This was no small decision. She decided to go after their golden boy, whom they had been grooming for years to take the position of Assistant Principal, and whom they had finally promoted to that spot. Come the Spring, the shit would hit the fan. Wait until the alumni base heard about this one.

As I said, Felicia and I had an outpouring of support once she went public as Jane Doe. What saddens me though, is that for the longest time so little public support came from the alumni base. Literally, the public support we received on the school's fan page was miniscule. Haters just loved to trash us. One alum called me a "noisy cow" and told me that "someone should shut me up." He posted this on the page and no one commented in support of me. Graduates were also publicly blaming Felicia's parents for a lot of what happened to her with Brother Ben and for a lot of what was happening currently. Typical comments were:

1. Her parents should have pulled her out of Prep- by keeping her there, they made it worse for Felicia;
2. Her parents should have taught her to just let it go and get over it - these things happen in life and girls need to just deal with it;
3. It was a big conspiracy with a crazy lady (me) to bilk the school for money and shame on her parents for allowing this to continue.

However, out of all the graduates who trashed us, one stood out among the pack of sheeple. His name is Arthur Freer, and he is a New York City Police Detective. Now, just for the record, it is no secret that Arthur is a cop. Arthur posted profile pictures wearing his badge on multiple occasions, and spoke about being a police officer on the alumni page. Why he so vehemently attacked Felicia and me on so many occasions we just could not understand. He actually called Felicia an "obnoxious loudmouth." It was as if he had a mission to debunk whatever we said. He called every allegation made by Felicia or reported by me "baseless." How he could ever say that was a mystery to us, because Brother Ben was removed from teaching for a reason. Nothing was baseless, so why was he trying to convince people of that? It didn't even matter that eventually, other people came forward on the alumni page confirming just about everything Felicia and I ever said - Arthur was going to try and shit on us to the best of his ability. After a while, he recruited help - his cousin Anthony Michael Freer. Anthony loved to make offensive memes about me and what I was discussing. It was his specialty, actually.

Here's one:

 September 24, 2014 at 5:36pm

Here's another:

 September 24, 2014 at 5:47pm

Classy, right?

After a while, Arthur's behavior began to strike me as suspicious. It was too targeted, too visceral, and he was constantly misrepresenting the current state of the lawsuits.

So I launched an Internal Affairs Bureau investigation into his conduct as it pertained to constant victim bashing on the alumni page for no apparent reason. Boy, did that shut Arthur up fast. Don't fuck with mama.

I want to make this clear at this point: What was happening publicly and what was happening privately during this period were two different situations entirely.

Publicly, Felicia and I were being trashed, called liars, and called phonies by the Kool-Aid-drinking-Scientologist-thinking alumni on the Facebook alumni page.

Privately, we were receiving an outpouring of support from people who knew we were telling the truth, and who had their own horrible experiences with teachers at Prep. Many of these people were giving me the names of other graduates to contact, who could fill in some blanks about predators I had mentioned in my blogs.

Almost 100% of these supporters had the same concern as Angel Amore: "Please don't tell anyone I told you, for fear of what the school might do to me or my family."

I understood, because who in their right mind wants to deal with Joe Diamonds, et al. No one would. I certainly didn't, but through all this, I felt a protective bubble of white light around me, so I kept on chipping away at Prep's reputation, keyboard in hand. Others did not feel this protection, and were not so sure I could protect them. So I honored their wishes. But quite frankly, I was sick of hearing how scared everyone was. It's hard to expose situations when you can't attach a name to what you've been told. A name gives a story credibility. Otherwise, it seemed to a lot of people that I was just making up stories. It was not an easy time for me, even though I was 100% telling the truth.

What made everything more difficult in general was that Felicia and I were being stalked:

- Her computer was hacked.
- My computer was hacked.
- I was getting phony emails from people pretending to be current Prep students, trying to get information from me about my sources. (It wasn't that hard for me to figure out they were fakes.)
- Someone tried to repeatedly hack Felicia's bank account and Macy's account. (They still are, to this day.)

- Some weird, skinny, young guy on more than one occasion was parked outside my house, working with what looked like a laptop or an Ipad in his car. Both times as I approached, he sped away.

Felicia and I didn't know what to make of it, other than somebody was trying to scare us and get some dirt on us. My thoughts were they wanted to trip us up, find something discrediting, and hurt us to make us go away.

But, we both knew it would never happen. Felicia and I weren't going anywhere, no matter what. Instead, we ramped up our game. That pissed our critics off even more. Too bad for them, the truth was on its way out, all the way out.

CHAPTER TWENTY-THREE
SEXUAL HARASSMENT IS A HUGE PROBLEM, IT SAID

By the time January, 2014 rolled around, St. Francis Prep had settled Marla Krolikowski's claims against it. That Queens County judge was just not going to let those pasty white old men off the hook for discrimination. He kept pushing the school to settle, and they eventually did. Thank god for that.

However, with settlement came Marla's confidentiality clause - meaning she couldn't discuss the settlement terms, and she couldn't disparage Prep in any way from the date of the agreement forward.

Well, good old Marla didn't give a shit about that clause. Marla, Felicia and I had been speaking continuously since Marla had overcome her motion to dismiss, and we continued to do so.

Marla had accumulated a ton of dirt about Prep in the thirty-two years she taught there and she told us all of it. She gave us names, she gave us dates, and she gave us places. She told Felicia she still had the director's cut of that documentary she had made about sexual harassment at the school, and she told Felicia she was free to use it in her lawsuit.

Marla had a few other things she wanted us to know. She wanted us to know how regretful she was that she hadn't done more as a teacher to protect students, and she cried hysterically about this on the phone with us often. The reason Marla carried so much regret was that she had her own incidents with inappropriate student-teacher relationships when she was a high school student at St. Anthony's, another Franciscan high school, on Long Island, New York. She knew up close and personal the damage evil men can do to a young person.

Now get this – Do you remember Michael Moran, the St. Francis Prep principal who was taken out of the school in handcuffs and arrested for child molestation in 1980? Well, that Michael Moran was Marla's (then Mark's) guidance counselor at St. Anthony's. And that Michael Moran, in exchange for a promise to expedite young Mark Krolikowski's college applications, suggested repeatedly that young Mark jerk him off.

Can you imagine being Mark Krolikowski, coming to work at Prep, and the current principal is the man who asked asked you to jerk him off in high school? This is exacty what happened.

As a result, Marla was vigilant at Prep about complaining to the administration about teacher misconduct. But, she had never called the cops. This was the reason for her tears. Yes, Marla had been a mandated reporter as well, and she, by her own admission, failed in her legal obligation to go to law enforcement about suspected student sexual abuse and harassment.

I want to state here that even though Marla never called the police, she did way more than 99% of the other teachers at Prep who knew students were being preyed upon. Those assholes did nothing. At least Marla tried to do something. But wow, after knowing what I know now, I really do wish she had called the police years ago. One call to the police could have changed so much. One call to the police could have saved a lot of future pain for a lot of kids.

There is one other thing I would like to say here, about my relationship with Marla. Marla was a great source of comfort and support to me during this time. She reassured me over and over again that I had to keep going. Her "public" hands were tied. Mine were not. She told me to keep blogging, no matter what. She told me people would stop her on the street, and ask if what they were reading in my blogs was true. "It's all true, every word," she would tell them. Word was spreading, people were talking, and the school was starting to hurt financially. We were getting to them in a big way.

With all this information about so many tragedies swirling in our heads, Felicia confirmed her decision to file a lawsuit against Prep involving her allegations of sexual harassment by Christopher Mendolia. She would also throw former music teacher Fernando Sicilia in for good measure.

Marla and I fully supported her decision. Now, let me say I didn't know Sicilig at all when he was a teacher at Prep. I can say, though, that I always considered Mendolia to be a big jerk. Specifically, I had four interactions with him during my four years as a teacher at the school that left me with an uneasy feeling:

1. In 2008, one of my Business Law students came to me distraught because she had failed a social studies quiz in Mendolia's class, and he had told her in front of the class that she" was a disgrace to her family";
2. While we both served on the Middle States Committee, he freely gossiped that one of the guidance counselors, a woman with a husband and two children, had been having an affair with the female school psychologist for years;
3. In a conversation with me, he made fun of the quality of student coming in to the school, complaining that many of them can barely speak English;
4. A student he had problems with had thrown peanuts on his lawn, knowing his toddler daughter has a peanut allergy, and he wanted to press attempted murder charges against this student.

As a result of the above, my personal feelings are that I do not think Chris Mendolia is a nice man. I actually think he is a horrible man with a big mouth and poor judgment, and displays an overall lack of caring or compassion towards others. But hey, that's just my opinion. You may think he's a swell guy, and good for you.

Once Felicia confirmed her decision, we were again smacked clearly in the face by the New York statute of limitations. The "alleged" acts regarding both Mendolia and Sicilia "allegedly" occurred in late Spring, 2008, so the statute of limitations for negligence had run three years later in Spring, 2011. It appeared we were out of luck at this point.

Appearances can be deceiving, though. And where there's a will, there's a way. And when the universe is on your side, who knows what you can do. There are no limits.

So even before Felicia spoke with Kevin about this potential lawsuit, I already had my lawyer hat on and was looking for angles we could use to file this suit.

One thing that leapt out at me right away is that Felicia said for her driver's ed class, her parents had signed a contract. She recalled that this contract stated that her teacher would be standing in loco parentis to her, which means acting as a parent would. If Mendolia had done what Felicia alleges he did, clearly, he was not acting as a parent and the school was in breach of contract.

The statute of limitations in New York for breach of contract is six years, which gave us until late Spring, 2014. We would make it by just a few months.

As an alternate cause of action, I suggested fraud, which is also a quasi-contract claim. It was my theory that the school had defrauded Felicia because her allegations would include that the school had prior knowledge that Mendolia and Sicilia had sexually harassed other girls. The statute of limitations for fraud was also six years.

When Felicia called Kevin to express her interest on suing about Mendolia and Sicilia, she pitched my two theories and Kevin thought it was possible. It would be a longshot, but a shot nonetheless. At this point, we wanted to take any shot we could that would lead to the end of student harassment and abuse at St. Francis Prep.

Kevin did some research, found cases to support these arguments, and called the school's attorney to let him know Felicia would be proceeding with filing a lawsuit regarding current Assistant Principal of Faculty and Instruction Christopher Mendolia and former music teacher Fernando Sicilia.

Now things got really crazy.

The school expressed an interest in settling right away. To move settlement negotiations along, Kevin asked Felicia to put together a narrative of her allegations so they would understand her version of what happened. It was scathing, but so far as my personal opinion is concerned, all true. I believed every single word Felicia wrote.

There was a settlement meeting set. Felicia had to really think about what she wanted, because any settlement agreement would likely call for a settlement of all her claims, including the sexual harassment by Brother Ben.

However, the day before the settlement conference, Phil Semprevivo dropped a bomb on Kevin. He said someone had emailed Felicia's allegations to some members of the school's Board of Trustees, and one big donor, and the school was not only not going to settle, but they were also going to sue her for defamation. These emails had the heading "Sexual Harassment at SFP is a Huge Problem," and that was one of the statements they were claiming was defamatory.

Felicia and I just about died and I almost vomited. Seriously, I was that sick over it.

But then we got angry. We were angry because she insisted everything she said in her statement was true, and I believed her. We were also angry because sexual harassment at SFP is a huge problem, and the administration damn well knew it. Again, they could go fuck themselves.

Then, about a week later, something bizarre happened. I received an anonymous email that said my and Felicia's emails had been hacked. Up to this point, I knew there had been several hacking attempts, but I never thought anyone actually got in. My brain started racing - I was thinking about all my personal financial information, etc., that someone may have seen. I almost vomited again. The stress was unreal.

There was really nothing left to do except change our passwords and make new email accounts, and wait.

Kevin filed Felicia's lawsuit a week or two later. We anxiously waited for the school's answer to see if a counterclaim for defamation would be in it. But it wasn't.

Were they bluffing?

No, they weren't. Two months later, at about 10:30 PM on a Saturday night in July, there was a knock on Felicia's parents' apartment door. It was a crackhead-looking, unkempt woman with a big envelope. Felicia was served.

Felicia was rightfully upset, and pissed. It was the most bullshit lawsuit I had ever seen. The absolute most ludicrous yet hysterically funny thing about it was Phil Semprevivo had attached a post from my website to the complaint. The user who had made the post was "Gerilyneatsmilliesbox."

Now, you are probably asking yourself, "What the fuck is that about?"

Let me explain. Gerilyn refers to Gerilyn Coccia, the woman who replaced Carolyn Szostek as Dean of Women. This is the same woman Mendolia said had a long-term affair with the school psychologist, Millie. I guess this rumor really made its way around over the years, all the way to a post on BRH.

That particular post by Gerilyneatsmilliesbox made reference to the email addresses for the Board of Trustees. The school was somehow trying to link all of this to Felicia, like a giant conspiracy.

I will tell you right now, Felicia says she didn't send those emails and I believe her. Besides, even if she did send them, it is my opinion that it's all true. As we know by this point, truth is an absolute defense to a defamation claim.

I do believe though that hacking was involved. This is why. As you may recall, back in January, 2013, I had uploaded a lot of documentation to the secret servers then hosted by the famous hacking group Anonymous for safekeeping. The date was January, 8, 2013, to be exact. How do I remember this so clearly? I still have the reply email with the confirmation link that was sent to me.

In addition, in June, 2013, Google had put a "this site may be hacked" designation on Prep's official website, sfponline.org. That designation was there for months and months. At the time I first noticed the designation, I googled what it meant, and it said "You'll see the message "This site may be hacked" when we believe a hacker might have changed some of the existing pages on the site or added new spam pages. If you visit the site, you could be redirected to spam or malware."

However, in June, 2013, I didn't put two and two together for some reason. I guess this was because all I had done was upload some information for safekeeping, and never heard another word about it.

But, after I received an email that my and Felicia's emails had been hacked, and the school actually sued Felicia, I had a feeling something bigger was going on. This is what I found on the website E Hacking News:

St. Francis Preparatory School website database leaked by Group Hp-Hack

by Sabari Selvan on Sunday, June 02, 2013 |

A new hacking group named "Group Hp-Hack" has found a way to break into the database server of St. Francis Preparatory School website and accessed the data.
Today, we received a notification from the team that they have hacked the sfponline.org website and leaked the data compromised from the server.
Talking to EHN, the group also provided a sql injection vulnerable link that gave them access to the server. The leak contains a list of username and password (plain text format).

To me, this explained everything perfectly. No, Felicia had not emailed the Board of Trustees - someone else did. Who, I am not sure, and I am not placing responsibility on any one particular person or group. What I am saying is, from this article, Group HP Hack (which is a Saudi hacking group, by the way) leaked all the email usernames and passwords. It seems to me any recipient of this information could have easily accessed Felicia's information when it was likely forwarded by Phil Semprevivo to certain members of the administration for review. I think this is common sense.

It is such common sense that Kevin filed a frivolous lawsuit claim against the school. Now Felicia had three lawsuits pending against them. It seemed they would never learn their lesson.

CHAPTER TWENTY-FOUR

JOHN, JUAN DIEGO, AND THE DEVIL

As the summer of 2014 progressed, Felicia, Mark Evangelista, and I got some bad news. All three original lawsuits were dismissed from federal court. Felicia's and Mark's were dismissed for lack of jurisdiction (the Court determined Prep does not receive federal funding and so Felicia and Mark could not sue in federal court) and mine was dismissed because the Court held Prep's letter about me to be a statement of non-actionable opinion and not one of fact. The good news was that Felicia could refile her lawsuit in state court, and I could file an appeal for my case. Mark, however, was out of luck. His only shot was the Title IX claim - he was not sexually abused by Stenger, so there was no possibility of using the Poly Prep strategy for him in state court. Poly Prep was now a common law precedent for sexual abuse only, and it would never fly. Kevin started working on Felicia's new filing and my appeal right away, and he was very optimistic, but for practical reasons it was a huge setback. Felicia lost over a year of time, and she was back at square one. As for my case, I would need to convince the appeals court that the district court was just flat out wrong in their decision.

I was very upset and discouraged. That lasted about a day. Then I decided that I was not giving up on holding this institution accountable for riding roughshod over so many people for so many years. They would be held accountable. It was not an option to me.

Then, out of the blue, the things I was hoping would happen began to come to fruition. From the start, I had an "If I build it, they will come," attitude about the website and the blog. Finally, now, during this summer, more victims were willing to talk publicly about their experiences and take action against the school.

The first was John Bennett. John had seen a social media post I made about the SFP abuse scandal, and contacted me via email. John had been molested by a deceased Franciscan brother at SFP, Brother DeSales Pergola, in the late 90's. DeSales was the school librarian, and I remembered him vaguely from my years as a student at the school, from 1983 -1987. I never interacted with DeSales much, I just recall seeing him in the library, and usually he was somewhat jovial.

John's story was so detailed, I knew he was telling the truth. He was DeSales' library aid during his years as a student. John remembered full conversations with DeSales, and inappropriate remarks and gestures that one would be hard pressed to make up. People often say "the devil is in the details." However, God is also in the details, and all the details were present in this man's story. For our purposes here, just let me say that DeSales was cunning and insidious. All his moves were calculated and planned. For example, he attempted to use getting John off the hook at the Dean's Office (regarding a minor rule infraction) as leverage for sexual favors. "Just give me a little feel," he told John. DeSales was evil in its purest form.

It was around this time that I was also put in touch with a young man whose Anonymous Shadowy Moniker on Facebook was, at the time, Juan Diego. Juan had been involved in an ongoing sexual relationship with Brother Dominic Quigley back when he was a 16 year old student in 2003. Brother Dominic was, for decades, St. Francis Prep's show brother. That is the best way I can describe him. He was charming, relatively attractive, funny, witty, intelligent, and all the other qualities that usually go with being a predator no one would suspect.

You may recall that Angel Amore clued me in about Dominic's propensity to be attracted to teenage boys in his messages to me. Well, Juan Diego's story confirmed all of it. Again, Angel hit the nail right on the head.

In short,
Brother Dominic asked Juan if Juan would penetrate his anus.
Brother Dominic asked if he could perform fellatio on Juan.
Brother Dominic asked to kiss Juan.
And one encounter took place in the room adjoining the school chapel.

Currently, Brother Dominic was not teaching at St. Francis Prep. He was teaching at St. Francis College, and also serving as sacristan at American Martyrs parish in Bayside, Queens. Yes, this means he was working with the altar boys.

I told Juan it was critical for him to come forward so we could make sure to get Dominic away from these children. Juan had his reservations about his identity being revealed, and I didn't blame him. People in general are not necessarily supportive of men who say they were harmed by predators when they were teenagers. The misconception is that boys this age are willing participants. Juan did not want to be attacked and have his name smeared by the Prep community. I assured him that I would keep his name private, and so would everyone else in the chain. I am a woman of my word and I take my word seriously.

I prayed for days that Juan would agree to come forward. The only other time in my life I prayed that hard was when Andrew was diagnosed with clubbed feet, and I wasn't sure whether he would ever walk correctly.

However, Felicia told me not to worry. She knew Juan would come forward. She didn't doubt it for a minute, actually. "Do you know the story of Juan Diego?" she asked me. I told her I didn't. So she told me to look it up and still see if I was worried.

What I found out is that Juan Diego was an Aztec Mexican to whom the Virgin Mary appeared on multiple occasions in the 1500's. As the story goes, Juan Diego was in the habit of regularly walking from his home to the Franciscan mission station at Tlatelolco for religious instruction and to perform his religious duties. His route passed by the hill at Tepeyac, which is now within Mexico City. At dawn on December 9, 1531, while on his usual journey, he encountered the Virgin Mary who revealed herself as the Mother of God and instructed him to request that the bishop erect a chapel in her honor. Juan Diego delivered the request, but was told by the bishop to come back another day after he had some time to reflect upon what Juan Diego had told him. Later the same day, Juan Diego encountered the Virgin again and announced that the bishop had put him off, and suggested she would do better to recruit someone of greater standing. However, Mary insisted that it was Juan whom she wanted for the task. Juan Diego agreed to return to the bishop to repeat his request. The next morning, he found the bishop more amenable to the idea. The bishop, however, asked for a sign to prove that the apparition was truly of heaven. Juan Diego returned immediately to Tepeyac and, encountering the Virgin Mary, reported the bishop's request for a sign. She agreed to provide one on the following day.

The next day, however, Juan Diego's uncle had fallen sick and Juan Diego was obligated to attend to him. In the very early hours of the following day, after his uncle's condition had deteriorated overnight, Juan Diego set out to Tlatelolco to get a priest to hear his uncle's final confession and to give him last rites. In order to avoid being delayed by the Virgin and embarrassed at having failed to meet her the previous day, Juan Diego chose another route around the hill. However, the Virgin intercepted him and asked where he was going. Juan Diego explained what had happened and the Virgin gently chided him for not having come to her for help. She asked: "Am I not here, I who am your mother?" She assured Juan that his uncle had now recovered and she told him to climb the hill and collect flowers growing there. Obeying her, Juan Diego found an abundance of flowers unseasonably in bloom on a rocky outcrop where only cactus normally grew. He gathered the flowers in his cloak and returned to the Virgin. Mary rearranged the flowers and told him to take them to the bishop. On gaining admission to the bishop later that day, Juan Diego opened his cloak, the flowers poured to the floor, and the bishop saw they had left on Juan's cloak an imprint of the Virgin's image.

Juan Diego found his uncle fully recovered, as the Virgin had assured him, and Juan's uncle recounted that he, too, had seen her, at his bedside. She had instructed him to inform the bishop of her appearance and of his cure, and she told him she desired to be known under the title of Guadalupe.

Juan Diego was on his way to a Franciscan mission? The Virgin Mary sought him out to help her? She performed miracles for him?

Felicia was right. No, I was no longer worried after I read this. God was watching, and God was on our side. God loves children, and he would see to it that they were protected.

I did not have to press Juan, or doubt that he would come through any longer. Within a few days of my having read this story, Juan contacted me to tell me he knew that God wanted him to come forward. He reached that conclusion all on his own, because God had given him signs.

The first sign came when Juan was riding the bus in Jamaica, Queens, a short distance from Prep. Guess who got on the bus? Yes, Dominic Quigley, whom Juan had not seen in over ten years. What are the chances, that on that particular day, both men would be on the same bus? Dom did not see Juan that day, but Juan saw Dom. And when he saw him, he felt sick to his stomach. He knew that coming forward was the right thing to do.

I think God wanted to make sure Juan got the message though, because this also happened.

The very next day, Juan was visiting the 9/11 memorial with his cousin. His cousin stopped at the wall of names to pay his respects. At this random spot where this young man stopped, the name Quigley was on the wall in front of them. There were thousands of names, and Juan's cousin randomly stopped there. God was speaking to Juan loud and clear.

When Juan told me he would come forward, I had him write a narrative of what happened so we could fax it to the bishop of the Brooklyn Diocese and get Dom out of American Martyrs. The bishop removed Dom that same day the fax was sent. St. Francis College also had Dom removed from his office and his teaching and administrative duties. They didn't even give him time to pack.

No one I know of has seen Dom after that day in September, 2014. But we would still hear his name, over and over again, for many reasons.

For the record, I want to say that ousting Dom from American Martyrs and getting him away from children was nothing short of a miracle. That is the main reason I know God's hand was in it. I say this because if he were still working for Prep, they very easily could have just tried to deny the incident, and pretend nothing ever happened, just like they had done with many of the allegations already made against them in the lawsuits. They could have, to save face, just kept Dom there, teaching teenage boys, and taken no action against him.

The bishop, however, is not an idiot. American Martyrs had already been hit with a huge sex abuse scandal once before.

In 2007, the New York Daily News reported that Monsignor George Zatarga of American Martyrs Parish resigned from his duties as Pastor as a consequence of admitting to sexual misconduct with several young people when he was a new priest in the Brooklyn Diocese in the 1970's. The article also stated that law enforcement was investigating more recent abuse allegations.

The bishop was familiar with the concept of potential liability. There was no reason for him to risk keeping Dom in his position of sacristan. He knew better.

However, I don't want you to think the bishop makes it easy to report this kind of thing. In fact, my experience is that the bishop makes it damn hard. The bishop has a 24 hour hotline set up to receive calls about sexual misconduct. However, it is only manned sporadically. If you want to speak with someone, you need to keep trying. I left multiple messages at first. No one called me back. I finally wrote an email to one of the other diocesan offices and asked them if there was another way I could report misconduct. They told me that the diocese will not take an email. They would, however, take a faxed statement.

Now, I think most everybody has email but perhaps not everyone has a fax machine handy. And if you are trying to keep a situation confidential, you are unlikely to take such a personal statement and trot off to the UPS store and ask them to fax it for you.

This was an unnecessary hoop, in my opinion. So long as an email has contact information, there is no reason not to take it seriously. Extra hoops discourage people from complaining. Maybe that was the idea.

Anyway, I faxed it, and the bishop and St. Francis College removed Dom, and the New York Daily News ran the story. The story was the color inset story on page 5 on October 1, 2014. The surrounding story was about a crazy Brooklyn Tech teacher named Sean Shaynak who was arrested for 36 counts of kidnapping and criminal sex acts against girls ages 13 to 19. Everyone read that story, so everyone read both stories. Dom's reputation was demolished. Thank you God.

Suddenly, the tide was turning. Felicia and I both knew it. We could feel it, and it brought tears to my eyes. God was working in mysterious ways - and what God wants, God gets.

CHAPTER TWENTY-FIVE
CONNIE COMES THROUGH

There was a lot more to the Brother Dom story, so of course, I blogged about it.

Do you remember the young man Angel Amore said complained to the school administration about Brother Dom making sexual advances toward him?

Well, that was not Juan Diego. That was a different young man. Juan Diego was sexually involved with Brother Dominic in 2003 and did not report it. It was a second boy who complained about Dom's advances in 2004. After this young man complained, Dom suddenly was scheduled for an extended leave to take a two year position in Rome. And in addition, the young man who made the complaint suddenly transferred out of Prep.

What does this sound like to you?

My question was, did Dom really go to Rome to take a prestigious position with the Franciscans after this boy accused him of sexual misconduct? Or did something else happen? The following is the blog I published on October 2, 2014, the day after the New York Daily News story came out:

When in Rome (Or Not): The Brother Dominic Quigley Timeline

In light of the student sexual abuse allegations reported in The Daily News... many St. Francis Prep alumni are inquiring why Br. Dominic

Quigley left St. Francis Prep in 2004, after having taught there for 33 years.

Well, I have been working on a Br. Dominic Quigley timeline, so the purpose of this blog is to let readers know what I've found.

First, let's make it clear that the young man alleges he had a sexual relationship with Br. Dom in 2003. This young man graduated in 2004. He did not report the relationship to the administration. I learned about the relationship from an alum who graduated with him. The first "reporting" happened in mid-September, when I sent documentation to the diocese to make them aware of the allegations. They removed Br. Dom from American Martyrs that same day. By the way, this young man is 100% on board with doing whatever is necessary to make sure Br. Dom is never around children again. I thank God every day for him and applaud his courage.

This begs the question, why did Br. Dom decide to leave St. Francis Prep in 2004? This is what St. Francis Prep told everyone was happening with Br. Dom:

*This screenshot can be viewed in my October 2, 2014 blog. It is the Fall, 2004 Grad News and this pertinent section reads as follows: "I know that many of our Alumni and friends of the Prep, would join with me in wishing **Brother Dominic Quigley** a fond farewell and extend our best to him in his journey as Secretary General of the International Franciscan Conference in Rome. Brother Dom worked enthusiastically within the Prep community serving others, saying "yes" when asked to help and raising his hand when offered the opportunity to lead. How about a Prep reunion in Rome! Also, our condolences to Brother Dom on the recent passing of his mother.

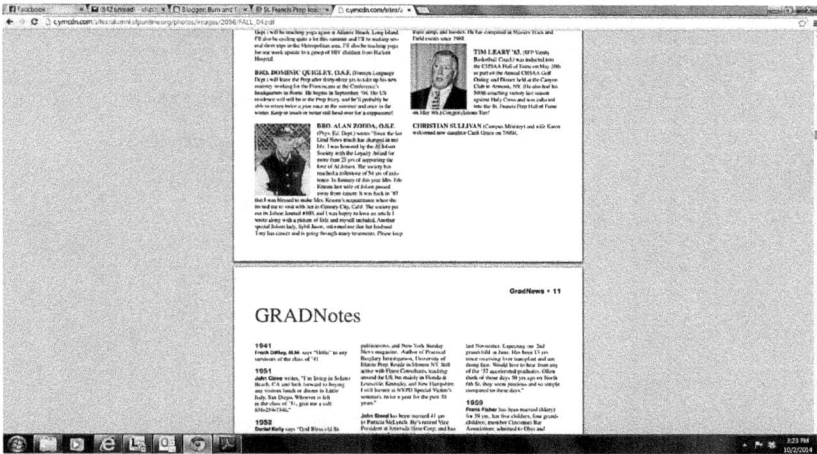

*This screenshot can also be viewed in the October 2, 2014 blog. It is another excerpt from the Fall, 2004 Grad News: **BRO DOMINIC QUIGLEY, O.S.F.** (Foreign Language Dept.) will leave the Prep after thirty-three years to take up his new ministry working for the Franciscans at the Conference's headquarters in Rome. He begins in September, '04. His US residence will still be at the Prep friary, and he'll probably be able to return twice a year once in the summer and once in the winter. Keep in touch or better still head over for a cappuccino!

I have some news for you. This never happened. Br. Dom never went to work for the Franciscan headquarters in Rome for any extended period of time. How do I know? I contacted them.

Here's my emails:

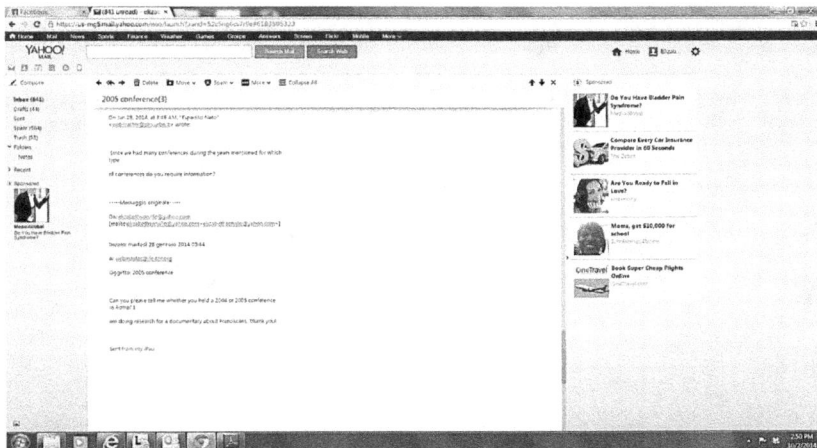

Controlled Burn:

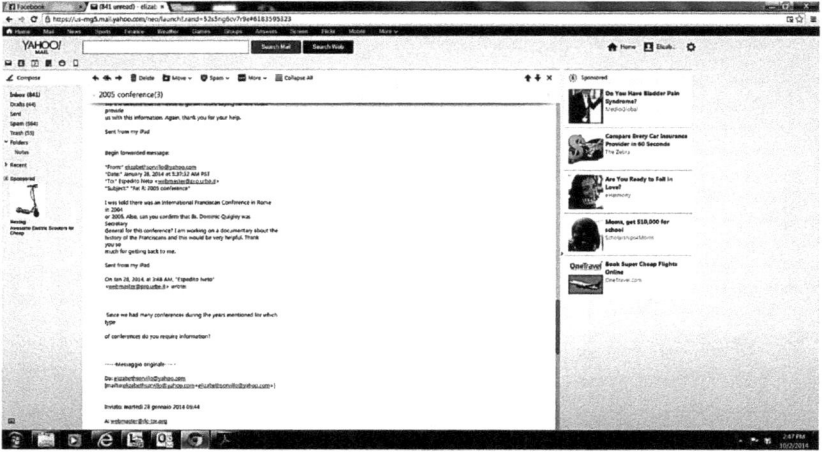

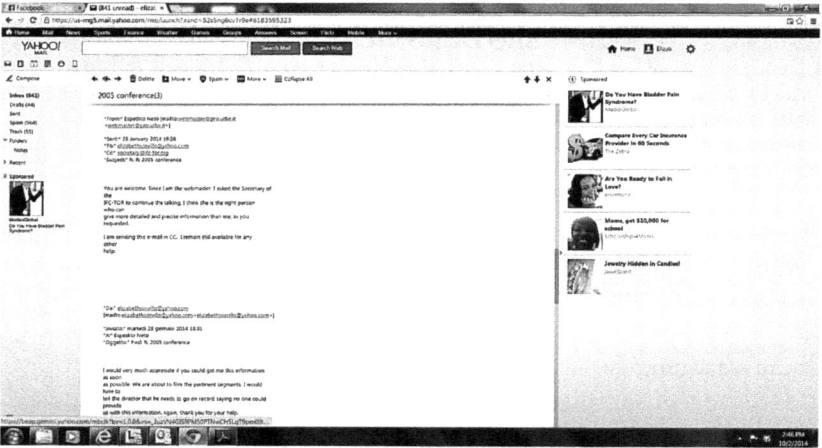

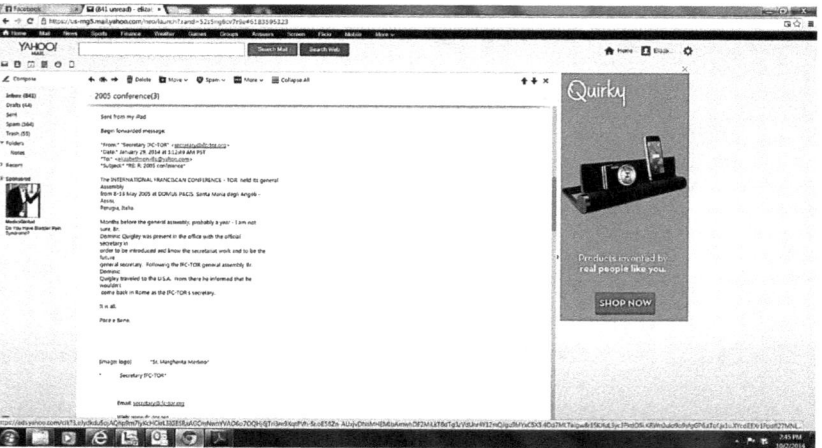

*The previous four emails can also be viewed in the October 2, 2014 blog. They read as follows:

28 gennaio 2014 05:44

Da: elizabethsorvillo@yahoo.com
A: webmaster@ifc-tor.org
Oggetto 2005 conference
Can you please tell me whether you held a 2004 or 2005 conference in Rome? I am doing research for a documentary about Franciscans. Thank you!
On Jan 28, 2014, at 3:48 AM, "Espedito Neto"
webmaster@pro.urbe.it wrote:
Since we had many conferences during the years mentioned for which type of conference do you require information?

January 28, 2014, at 5:37:32 AM PST
From: elizabethsorvillo@yahoo.com
I was told there was an International Franciscan Conference in Rome in 2004 or 2005. Also, can you confirm that Br. Dominic Quigley was Secretary General for this conference? I am working on a documentary about the history of the Franciscans and this would be very helpful. Thank you so much for getting back to me.

January 28, 2014 19:28
From: Espedito Neto webmaster@pro.urbe.it
You are welcome. Since I am the webmaster, I asked the Secretary of the IFC-TOR to continue the talking. I think she is the right person who can give more detailed and precise information than me, as you requested. I am sending this email in CC. I am available for any other help.

28 gennaio 2014 18:31
From: elizabethsorvillo@yahoo.com
I would very much appreciate it if you could get me this information as soon as possible. We are about to film the pertinent segments. I would hate to tell the director that he needs to go on record saying no one could provide us with this information. Again, thank you for your help.

From: "Secretary IFC-TOR" secretary@ifc-tor.org
January 29, 2014 at 1:12:49 AM PST
The INTERNATIONAL FRANCISCAN CONFERENCE – TOR held its general Assembly from 8-13 May 2005 at DOMUS PACIS, Santa Maria degli Angeli – Assisi, Perugia, Italia.
Months before the general assembly, probably a year – I am not sure, Br. Dominic Quigley was present in the office with the official secretary in order to be introduced and know the secretariat work and to be the future general secretary. Following the IFC-TOR general assembly Br. Dominic Quigley traveled to the U.S.A. From there he informed that he wouldn't come back in Rome as the IFC-TOR's secretary.
It is all.

Pace e Bene.

So, it looks like he was with the Franciscans in Rome for a few days in 2004, and possibly a few days in Assisi in 2005. So where did he go for two years? There is a big, gaping two year hole in his LinkedIn profile:

http://www.linkedin.com/pub/brother-dominic-quigley-o-s-f/8/27a/314

If anyone knows where he was or what he was doing during that period, I would appreciate it if you would either comment on this blog or send an email to hell@burnandrotinhell.com.

Since I published the September 18th blog (Atomic Blog) two teachers contacted me to tell me that in 2004, a young man reported to the St. Francis Prep administration that Br. Dom tried to kiss him. They both said the young man wound up withdrawing from SFP and not graduating. I am looking into these allegations at the present moment.

In 2006, Brother Dom resurfaced and began to work at Bishop Ford High School in Brooklyn. He worked there for 4 years, and then began to teach at St. Francis College. I wonder why after his extended leave he did not return to SFP, since that had been his "home" for so long.

I am pretty confident that I will get some answers to all these questions soon. The reason I am so optimistic is that a very special alum granted me a wish. This graduate has offered to pay for a full 30 year investigation of St. Francis Prep. I am absolutely ecstatic about this. All I need to do from my end is pass on the documentation I have compiled so that the chosen investigation firm has a good starting point. I think a good starting point would be early 1980, when former St. Francis Prep principal Br. Michael Moran was taken out of the school in handcuffs and arrested for child molestation.

I am very grateful for this offer as I must confess that I need the help at this point. I do not have the resources on my own to dig deeper. This firm, I am told, has contacts in the CIA, FBI, NCMEC, and law enforcement agencies across the country.

I think the coming weeks will be very, very interesting. Do you?

This blog went viral and thousands of people read it the very first day it was published. What I didn't anticipate was that this blog provided a new avenue for my fan base to contact me - via my personal email address.

It hadn't even dawned on me that they would use the email address in the screenshots to reach out to me. Everyone had to date either messaged me on Facebook or sent an email to my BRH email address. It seemed having my personal email address in the public domain added a new dimension to this whole cause - it made me more real and humanized me.

A few days after this blog was published, I received an email sent to my personal email address that was the most upsetting email yet. It was about a woman named Connie Lord who, when she was a sophomore, had a sexual relationship with her Prep biology teacher, Rodney Alejandro.

The person who emailed me this information refused to identify herself. The most she would tell me was that she is very close to someone who was very badly hurt by someone from Prep and the victim begged her not to reveal her identity.

I was used to this type of communication at this point, so we kept emailing back and forth, and I found what she was saying to me to be credible. She told me Connie would have graduated in 1990 - which would have made her a freshman when I was a senior. Luckily, I still had my yearbook from 1987. In those days, each homeroom took a picture. I found Connie's homeroom and there she was.

Next, I turned to my usual next step - seeing if I could find this person on Facebook. There were a few women named Connie Lord, but only one had the forty-one year old version of that thirteen year old girl's face from the St. Francis Prep 1987 yearbook.

Still, like any good investigative journalist, I wanted to have as much information as possible about the situation before I reached out to Connie. So, I googled Rodney Alejandro. I saw that he was teaching at a New York City public school in 2010. I also found a link to a book he self-published in 2010. What was most interesting, however, was a review written on November 19, 2012:

> **Rodney Alejandro.. Well, well, well... I'm wondering why in your short bio, you excluded the fact that you were a teacher at St. Francis Preparatory High School in Queens, New York, seduced and had a relationship with one of your 15 year old students, forced her to get several abortions (at the same time quoting the Bible), and pretty much ruined her life. You were fired from St. Francis Prep when I made that relationship known to the school. What a phony piece of garbage you are. What you did to my friend was unforgivable. I hope you rot in hell.**

All the pieces fit. There was no question in my mind that what I was told indeed happened. The next step, therefore, was to think about what I should say to Connie. This was obviously a sensitive and very disturbing situation. The emails I received said Connie left Prep at the end of her sophomore year. Bad things happened that ended badly. That much was obvious.

I clicked the message button on Connie's Facebook profile and I simply asked "Did you ever attend St. Francis Prep?" Then I waited.

Weeks went by, and Connie had not responded to me. However, despite this, I felt I had gathered enough information that would justify contacting the New York City Department of Education in order to inform them of the very disturbing situation they had on their hands in 2010.

I spoke to the department that handles complaints against teachers, and they issued me a complaint number. Then they said they would refer the case to an investigator, and someone would be in touch with me. Shortly thereafter, I received a call from DOE Detective Derrick Dottin. Detective Dottin had two interesting things to tell me: 1) Rodney Alejandro was fired from the NYC public school he taught at in 2010, and 2) Dottin was familiar with St. Francis Prep in that he had been there investigating another matter about a decade earlier. I could only guess what that matter had been about.

Detective Dottin asked me if I had been in touch with Connie. I said that I had a message out to her but had not heard back. He told me he was very limited in what he could accomplish unless he could speak with her. I told him I would see what I could do.

But I didn't have to do anything. The day before Thanksgiving, five weeks after I had messaged her, there was a message from Connie in my Facebook inbox:

> **i went there for 2 years and failed out because a teacher seduced me and screwed up my high school career. sorry didn't graduate but i'm a musician. who are you?**

Suffice it to say, I explained who I am. This started a series of long conversations with Connie and her best friend, Chris Murphy, who had not only written that toxic review of Alejandro's book, but who also reported the sexual relationship between Connie and Alejandro directly to then principal Brother Leonard Conway in 1988.

Both women were both fully committed to making sure Alejandro never teaches again. To that end, I put them in touch with Detective Dottin. I also contacted Queens Assistant District Attorney Ken Applebaum.

Mr. Applebaum had been assigned the Brother Dom case after I had faxed Juan Diego's statement to the bishop. Unfortunately, because Juan is over twenty-three, Applebaum could not file criminal charges. This was very upsetting, because two more men had contacted Applebaum about Dom's predatory behavior right after the story was published in the Daily News. I thought in Connie's case, the sexual misconduct was so egregious that perhaps there was a way to file charges against Alejandro. One could only hope and try.

Both Detective Dottin and ADA Applebaum wanted to interview Connie and Chris personally. So in preparation for that, I asked Connie to write a narrative of what happened to her. This is what she wrote:

"It started when he had me play a strip poker game with him on a computer. It was cartoon characters stripping. He did this in the back room of the lab adjacent to his classroom...

January 24, 1988 is the first time Rodney Alejandro raped me. I lost my virginity that day. I was sitting on the floor and he became very aggressive and jumped on top of me and started kissing me with his tongue. He took a condom out of his pocket. Next thing I knew my clothes were off and he was on top of me. He penetrated me hard and broke my hymen. He covered my mouth because I was screaming. I was very scared. I went to the bathroom and discovered I was bleeding a lot. I just wanted to leave. I wanted to go home and crawl into my bed and pull the covers over my head. I asked him to take me home. He drove me home in his little red Hyundai. He was paranoid because he saw how upset I was. He kept asking if I was ok. He dropped me off a couple of blocks from my house and I walked home...

I always called him Mr. A because he acted like an authority figure and was very intimidating. He scared me...

After school at SFP he would wait for me and pick me up and take me back to his apartment. I couldn't look him in the eye when he took off my clothes and raped me. He tried to seduce me and make me fall in love with him but he couldn't so he forced himself on me. He wanted me to look him in the eye romantically and I didn't feel that. After that I became afraid to look anyone in the eye...

One day after school he came to my house. He knew no one was home. My back door was always unlocked. He opened the door and ran in and saw me trying to run up the stairs. He grabbed me down and forced me into his car and took me back to his apartment again... In the summer of 1988 I got pregnant for the first time. I failed out of SFP. He passed me with a 75. He forced me to get an abortion because he was afraid of going to jail. In January of 1989 I became pregnant again... I was severely depressed. He was the cause of my failing out of SFP...at this point I was suicidal...

RA always told me women are to be subservient to men. Every time I stood up to him he would point his finger down and say "Satan." Other times he would just point his finger down and say nothing, because he knew I knew what that meant."

When I first read this, I cried. Girls like Connie were the reason I was doing all this in the first place. I wanted justice for her in the worst way.

Connie and Chris met with Detective Dottin and ADA Applebaum. They both found the women sincere and credible. Dottin said his investigation would ensure that Alejandro would never teach in New York City ever again.

Applebaum, on the other hand, said the timeframe of Connie's rapes did not fit the statutory scheme in such a way that he could prosecute Alejandro.

The victory for Connie was much smaller than I would have liked, but a victory nonetheless. She would have some justice, and everyone would know her story.

I published it on December 22, 2014.

It is the second most-read blog I have ever written, second only to the original "I Am EC" blog.

Connie, thank you for being a hero.

CHAPTER TWENTY-SIX
THE BISHOP, THE CARDINAL, AND E

Felicia Mooradian, John Bennett, Juan Diego, Connie Lord - their stories touched me so deeply and simultaneously enraged me so much that I decided to take this whole endeavor for justice to the next level.

I would leave no room for doubt in anyone's mind about the extent of child sexual abuse, child sexual harassment, and corruption that has taken place in the halls of St. Francis Prep.

What I could not fully process mentally and what upset me the most in all this is that even when men were reported to the St. Francis Prep administration for these abuses, they still walked out the doors of the school without consequence. It made me so sick to my stomach that many a night I lied awake, playing these scenarios over and over again in my head, unable to believe some people would be so uncaring as to permit this.

St. Francis Prep does not like to fire teachers. In fact, they will do anything possible to avoid it so as to not be subjected to a wrongful termination suit. Typically, what Prep will do is what most corporations do: ask the employee in question to resign, and if they refuse, tell them they will be terminated. I have heard this over, and over, and over again from so many sources at the school that I have lost count. They did this with Rodney Alejandro. Connie remembers clearly the day Rodney came home, and told her he was given the choice to resign or be fired. What a nice offer for a school to make to a child rapist.

Of course, most teachers chose to resign over the years. That is the "smart" move for the vast majority of people. If you are terminated, you carry that with you for a good, long while. It goes on your record, and could be disclosed to future employers, should they call for a reference. A termination has the potential to open up a can of worms, and when you have a family to feed, that can be quite scary for your future.

What is interesting is that Marla and I were two who chose to be terminated. The ones who choose to be terminated, well, those are people who obviously don't give a shit. People who don't give a shit are just about the scariest people on earth, and they can wreak all sorts of havoc if it means taking a stand for something they believe in. It's a badge of honor, in my book.

This being said, in my mind it was clearly time for the administration of St. Francis Prep to come to Jesus.

Although Bishop DiMarzio of the Brooklyn Diocese had removed Brother Dominic from American Martyrs, to my knowledge he had not attempted to force the resignation of the current St. Francis Prep administration, or admonish them in any way. I heard from sources inside the building that the Bishop was greatly displeased with the humiliation he had been caused by the publicity surrounding Brother Dom, but that was about the extent of it.

This bothered me a great deal. Why was he so hands off?

If you asked the Bishop for the talking point response, I am guessing he would probably say that since St. Francis Prep is operated by an independent Board of Trustees, there is nothing he could do. St. Francis Prep does operate independent of the diocese and is not technically under diocesan control.

However, the diocese pays the teacher pensions. In addition, the diocese holds the lease on the building which houses St. Francis Prep. Yes, that's right. Prep does not own the building. The Brooklyn Diocese owns it.

In 1976, when the Brooklyn Diocese was under financial strain, it made agreements with six Catholic Schools, including St. Francis Prep, to turn over operations to independent Boards of Trustees, in exchange for holding the leases on the buildings. In fact, in 2013, the Brooklyn Diocese sued Christ the King High School in Queens for violating its lease.

I decided to try and force the Bishop's hand. I began a relentless mission of sending disturbing information about Prep to him. I also decided to bring Cardinal Dolan into the loop.

Here is what I sent the Cardinal. (Please note that at this time, there was no direct way to email him. The only way to reach out was via the general communications mailbox on the archdiocese website that I had used two years earlier):

St. Francis Preparatory School lawsuits and former SFP teacher Br. Dominic Quigley removed as Sacristan of American Martyrs Church

Elizabeth Sorvillo <elizabethsorvillo@yahoo.com>
09/24/14 at 9:30 AM

To: communications@archny.org

Dear Cardinal Dolan,

I wrote you almost two years ago to inform you of ongoing problems at St. Francis Prep in Fresh Meadows. During these last two years, several lawsuits have been brought against the school by former students, and more alumni continue to come forward with their stories of sexual abuse and sexual harassment.

To date, I have received complaints about the following Franciscan brothers: Br. Michael Moran (former principal of SFP arrested for child molestation in 1980 - now lives in Mission Viejo, CA), Br. Joe Mussa (former coach/teacher who molested boys on the SFP hockey team, was removed from SFP and transferred to Xaverian HS, now lives in friary on Remsen Street), Br. DeSales Pergola (SFP librarian who sexually harassed and molested boys for decades), Br. Ben O'Reilly (sexually harassed female students for decades, was removed from teaching in 2006 because of a complaint by a student, lawsuit pending in state court), and Br. Dominic Quigley (former SFP teacher who had an ongoing sexual relationship with a 16 year old boy in 2003. Please note, he was the Sacristan of American Martyrs parish in Bayside, Queens, up until last Thursday, when he was removed because of the 2003 victim's complaint.

Please be aware that I have exchanged emails with Jasmine Salazar at the Brooklyn Diocese victim services office regarding the situation at St. Francis Prep. By the way, since I last emailed her two more men came forward about Br. DeSales and and Br. Dominic. I am writing to let you know I consider the Brooklyn Diocese on notice about the problems at St. Francis Prep. Although the school is operated by an independent Board of Trustees, the diocese pays the teachers their pensions and also, I believe, holds the lease on the building. If more children continue to be preyed upon by their teachers at this school, I will hold the diocese accountable.

> I gently suggested to Ms. Salazar that the diocese take this opportunity to step in and investigate the school and perhaps appoint new leadership before this snowballs out of control, possibly leading to the demise of the school. I hope you seriously consider this suggestion.
> I would be happy to assist in any way I can.
>
> Regards,
> Elizabeth Sorvillo

Of course, the Cardinal did not respond to this. I didn't expect him to, considering his history as Archbishop of Milwaukee. However, that didn't stop me. I would continue to email Cardinal Dolan and Bishop DiMarzio with every ounce of information about Dominic Quigley and the abuse of students at St. Francis Prep that would come into my hands.

On October 6, 2014, I also sent the Bishop (via his assistant) Joseph DiSomma's criminal background. Here is some of what I said:

> I want you to know that I am sorry that I am bombarding you with emails, but I need to make sure children are protected at St. Francis Prep. Therefore, on another note separate from the Dominic Quigley issue, I would very much appreciate it if you passed the below criminal history of the financial controller of St. Francis Prep on to Bishop DiMarzio. Joseph Disomma spent almost 5 years in federal prison and his court cases reflect a history of gun possession. I don't really think he should be around children every day. If the Bishop Googles Joseph DiSomma all the information will be right there on various legal sites.

Then, in December, I decided to send the Cardinal Connie's story. What surprised me was that the Cardinal had suddenly created a "Safe Environment Program" to handle these types of abuse inquiries, and named a director to address concerns. So here is what I sent Edward Mechmann, Director of the Safe Environment Program at the Archdiocese of New York:

> Fw: Rape of St. Francis Prep student by her teacher
>
> Elizabeth Sorvillo <elizabethsorvillo@yahoo.com>
> 12/27/14 at 3:36 PM
> To: emechmann@archny.org
>
> Dear Sir/Madam:

I am writing to report that a 15 year old St. Francis Prep student was raped, impregnated multiple times, and forced to have abortions by her St. Francis Prep teacher in 1988. I am the former St. Francis Prep teacher who caught this pederast who was working as a sacristan at American Martyrs Church in Bayside, Queens:
St. Francis teacher accused of abusing student

St. Francis teacher accused of abusing student

A Franciscan brother was removed from his job at a Queens parish as prosecutors investigate charges he sexually abused a student while teaching at St.

View on www.nydailynews.com   Preview by Yahoo

After this article was published, I was contacted about a woman named Constance Lord who is the subject of this email. Connie has gone to the authorities about the rapes, and she would like to work with the Cardinal to make sure children are protected at the school that bears the Pope's name. She is not convinced ANY child is protected at the school, because Brother Leonard Conway, who was in charge while she was being raped by her teacher in 1988, is still in charge there.

I understand that St. Francis Prep is under the supervision of its Board of Directors, but the Brooklyn Diocese holds the lease on the building, and the Brooklyn Diocese contributes to teacher pensions. Therefore, the Diocese has at least some responsibility to make sure children are not sexually harassed and abused at the school, as they have been for 30 years. It cannot turn a blind eye to the safety of children who attend this school.

I forwarded the below email to my contact at Bishop DiMarzio's office. I hope to hear from someone there or from your office regarding a course of action to make sure policies and procedures are put in place that will ensure that children have a voice and are not being victimized at St. Francis Prep. Their current policy calls for an investigation by the principal in the event a child complains about sexual harassment or abuse. For many reasons, I honestly can't think of a worse policy from a victim's perspective and I would be happy to discuss them.

I look forward to hearing from you.

Sincerely,
Elizabeth Sorvillo

----- Forwarded Message -----
From: Elizabeth Sorvillo <elizabethsorvillo@yahoo.com>
To: Jasmine Salazar <jsalazar@diobrook.org>
Sent: Wednesday, December 24, 2014 11:57 AM
Subject: Rape of St. Francis Prep student by her teacher

Ms. Salazar,

The Bishop should know that a woman named Constance Lord was raped, impregnated, and forced to have abortions by her St. Francis Prep teacher when she was 15 years old in 1988. She has come forward to support all the other victims of sexual harassment and abuse at St. Francis Prep, and has gone to the authorities.

Please ask Bishop DiMarzio to read this:

Burn and Rot in Hell: My Name Is Connie and My St. Francis Prep Biology Teacher, Rodney Alejandro, Raped Me

Burn and Rot in Hell: My Name Is Connie and My St. Franc...

This was not a fun blog to write, but I believe everything that led up to this blog happened for a reason, and that God wants me to do it, so here we go.

View on blog.burnandrotinhel...	Preview by Yahoo

It would be nice for the public to know that something is being done to make sure children are protected at St. Francis Prep. The woman who contacted me about Connie is also a victim of abuse she experienced at SFP and she is considering coming forward in the near future.

Regards,
Elizabeth Sorvillo

(Notice I sent my blog about Connie to the Bishop's office as well. I wanted both the Bishop and the Cardinal on the same page about what has happened at SFP over the last 30 years.)

This was Edward Mechmann's prompt response to me:

RE: Rape of St. Francis Prep student by her teacher
People

Edward Mechmann <Edward.Mechmann@archny.org>
12/29/14 at 8:36 AM

To
Elizabeth Sorvillo
CC
jsalazar@diobrook.org

Dear Ms. Sorvillo --

Thank you for your email. I am the Director of the Safe Environment Office of the Archdiocese of New York. Our jurisdiction does not include institutions located in Queens, so unfortunately we cannot offer any assistance with this situation. I see from the email chain, however, that you have corresponded with Jasmine Salazar, who is the appropriate person in the Diocese of Brooklyn to handle these kinds of allegations. I am confident that Ms. Salazar will be able to help you as best as she can.

Sincerely in Christ,

Edward T. Mechmann, Esq.
Director of Safe Environment
Archdiocese of New York
1011 First Avenue
New York, NY 10022
646-794-2807

"Whatever you do, do all to the glory of God." (1 Cor. 10:31)

Check out my blog: http://blog.archny.org/steppingout/

What made it even more disturbing was the line after Mechmann's contact info: "Whatever you do, do all to the glory of God." This presupposes that one ACTUALLY BE WILLING TO DO SOMETHING. Apparently though, the Cardinal's office was not willing to proactively do anything to help ensure the safety of the children of St. Francis Prep.

And it appeared neither was Bishop DiMarzio. I was sick to my stomach.

CHAPTER TWENTY-SEVEN

THE TEN THOUSAND DOLLAR TUITION PROBLEM

Once Connie Lord went public with her story, things got even crazier, to say the least. Don't forget that at this time, Felicia Mooradian was still a defendant in St. Francis Prep's defamation lawsuit against her. Please also don't forget that one of the statements the school was saying is defamatory is "SEXUAL HARASSMENT AT SFP IS A HUGE PROBLEM."

Connie and her friend, Chris, were both willing to testify about what Connie had endured while a student at the school.

After the school learned of this, Felicia received Snapchats on her phone saying truly disgusting things about her history of abuse that only someone who had seen Felicia's medical records would know. If you recall, those records had been sent to the school in conjunction with filing her lawsuit regarding Brother Ben. Therefore, I am guessing that someone who works for the school or who knows someone who works for the school or was hired by someone who works for the school sent her those Snapchats. The information is way too personal to share here, but suffice it to say that the tone and content was as vile as the Burn that was posted about my wife, son and me that I included in a previous chapter. In fact, that Burn about my family and the Snapchat Felicia received are written with the same syntax and in the same style. I would bet they were written by the same person. I have a guess who this person is. Do you?

I can tell you the Snapchats said over and over again that Felicia "ruined the school." In addition, Marla Krolikowski received a voicemail message stating "Your little whore girlfriend, Felicia, ruined the school. Good job, asshole!" This led me to conclude that they were not too thrilled about Connie going public and supporting Felicia.

Discovery was proceeding in the school's defamation lawsuit against Felicia, and her frivolous lawsuit claim against them. Therefore, Kevin Mulhearn submitted his document requests to the school. They included requests for all documents related to the sexual harassment of students over a thirty year period, and the following:

> "8. All documents which discuss, relate to, concern, pertain to or contain Felicia Mooradian's complaint or complaints to St. Francis Prep (and its administrators) about the conduct of Br. Ben O'Reilly, ("Brother Ben") towards her, including but not limited to any psychological reports or assessments of Brother Ben's fitness to teach children (particularly girls), and any disciplinary records which demonstrate or relate to St. Francis Prep's response and reaction to Felicia Mooradian's complaints about Brother Ben and/ or reports or assessments of Brother Ben's fitness to teach children (particularly girls)."

Well, guess what? St. Francis Prep refused to hand over anything. In fact, in their response, they said that asking for Brother Ben's file constituted harassment against the school and its former employee.

I have never, in all my years as an attorney, heard of a plaintiff refusing to hand over any documents for discovery in its own lawsuit. Usually, plaintiffs want to run to the courthouse screaming "Here's what I've got! Let's go!" and move ahead as fast as possible. But the case here was the opposite. To me, this was a clear sign that Prep knew it had made a mistake in suing Felicia. They knew that if they handed those records over, they would lose. So, they were going to try anything within their power to prevent that, even if it meant stalling their own litigation.

As this discovery drama was unfolding, I was receiving inside information from my sources regarding the state of the school. Specifically, what I was told was:

1. Seventeen faculty and staff members had suddenly retired/resigned in June, 2014 and close to an additional dozen were leaving in June, 2015.
2. Donations were shrinking tremendously.
3. Enrollment was falling to its lowest point in 30 years, to under 2,600 students.
4. The Board of Trustees had passed a resolution to increase tuition and fees to nearly $10,000 for incoming freshmen starting in September, 2015.

When I heard about the tuition increase, I knew they were in dire straits. It seemed to me that they were repeating the exact mistakes the administration of Bishop Ford High School made. Bidhop Ford was another Franciscan-run high school located in Brooklyn. While Prep's scandal largely involved allegations of sexual harassment and sexual abuse of students, Bishop Ford's scandal involved allegations of embezzlement by its President, Ray Nash. This scandal ultimately resulted in the closing of the school.

Here is the letter that was being circulated among Bishop Ford's alumni in 2012:

AN OPEN LETTER TO THE BOARD OF TRUSTEES OF BISHOP FORD CENTRAL CATHOLIC HIGH SCHOOL: We were shocked and dismayed to learn that Bishop Ford Central Catholic High School President Raymond P. Nash has admitted to misappropriating over $50,000 from the school's Development Fund. What is even more disconcerting is the fact that this $50,000 personal loan to his son has involved our alma mater in an outside, Federal investigation. To make matters worse, the Board of Trustees concealed this entire matter from the Bishop Ford Alumni Association and other interested parties and has allowed Mr. Nash to remain President for two years after his unfortunate error in judgment, with only a written reprimand. Misappropriation of funds over $50,000, whether paid back or not, is a Class C Felony. Although Mr. Nash has done a great deal for Bishop Ford Central Catholic High School over his many years of service and employment, allowing him to remain in his current position is unconscionable. There could be dire legal and financial consequences that could ruin the school's reputation and hinder its ability to function successfully if Mr. Nash continues to serve as President. At the very least, Mr. Nash should have been temporarily suspended from his duties and an Interim President brought in until the legal investigation Bishop Ford has now been dragged into was concluded. If Mr. Nash cares about our school and its reputation,

instead of hiring a PR firm to bolster his image in the media (which could be construed as once again using school funds for personal reasons), he would step down from his position as President. His refusal to resign and his silence in response to our many demands for an explanation speak volumes. The Board of Trustees is charged with the responsibility of ensuring that all incoming funds are used in the best interest of Bishop Ford students. The Board has failed to meet this responsibility. Our school community is more important than just one person. We urge the Board to reconsider its decision to allow Raymond P. Nash to continue acting as President and demand Mr. Nash's immediate resignation. We each continue to pray for Mr. Nash, the members of the Board, and their families. Today is indeed a sad day in our alma mater's history.
Sincerely,
CONCERNED ALUMNI OF BISHOP FORD CENTRAL CATHOLIC HIGH SCHOOL

Nash eventually resigned, stating that the allegations against him "were blown out of proportion." By that time, the writing was largely on the wall. Bishop Ford was raising tuition despite falling enrollment, and it was on its way to closing.

Prep was doing the same thing. They had a chance to move forward, but didn't want to take it.

I had published my proposal to save the school several times on the school's Facebook alumni page, but the school never made a move to accept it.

What I was proposing was simply this:

1. Five specific resignations, namely, Leonard Conway, Patrick McLaughlin, Joseph DiSomma, Christopher Mendolia, and Robyn Armon;
2. Better policies put in place that protect children;
3. Settling for reasonable amounts of money with victims. (Notice here, that I never mentioned settling with me. That was the least of my concerns.)

I thought this proposal was fair, reasonable, and a good way for the school to have a new lease on life. Obviously, they didn't agree. That didn't surprise me.

Something else needed to happen to push this cause forward. So, I reached out to a former classmate of mine named John Cardillo who had been sexually harassed by Brother Dominic and verbally threatened by Brother Ben. He was now a well-known investigative blogger, and he was willing to assist me.

I sent him a lot of the information I had gathered for him to review and evaluate. In January, 2015, he blogged about the "Decades Long Sex Abuse Scandal at America's Largest Catholic High School." His blog got over 500,000 hits and over two hundred seventy comments, mostly by people who had witnessed or experienced teacher sexual misconduct at St. Francis Prep.

Now, the cat was really out of the bag. Calls and emails were coming in from alumni all over the United States. The truth shall set you free.

This I did expect. I was not surprised at all by this response. There were hundreds of victims waiting to speak their mind. It just took a while to reach them. In fact, so many victims came forward that I was named to the list of Catholic clergy abuse whistleblowers on the website BishopAccountability. org. To be in the company of such great and brave people is an honor I will treasure forever.

What I didn't expect was what came next. In February, 2015, I received a call from a private investigator named Jim Murphy of Sutton Associates in Hicksville, NY. Jim was hired by the Franciscan Order to investigate Brother Dominic Quigley, whom I had reported to the Bishop six months earlier. Right from the beginning, Jim was affable, respectable, and forthright. He is also a former FBI agent.

At first, I didn't know what to make of his contacting me directly since I was still involved in pending litigation with Prep. I also didn't know what to make of the whole idea of an investigation into Quigley, given that all signs pointed to the high probability that the Franciscans knew he had "problems" for decades. However, I complied. I gave Jim all the information I had that I felt would not be violating any confidences.

The investigation is still open, but Jim Murphy told me unequivocally that when he issues his report, it will show that his investigation had determined that Brother Dominic Quigley is not technically a pedophile, but someone who has a strong sexual attraction to teenage boys. He also said that he would be absolutely shocked if anyone ever let Brother Dominic Quigley around adolescent boys again, or reinstated him to any kind of position at a school or with the Brooklyn Diocese.

That was music to my ears. Thank you, God.

CHAPTER TWENTY-EIGHT
BYE BYE MARLA

Life is so strange and takes so many unexpected twists and turns, there is just no way to stay ahead of the curve. After Marla settled her lawsuit with Prep, she obtained a position at Estee Lauder, the cosmetics company, as an assembly line supervisor. Marla was sixty at this point, but still wanted to work. She was not one to sit around the house relaxing all day. She wanted to be productive.

At this point, everyone knew that Marla was going to be one of Felicia's key witnesses. Marla spoke frequently with several teachers still working for the school, and had told them that she would do whatever it took for her to help Felicia. This included making sure a provision was included in her settlement agreement giving her the ability to testify in court for Felicia.

In early September, 2015, Marla retired permanently. She had made the choice to leave Estee Lauder and pursue becoming an advocate for transgender rights full-time.

Then she died suddenly on September 20th, 2015. The Trilogy of Terror was no more.

Marla had been at an art show hosted by a former St. Francis Prep art teacher when she collapsed to the floor and died within seconds. The cause of her death is unknown, and her family chose not to do an autopsy.

Felicia and I could not believe it. We had just spoken to her a few days prior. She sounded great, and she said what she always said to us "Do not stop, do not give up. People know you are right. We will get these bastards."

Now, with our star witness gone, Felicia and I were wondering exactly how we would get these bastards.

Then the phone call came. A member of Marla's family reached out to Felicia. Apparently, Marla had left Felicia a very special gift. It was the unedited documentary Marla made in the 90's, with a dozen or so St. Francis Prep sexual harassment victims telling their story. The truth was determined to come out.

Thank you, Marla, for all you did for us.

Chapter TWENTY-NINE

DANNY

Anyone who knows me will tell you I believe in miracles and I do not give up. I keep fighting because of people like Danny.

Do you remember that blog I posted in 2013 about the sexual abuse survivor who was molested by former St. Francis Prep teacher Brother Joe Mussa, the well-respected hockey coach?

Well, two years later, just around the time Marla died, Danny commented on that particular blog that he was molested by Mussa as well, and he asked for my help. He posted his phone number right on the blog, so I texted him.

Danny told me he was seeking closure and validation of what he had been through. He had confronted Mussa and the Franciscan hierarchy in the past, but they would not admit a thing. He now had litigation on his mind.

Of course, after discussing dates and places where the offenses occurred, I had to explain to him that there would be no litigation. New York's awful and unjust statute of limitations would prevent that.

The best I could do was let Danny be heard. The result of those conversations is one of the most detailed, compelling, and disturbing narratives of being groomed and molested by a Catholic cleric that a child sex abuse survivor has ever written.

I am warning you that Danny's words are raw, angry and heartbreaking. As you will see, eventually he stops using a capital "M" for Mussa. He says the man who sent his life on a downward spiral is not worthy of that respect.

Here is his story, just as he wrote it:

"It was right before Easter 1976, I was in the 5th grade at Holy Name of Jesus Catholic School in Brooklyn, New York. I was 11 years old. A student from Mr. Joseph Mussa's 8th grade class came down to my classroom and told my teacher that Mr. Mussa needed two volunteers, one boy and one girl, to help him decorate the bulletin board in his classroom . Everyone's hand shot up. Mr. Mussa was the coolest teacher in the whole school. He was Joe cool. He ran the intramural hockey and football leagues at the school. If you had Mr. Mussa as a teacher you were considered very, very lucky. A lot of teachers at Holy Name were nuns and a handful of Brothers, for the most part they were all considered to be very strict and mean, and quite frankly they were. During my grammar school years there was also a decline in nuns and Brothers being teachers, they seem to be fading out. Now there were some regular people teaching, and they seem to be more easier going and pleasant then the men and women of " the cloth." You would think it would be the other way around, you know with the GOD thing and all ! So when I was picked as the boy student to go up to Mr. Mussa's classroom, I was thrilled and the envy of all the other kids in my class. And when my teacher picked the prettiest girl in all of the 5th grade I was thrilled and envied even more. Looking back now all these years later..........I wish I never raised my hand on that day. But at the time it was akin to Charlie finding the golden ticket for a day at the chocolate factory with Mr. Willy Wonka himself. The girl, Michelle, and I spent that afternoon decorating Mr. Mussa's classroom for the upcoming Easter holiday. We joked around and laughed the afternoon away. I was nervous about meeting and interacting with Mr. Mussa , but as I soon realized, he was not like the other teachers at Holy Name, He would pal around with you, put you in a playful headlock and give you a few nuggies on the head, way different than any of the other teachers . He would even tell me to call him Joe. Mr. Mussa had noticed me when he would be in the schoolyard refereeing the flag football games. At one game I was picked to be the kid who was in charge of the clock that kept the time for the games. It was a position everyone who wasn't in the game jockeyed for, and a job Mr. Mussa would assign someone at each game. I would watch the older boys like John C. and Bart P. jump into his station wagon after the games when he would take them down to Burger King for some burgers. I would hear the stories the next day of all the laughs they had and I wanted to be a part of that fun. For the next two months after our afternoon decorating his classroom, Mr.Mussa, or Joe as I was allowed to call him, would hang around the schoolyard after school and throw a football or baseball around, talk sports and would joke around the neighborhood kids who played there after school. I only lived two blocks away from the school and spent lots of time there. One day I received a letter at home from Mr. Mussa. I was surprised. In the letter, from what little I remember, Mr. Mussa told me how happy he was to meet me and how special of a kid that I was. He also said that we were going to be very good friends. I remember how in the beginning of our friendship he would always repeat those same things to me. How special I was, and how we were going to be good buddies. That really made me feel good about myself. There were even a few kids, me being one of them, that Joe was taking a liking to. Kids my own age, kids in my class. We were finally being the ones he would take for burgers or ice cream. He even took me and another classmate home to his parents' house to look at his record album collection. I remember going there specifically so he would show us the clues that were hidden in the "Paul is dead album" which had rumors about the Beatles' Paul McCartney. They claimed Paul McCartney was dead and replaced by a lookalike, with hidden clues on album covers and inside album jackets and you could even hear someone saying "Paul is dead" by playing one of their albums backwards. Mr. Mussa knew and showed us where all these clues were.

The end of the school year was coming. At that time I got average grades of B's, C's and D"s. School was a bit of a struggle for me. Summer was coming and I couldn't wait to go the CYO surf club in Coney Island where me and my family spent the summers BBQing and swimming with other families from Holy Name Parish. I was starting to gain confidence in myself. My self esteem was starting to grow. Mr. Mussa had taken a liking to me that made me feel like I was the most special kid in the world. He promised me more trips to Burger King for french fries and hamburgers and to Carvel for ice cream. We had been there several times, mostly with other boys from school, but the last couple of times it was just Mr. Mussa and myself.......
Summer arrived and Mr. Mussa sent a couple of more letters to me and then all of the sudden they stopped. Summer went and no sign of Mr. Mussa. I was devastated. I thought I may have done something wrong. Was he mad at me? These thoughts ran through my mind. My self esteem and confidence which was picking up steam was now dissipating. I was baffled and confused. No Joe Mussa !! Where did he go? He was a fixture at the school, active in sports programs and very much liked among the student body. Sixth grade was beginning soon and I was anxious to see Mr. Mussa if only for one thing, to find out what I did wrong, and why at one moment I was his new little pal and then the next I wasn't.

I spent the summer wondering where he was...... spent the summer waiting for one of those letters that were also like a golden ticket to Willy Wonka's chocolate factory............ . very few kids got personal letters from him, but if you did you felt as part of an elite group. Mr. Mussa was your buddy.....a school teacher went out of his way to see you, you were friends to the envy of your classmates. And he has such a distinctive handwriting that you would be able to tell it was a letter from him without even reading anything on the envelope. It was that distinctive. You could even tell if someone else had a letter from him at a quick glance of it from across a room. He was already having a bad effect on my life and I only really knew him for two months. It's as if I was raised up past all my peers and put on some sort of pedestal only to be tossed aside and forgotten. The worst part......I had no idea or explanation as to why. Me and my schoolmates speculated as to what happened and where he was. Then school started up, and he never showed up. We were told he wouldn't be teaching at Holy Name. He was being replaced, gone. And no one seemed to have a clue as to where he went. Sometime towards the middle of the 6th grade, the girl who lived downstairs in the building I lived in solved the mystery. There he was, a photograph in the Tablet, a Catholic newspaper. There was a picture of him with a few other men in a semi-circle all dressed in brown robes with a headline above the photograph announcing them all as new Christian Brothers in the Franciscan Friars order of the Catholic Church. Mr. Joseph Musa had become Brother Joe. I was disappointed when I saw it. Why would the coolest teacher in the world join a group of men that the students were all frightened of? The few Brothers that were at Holy Name all had a reputation as being strict hard-nosed men and they did nothing to make you believe otherwise. (From this point forward I will refer to Mr. Mussa as just mussa, the m in lowercase and I will never refer to him as Brother. He is not deserving of respect that I would show any man by referring to them with Mr. , and I will not refer to him as Brother in respect to myself for my own feelings in regards to Brothers in general .) Me and my classmates were in shock over this bit of information, I couldn't understand it. To me mussa had joined a group of mean spirited men who walked around in heavy brown robes with a thick bright white rope tied around their waist, who ruled with an iron fist carrying around a ruler to discipline out of line students with. At least that's the impression we younger kids got from the older ones. During my 8 years at Holy Name, the lay people, as they were referred to as (people who were not members of any religious order) were just starting to gain numbers over the nuns who in turn outnumbered the Brothers in my school. There still were several nuns at holy name and if my memory serves me right, I can only remember there being two Brothers teaching in Holy Name, Brother John and Brother Tom. And in contrast to a student being considered lucky to have mussa as their teacher, you were considered not as fortunate to get either Bro. John or Bro. Tom as your teacher. Their class was rigid and strict. In my eight years there I never had a

Brother as my primary teacher. I think maybe once I had a nun as a primary teacher as well as the art teacher and the librarian who were both nuns and whose interactions were limited to an hour each a week. Then somewhere towards the middle of my 6th year at Holy Name when I came home from school and I received a letter from mussa......instantly upon seeing the envelope, I recognized his distinctive handwriting and the bright blue ink (he always used a specific bright shade of blue ink) I was nervous and tense about getting his letter. In fact it took several hours before I opened it and read it. Inside the letter mussa told me about where he was for the last year and how he was ordained as a Brother, and what changes that is having in his life. mussa also told me that those changes would not have any effect on our friendship and that his movement were restricted while he was studying to become a Brother and now he had more freedom to come visit his "little buddy" which was what he called me all the time. He use to always sing "oh Danny Boy" to me all the time, I find it very difficult whenever I hear that song now. I wrote back to him, I had many questions. I put the letter with the others in a shoebox under my bed. I was acquiring quite a collection. And now that he wasn't on any restriction, the letters started coming pretty much on a weekly basis. One of the first things I was worried about was what mussa was going to be wearing. The brown robes and sandals disturbed me. How were we going to go to the movies or to Burger King? I was concerned about being seen in public with a Brother, and what was I to call him? Should I call him Mr. mussa or do I have to call him Brother Joe (I know i said i wouldn't but I had to refer to him as mr. and Brother, but that's really the last time ever!!!!) mussa assured me that his being a Brother would not affect our relationship. As a matter of fact I was told from here on out I was to call him Joe just like before. Never his surname and never refer to him as Brother, I was he little buddy. We were friends. I cannot tell you how important that makes a young kid feel when a teacher at your school who everyone had to address them with respect with now using Brother before his name, where I was allowed to call him Joe. He liked me better than you, it was euphoric. Also mussa told me that when we hung out he would always be wearing street clothes. Him being a Brother was just his job, the robe was his uniform. When he wasn't working he wasn't required to have his uniform on. He compared himself to a policeman. When they were on duty they were required to wear their uniforms. They weren't allowed to wear them when they were off duty and that included traveling to and from work. I only remember seeing him wearing his robe only once, and the sight of him wearing it made me uncomfortable. mussa was big on the Muppets, he took me to the Muppet movies, bought me a Miss Piggy doll and a Kermit the Frog doll. He surprised me with these things and I was really embarrassed about them, so much that I kept them hidden in my closet. We also would take trips to Sam Goody, a record store in Kings Plaza Mall. In total I had 171 record albums that mussa had bought for me over the 2-½ years of my encounter with him. Whatever I wanted he would buy it for me, a boom box, electric toy car, a Kiss make up set that you can make yourself up as any of the members of the band...movies, baseball games, Burger King , McDonalds, Baskin Robbins, Carvel. As I look back that 1st year mussa never touched me in a bad way. He would pat and rub my back affectionately, mess up my hair and squeeze my kneecaps in an attempt to razzle me, it's akin to hitting your funny bone. Then all of the sudden all that changed. mussa would start to put his hand on my knee and then start moving his hand up my thigh rubbing my thigh as if to say "Hey buddy, good to see you." I became very tense and uncomfortable. I really didn't know what he was up to. I was very confused! The last thing I think he would do, is try to go to my private area. But his hand continued up my thigh. At this point I placed both of my hands on my lap, placed in such a manner that blocked the path I was sure now he was taking. He was heading for my penis. God-damn-it, they were right. The rumors were true, the teasing somehow justified. Ever since I started hanging out with mussa, some of the older kids who were in his class in Holy Name or were on the intramural hockey or football teams said that mussa liked little boys. They used to tease me when after that 1st interaction with him, decorating his bulletin board. The older kids would say he was lining me up to be his next boy toy. That's all I thought it was ....teasing, I don't know if I didn't want to believe it or not. At the time I was hearing these "rumors" I had nothing but good memories of spending time with him. Besides I really wasn't clear of what the meant at that time. But as the year went by I was beginning to understand. In 1976 I was 10 years old. A very little boy, physically and mentally. I was ALWAYS 2nd in line, weather it was lining up in the school yard every morning for class, or my 1st Holy Communion or my as yet to happen at that time, my Confirmation (for which I picked the name Joseph after mussa.) I was always behind Richard R. who held the prestigious honor of being the shortest for our 8 years together at Holy Name. But today as I write this and over the years I would look at young boys that were 10,11,12 even 13 years old and think how can anyone do something like touch these babies the way mussa was starting to touch me. How the fuck could they do such a thing?! I can't remember exactly what had happened that first attempt at molesting me. Whether he succeeded at getting to my penis or not, it really is irrelevant. I do know from that day forward my life was completely changed. I was an 11 year old boy who wasn't even close to puberty. I didn't see my 1st pubic hair until I was 18 years old, (all the boys around me were showing obvious signs of manhood, I really thought that I was physically damaged from the sexual abuse and I'd never see puberty. High school gym was an absolute HORROR for me) just a young kid whose adolescent years were robbed from me. I was involved in an adult activity that I had no idea what it was about, it was frightening and it was disgusting. It was ugly and it was incomprehensible. I just didn't understand. And most of all I was ashamed ! He romanced me for that first year, groomed me and isolated me. I stood up for him if someone was to say something in regards to him and young boys. mussa would spend the spring of 1977 manipulating me with a false love and gifts, there was never two words said between us when he was attempting to abuse me and when he abused me. It's almost as he wasn't aware of what his right hand was doing. He just would drive the car to wherever we were heading while nonchalantly putting his hand on my knee, making its way up to my crotch and manipulating my zipper on my pants. Mind you , I was trying my best to not allow him to get to my zipper. It was a silent war between us. He would try to go under and over my hand, back and forth I would shift down, he would try to go deeper under my hand. He would then go over, then go over and quickly go under as if to trick me up when I thought he was going one way. And I had so much time invested in our friendship that I didn't know what to do. I was too scared to tell my parents, thinking of how they were starting to be concerned about the things I was bringing home, and I defended him or at least I defended the gifts. I was being molested in his car, in the movies, in the schoolyard. It started happening more and more. And the more he molested me the more things he bought me. Times were a lot different then, I'm sure that if it was going on today, as far as my parents are concerned, they most definitely would have stepped in. People are more educated today, these whispers about shady scoutmasters or camp counselors, teachers, priests or the neighborhood adults who tended to gravitate around the young children. People today are more aware of the characteristics and tell tale signs of potential pedophiles. Also both my parents were the product of the Catholic school system, both my parents attended Holy Name. So I can imagine what they went through, how they viewed these men and women who are drawn to this life of celibacy, vow of poverty. When they were students all of the staff were priests, nuns, and Brothers. And when I made a stink about defending him, (when I did he hadn't touched me yet), so I legitimately defended him. I was afraid that I was going to have to return things back, too. Then when mussa started touching me in an inappropriate way, when he started to force his way into my pants so he could fondle my genitals I then felt responsible, somehow now I was complacent in allowing him to abuse me. He groomed me to feel this way. I mean at the end of the day, I did take the record albums, the cars, the footballs, the baseball gloves, clothes or any movie I wanted to see no matter what the rating of the movies were, no matter how inappropriate they may have been for the minor that I was (i.e. Kentucky Fried Movie, Saturday Night Fever, Exorcist to name a few).There were 2 parts of my relationships with mussa, 90% of it was great and 10% an absolute fucking horror. I felt like I was a whore, allowing mussa to touch me inappropriately in exchange for gifts and money. Yea he would even give me money every time we got together $10 - $20 bucks after every visit. Hush money I freely accepted in return for my silence. My parents say they gave me a Catholic education that they believed was the best thing for me and for my other siblings it was. They were fortunate enough not to meet the monster that I met in school. I was a small, timid boy in grammar school that was bullied and teased by the bigger kids in class which turned me introverted even more. And problems at home that were developing were a direct result of my friendship with mussa. I became withdrawn , my grades took a nosedive from a struggling point to start out from..My respect for the entire education institution had become jaded, the Catholic church and GOD even deeper ensnared my belief system. The punishing God that was embedded into our young minds was taking his wrath out on me. How else can you explain one of his own doing what mussa was doing to me, to me the protocol was nuns, Brothers priests then GOD !! That summer of 77 I was given a break from the manipulation and abuse from mussa. My parents, brother, and two sisters along with myself all piled into the family wood paneled station wagon, and headed west to California, I hold this trip dear in my heart and have cherished memories of it. The places we saw along the way, camping out every night at some of the coolest campgrounds with these fantastic playgrounds. Falling asleep in the tent and waking up in the back of the station wagon every morning because my Dad would gently carry his sleeping children there so he would get an early start on the road. Seeing such majestic places like the Grand Canyon, Mt. Rushmore, Hoover Dam, the Rocky Mountains the great Salt Lake, the Pacific Ocean, Hollywood, Disney World. Even though I was damaged goods at that point, I had a tremendous sense of relief that I wouldn't have to see mussa for a while. In essence it was my last real childhood memory. I knew when I got home I had to somehow end this relationship. But until then I was going to try to enjoy my trip to California. I remember trying to come up with a way to stop seeing him all together. . The stress that had put on me....how was I going to stop him, I couldn't go to my parents, the last thing was to go to my teachers. Not only was I becoming a troubled student who was getting failing grades and acting out I just didn't trust them. Did not trust the nuns, didn't trust the priest. Was so alone with only my thoughts to rely on, and they told me not to trust anyone. That trip to California was truly, truly the end of my childhood, my innocence and youthful spring in my step was now to become a dark scary outlook on people and an even darker outlook on life. I hold dear to my heart that trip. That was the last time I was Danny Cunningham. A little dramatic? You may think so if you have never been through this overwhelming internal tug-of- war that goes on deep inside your gut, deep into your soul a soul that has yet to know the cruelest and sickest parts of human nature. Realizing how cruel and selfish people can be, how blind to someone else's pain. How completely selfish and self centered one person can be towards another human being without any concern for their well being, their mental state. Do you know how difficult it is to hide the pain I was living, to walk around with a knot in your stomach that felt the size of a softball? How hard it was to hide the pain from everyone? No adult should have to go through such turmoil.....let alone a child. THE CONFLICT THAT I HAD TO ENDURE WITHIN MYSELF< I WAS LITERALLY INTERNALLY ARGUING INSIDE MY HEAD, ASHAMED AS A FUCKING 11-12 YEAR OLD BOY.

When I should be playing baseball or trading cards, playing war, fort, or cops and robbers with my friends instead I was stuck in a friendship having been tricked into and for the most part having sex with a full grown man. A child involved in adult activities that that child had no fucking idea what that meant or the damage that it would cause me for the rest of my life. Almost every waking moment at that time my thoughts were consumed with what he was doing to me, in class all of the sudden having images in my head of him touching, in the middle of eating a sandwich an image flashes in my mind, playing at the playground another flashback. Consumed with the worry of people finding out what he was doing, feeling like a cheap streetwalker because I was accepting money and gifts. And the fear of not being able to turn him away when he was touching me, it was done in silence. Two words were never spoken between the two of us. I would have what would be some sort of outer body experience, like I rose above the event and watched from above as if it was someone else he was abusing.

I was afraid to see him.

Seventh grade was a nightmare. We returned home from our road trip to California. The end of my childhood. A letter from mussa arrived days after our arrival to Brooklyn . I took that letter and put it aside, not opening it for days. I'm guessing that mussa was catching on that I was trying to distance myself from him. Because his next move was one for the books. He finally reached me on the phone, the house phone, at that time that's all there was. No caller i.d. ,no answering machine. Just a standard ringing phone that had to be answered in order to find out who was calling. This time I found out it was mussa. There was also a strong attachment to mussa. I really,

really, really liked this man, you could say I loved him, and believe me he conditioned me that way. It was if I was a ball of clay and was molded into precisely what he wanted and needed to get away with his crimes. And he was brilliant at masking these crimes. When he saw me distancing away from him he sensed my discomfort I guess when I was silently struggling with him trying to keep him from my genitals. He started laying on me a line about all of the touching was necessary that he had a real reason for doing it. He asked "I'm a teacher, right?" and yes he was. "Well I was trying to teach you sex education. What everyone your age should be taught, really I taught." That started to bring my guard down, I wanted a reason why .....a good reason. And even though it didn't explain everything he was doing 100%, at least I felt 60% of it maybe being the reason. And that's all I needed. He had convinced me in my 11 year old mind that he had me ask my mother if it would be ok if he taught me sex education. That was one of the classes he taught at Nazareth high school which was now where he lived and worked. Along with teaching me sex education which he got the ok from my mother for him to do, he also was going to teach me how to drive, which mussa thought we should keep it between us for the time being.........Now let's look at this perfect execution of manipulating an 11 yr. old boy. The abuse was educational, after all he is a teacher and in order to continue that education he had gotten permission from my mother. IMAGINE THAT ....HE HAD MY MOTHER'S PERMISSION TO PUT HIS HANDS ON ME SEXUALLY. The sex ed class he gave me after he got permission to give it to me took place inside his car in Holy Name school yard. And it was hands on and it involved pornographic photos him showing me his "full grown" genitals and him forcing me into showing mine so we could compare the two. Outstanding, well played mussa! Now you had an even shorter leash on me, and knowing that I wouldn't go to my parents because now he had permission.

He was crafty...then came the driving. The classic of all the mussa mind games. His promise of letting me drive his car, to teach me how to drive safely and correctly. Like most pedophiles , mussa knew how to lure me in, how to gain my confidence only to be conned. mussa driving academy consisted of me sitting on his lap, feeling his erection while he controlled the foot panels and me the steering. And this was done in an isolated area down on 2nd Ave and 32nd Street in Sunset Park. We went down there for one, the obvious reason. So I didn't get into an accident, but as I suspected, so he could get away with abusing me. With my hands doing the steering, that freed up mussa's hands to do the abusing, all while I sat on his erection.

My behavior had started to become very bad. I was acting out a lot more. I had all this confusion and anger going on inside of me. This conflict internally would in turn become the conflict externally. My parents would yell at me at home. I would yell back and storm out of the apartment, cursing and screaming, teachers would discipline me for acting out or spacing out in class and mussa would keep sexually abuse me. I was drifting apart from everyone, I became withdrawn. The problems grew bigger and bigger. I was a little time bomb ready to explode. And from time to time that's exactly what would happen. I once threw chair at a science teacher, was having fights in class,   I had become a chronic bed wetter (which lasted to my mid twenties), my school grades absolutely horrible. The stressors that I was dealing with just withdrew me deeper into depression. I was trapped and I felt as if I had no one to turn to. I was manipulated into believing that. Here's a funny thing. Around the time that mussa started to abuse me every week or every other week I would be taken out of class to go and talk to this nun in a tiny office on the 1st floor. Don't remember her name, she was some sort of counselor. She would ask personal things about my family what I did outside school. Thing is, my parents never knew anything about these meetings with this nun. Had no idea I was taken out of class on a weekly basis. No letters to them informing them of their intentions, no phone call asking for their permission to pry into their son's mind. They took it upon themselves to take a look at me in a prying and personal matter. And at no time were my parents notified or brought up to speed on what they were doing and the results of these sessions that were very exhausting for me. I remember discussing mussa with this nun, what did she think about a former teacher from this school still returning to the school to spend time with a student that was never in one of his classes. I know that if I was told to evaluate a student's behavior and try to find some signs of why he would be acting out, what is it that could be causing him to be withdrawn and struggling with his schoolwork, I may take a harder look at a relationship he appears to be having with a past school employee where there was never any academic connection with said student. What conclusion did she come up with? I'm sure I was discussed by my teachers prior to these sessions. They must of had some concern for me to bring in someone who was never at the school before, bring them in to see me. My name wasn't just pulled out of a fucking hat to see this lady. I'm sure she had to report to her superiors on what conclusions she came to. I WOULD LOVE TO SEE THAT, would love to see what came of it. My guess is they went on a fishing expedition and threw a net and dragged up something they thought was rotten and threw it back in. Threw it back in with no concern for any future regard for it and the damage it may cause later on. The only concern for the reputation of the institution as a whole. A true collateral damage in the wake of one of their own. Now this is only speculation on my part, then again I am the person who went through this experience first hand and am sure I'm not too far off the mark. The faculty and staff had to have had a reason to pull me from academic classes for an hour a week or bi-weekly, whichever it was is not relevant as much as why they did is. I'm sure my teacher and principal were involved and had discussed me, had decided not to inform my parents of this decision and take action on their own, and then come to some conclusion. And I'm sure if they felt the problem was at home they would have had someone take a closer look into it, but maybe they found the problem was in-house and decided to turn a blind eye to it. Again, speculation. But I lived through it and it is my speculation. AND IT'S THE FIRST OF MANY DECEPTIVE LOW BALL BULLSHIT THAT I WOULD DEAL WITH WHEN DEALING WITH THE MEN AND WOMEN OF THE CATHOLIC CHURCH.

The summer of 1978 had brought tremendous changes in my life. Changes that may not have been the best thing for me in the long run. But they were definitely what I needed for the short term solution for the problems I was going through in my young life, the pain and turmoil I experienced every day of my life, fantasizing of swinging a bat to mussa's head and ending my life. I should have been dreaming of girls, instead I was dreaming of assault. My parents had purchased a house down the block from where we were living at the time. 9 ½ blocks away. From one parish into another parish. From a very close-knit Catholic proper neighborhood into a more diverse mixed rougher area than the one in which we were currently residing. We lived in Brooklyn to start off with, so rough was pretty much the norm. But it was definitely more colorful living down at the bottom of the hill in Windsor Terrace. It might as well been a hundred miles from up the hill...

My neighborhood was cut off by the Prospect Expressway to the north and Prospect Park to the south. At the top of the hill there is 9th. Ave, and the bottom of the hill there's Greenwood Ave. This is my neighborhood, my boundaries. Windsor Terrace is of course much larger. This is the area I spent my childhood/adolescent years in. This included the apartment we lived in for the first 13 years in my life on the Circle and the house my parents bought down the hill on east 7th Street. Down the hill had a much more diverse group of kids in it. It was a little more the wild, wild west in comparison. Prospect Ave was a tiny business strip at that time. There was a butcher, deli, candy store named Blondie's, a luncheonette called Angie's, a plumber, Kingsbrook Printers where I had a small job at as well as a job delivering pizzas at Laura's Pizzeria.

Prior to us moving down the hill, I was on a baseball team for the Holy Name Father's Guild. I was lousy at sports, but my coaches were pretty cool younger guys. The coach, Tommy S., took a liking to me and sensing I was a bad player sort of made me his assistant. So here I was carrying a clipboard for another coach. But this dude was a lot more a ladies man. Where mussa would surround himself with young boys, Tommy S. would have pretty girls surrounding him. While mussa was into Helen Reddy, Barry Manilow and the Muppets, Tommy S. was at the other end with Led Zeppelin, The Who and smoking weed. When he and his assistant coaches, Ritney, Chris with the lazy eye, and Sidney, needed to take a pot break somewhere in the middle of the game, I would take over for all of them. Well when my family moved down the hill unbeknownst to me these guys all hung out there. I started hanging out with them, and I started to understand that what was happening to me because of mussa was wrong. Up until this point I was very uncomfortable with what mussa was doing to me. I felt very confused and scared by his actions, but I wasn't aware that what he was doing to me was against the law and I was becoming aware of it more and more, especially hanging out with these older dudes. That was giving me an education in itself.

And that goes as well for all the kids at or around my age that were in this neighborhood. They were drinking alcohol and smoking cigarettes and weed. They were way ahead of where I came from. It was at this time that Slats gave me my nickname "Ziggy" and I was reborn. I was almost like another person. Danny was put away and I let Ziggy take over. That summer I saw mussa a handful of times, as I was gaining new friends, bad kids. With my new friends I was shutting down from the lifelong friends I had in Holy Name. I was resenting everything about the school, students and faculty, the church, priest nuns and of course Brothers... But this didn't happen overnight. mussa still forced his company on me, as well as bribe me to be his friend. That summer we did two things...well he tricked me into these things ,,,one was floor seats to a Kiss concert, there was no way I was saying no to that especially after he surprised me with the tickets. The second was a trip to the Baseball Hall of Fame in Cooperstown, New York. Two very damaging points in our dysfunctional friendship we supposedly had. The KISS concert, at that time I lived and breathed KISS, they were the greatest band in the world to me at the time. Had all their albums to that point and now had tickets a foot from the stage. There are two things I remember very clearly about that show. The first was when the band came up through the floor, two on one side, two on the other, with an announcer saying over the P.A. "You want the best, you got the best, the greatest rock-n-roll band in the world, KISS!" Pyrotechnics were going off, their fist raised above their heads. It was so cool. The second thing I remember was the look from the guy who was sitting in front of us, or rather standing in front of us. The look on his face when he saw mussa putting his hand in my pants while he had me sitting on his shoulders. The guy was probably 18 to 20 years old. He didn't do anything to stop it for whatever reason, but he was horrified at what he was seeing.......that's my memory of that show. The guys exploding on to the stage and then me being molested in front of 17,000 people. The trip to Cooperstown to the Baseball Hall of Fame was a very traumatic experience for me that I just as soon not remember. I know that someone else was on that trip with us but I blocked a lot of it out that I have no idea who that person was. And the biggest thing that I remember about the trip was a dark creepy building that looked like something out of the 18th century. It was some monastery between Brooklyn and Cooperstown, NY. Don't know where it was, all I know was that was where mussa forced his way into the shower with me offering to wash me. Him grabbing my genitals and massaging them. And then him grabbing my hand and having me touch his penis in some warped attempt to jerk him off......I was so frightened, trying to pull away from him. Don't remember how it ended, the shower that is. I know after when it was bedtime that he got into bed with me. I was horrified, being in this large damp building with all these monks walking around in their brown robes, not knowing where I was, blaming myself for putting myself in this situation. I remember him tickling me and me not wanting him to, as if he was trying to inject humor into this assault on me. Then I remember having a sort of out of body experience, as if I was watching someone else in the bed with mussa, someone else being violated by a grown man. And that is all the memory I have of that. Couldn't tell you where this other kid was during this.

Since I had spent 7 years attending Holy Name my parents thought I should spend my last year there and graduate with all my classmates who I spent the last 8 years with. My younger sibling went to a different Catholic school. When we moved, we moved into a different parish. At this point I was totally damaged goods. When I got home from that trip to Cooperstown, I now trusted no one, every teacher, every storekeeper, priest or relative was treated as a potential abuser.

I don't remember exactly how my relationship ended with mussa. There was no defining moment. It just ended, I was tired of being touched, I was embarrassed. I was sick of going to the movies only to be molested time after time after time in a dark room, mind you, full of people unaware of the crime being committed before them. At this point I was terrorized each and every time I got in the car with this man. That's where he would molest me all the time. The same pattern over and over and over. The rubbing on the kneecap then move on to the upper thigh, then force his way to undo my zipper and fondle my genitals. Only once did I wear a pair of shorts in his company after the abuse started. That was like a field day for this pedophile. He would always make a comment on the long pants I was wearing, suggesting i was probably way too hot and should be wearing shorts. Imagine that, being a 12,13 year old boy who made wardrobe decisions based on whether or not I was spending his day with a child molester. I would layer clothes with 2 pairs of underpants two jeans extra shorts over underpants over long pants. All my waking moments were consumed somehow with the sexual abuse I was enduring. How to prevent it, how to avoid it and most importantly how to fucking stop it !! He knew I was becoming more and more defensive and I started to voice my uncomfortability with him and with what he was doing to me. After what had taken place that night we spent in that monastery on our way to the Baseball Hall Of Fame , I drew a line . And when that weekend was over, I started my retreat from mussa. The walls came up. After spending a weekend with a man who would not leave me alone, not just in a sexual way, but in a way that he would hover over me wanting to be sure that I was ok. His guilt making him paranoid because I was now reacting to what he was doing to me. He knew damn well I was beginning to resent him more and more as time went by.

Back at my new neighborhood, I was being schooled on the streets and it was making me aware of what he was doing to me. And what he was doing was not right. And I was beginning to see some of the bad effects it had in my young life. It was destroying my social skills, my school grades, my home life everything had been affected by it. It had a huge snowball effect, problems grew larger and larger to the point where I was totally isolated, which was, in fact, exactly the position that mussa wanted me to be in. From that afternoon in his classroom when Michelle and I decorated his bulletin board he had seen in me the potential of being a target for his abuse. What motivated him I don't know and I don't care!! What I was learning from the streets at that time was that mussa was doing to me is a crime , and my last visits from him, however they faded out, he felt me resisting more adamantly and standing my ground. I stopped answering his letters and his phone calls. And as hard as it is to admit, it really was painful to have to do it. It's so hard to explain all of emotions that I had to deal with . How one emotion would contradict another. I felt guilty all while feeling angry. I was relieved but at the same time burdened.

Since mussa wasn't getting what he wanted he finally left me alone and moved on. He got the message. The phone calls stopped, no more letters in the mail. mussa went on to live his life as a prince of the church. Setting himself up as the perfect pedophile would. Teaching high school students. Working the boys locker rooms like a sick pervert that he is. Coaching several high school hockey teams and and I'm sure whatever else he could do in the shadow of Catholic education, to gain access to the boys he was entrusted to care for. He moved on to his next victims. What mussa left in the wake of our relationship was a damaged young man. I was traumatized by our friendship. the most eventful thing so far in my short life, being his buddy, was a lie. This man tricked and manipulated and painted me into a corner having me believe I had no way out. My emotions were shattered. The person who I met that was supposed to be an important role model and authority in my life at the time, to take me under his wing and treat me in a way like I was his own son. Raising me up above everyone else, isolating me. Then abuse me for as long as he could get away with it then toss me aside like the morning's trash. I cannot begin to tell you what that dose to a 13 year old boy's self esteem, his feelings and his outlook on life.

I was emotionally crippled and extremely angry with it all being masked by a false sense of self. I literally changed into someone else in order to protect the little boy that I still was inside my head. Some if the behaviors I conditioned in myself have become a liability over the years. I blame mussa for causing the end of my childhood and directly putting me on a road to self destruction, self loathing self hate and self medication, I blame the friars as well for they could have helped me many years ago when Iwent to them for help, The help they were offering me was not the help I was looking for. It's not like I wanted to go to the Betty Ford clinic, I asked Brother Grady to send me to a rehab. I did not want to be around the friars. I had good reason to not want to be around them. My experiences with them have been nothing but bad. I was told I had to take what they were offering me. Like I was going to them as a beggar, them seemingly having the authority over my life and any decisions. Their way or the highway. They did nothing of what I was looking for. The main thing was to have mussa admit what he had done to me and apologize to me. I AM CONVINCED THAT THEY ARE COMPLETELY AWARE OF WHAT THAT MAN WAS UP TO... And they decided for the good of the church they were going to keep it quiet, no concern for well-being of any of his victims. Even as far back in grammar school. Someone somewhere had to have come to the conclusion that there was trouble in my life. They found it necessary to have a counselor come to my school and remove me from class and pry into my personal life and dig around for something that was the cause and effect of my behavior, mind you all the while without my parents knowledge let alone their permission. That leads me to believe that they were suspicious of them being the cause and effect of my troubles, but they were never contacted or were confronted by anyone about anything. It wasn't until I was in my forties that I told my parents about these unauthorized therapy sessions and it was a complete surprise to them and it made them very angry that they did this to me and without their permission or consent. I do remember that when I told this nun about my ongoing relationship with mussa she became very attentive and inquisitive about it. She was prying so much that I remembered that I thought I was getting him in trouble. I wonder what conclusion that that nun arrived to and who she discussed that situation with. Was there a report, a meeting that discussed me? Or did they just sweep it under the rug and look the other way so they could protect the distorted ancient lifestyle and all the riches that are attached to it for the better of the church. That right there is what has motivated me over the years to keep pressing the issue. I did manage in 2001 to report mussa to the Brooklyn DA, where at that point he was removed from teaching and interactions with kids. I just couldn't believe this man was still teaching kids. The man is a fraud - he is in it for the boys, the young men he can hunt and take advantage of their weakness and find a vulnerable boy to help as if he is a good man when in fact he is a man whose only intention is to molest and control them.

Now at almost 50 years old I'm way too exhausted from the tremendous job it is to keep on trying to get through life with all its shortcomings that at times get the best of me, and if mussa and all of his supporters want to still deny me my healing and closure on this matter then I have no other choice than to approach it this way in a no holds barred meat and potatoes way, what he did to me and what it did to my life. As well as my dealing with the friars. They rejected me and treated me like I was some rotten person who is just out to harm this good man's reputation. Yea that makes sense. A man who was at once a great friend to me , who bought me all sorts of things and took me to many places , I am so very grateful to him that I want to destroy his life. The MAN DESTROYED MY LIFE BY PUTTING HIS HANDS ON ME SEXUALLY. If I was just not the one who raised his hand and met this Monster, all of the struggles and problems I had in my life would not be an issue. I know things would have been different. I would have problems of course, but nothing in comparison to the mountain of problems that come from surviving sexual abuse from someone you loved, admired, defended and respected. What mussa did to me was put out the fire I had in my life, the fire in my heart. And there is nothing but darkness when the fire is gone. And , if it was true , as I was taught in my Catholic education, that man was made in god's image, well then from that point on my relationship with god was extremely, extremely fractured. I can only imagine how my life would have turned out if I never met this mentor and role model who was really just a wolf in sheep's clothing.

For thirty years I knew that there would be were others abused by mussa. Around October, 2014 I googled Brother Joe Mussa, as I would from time to time in my quest and belief that someday somewhere other victims would surface. I was vigilant . The Container Diaries would always come up in the past as it did this time. Container Diaries is a website created about Holy Name and the neighborhood. Container is reference to the to-go quart of Budweiser (container) that you can get at Farrells Bar. When I was growing up that's what the neighborhood centered around. Holy Name church/school and Farrells Bar. The posting about mussa was brief. Just people's comments saying what a great teacher he was at Holy Name and how he would referee the basketball and football games in the school yard. Someone even made a comment at how good mussa was at picking out "at risk" kids. That pissed me off to see people praise him when I had these bad memories of him and all the things in a sexual nature that he did to me.

I have given mussa the chance to come clean with me. As far back as 1992 I have had encounters with the Catholic church and my desire to heal the wounds that this man has caused in my life, always to be denied and cast off as some degenerate who was looking for a payday. THAT WAS NEVER THE CASE!!! Several times I went to the church and asked them for help with a crippling drug addiction. An addiction that I blame mostly on mussa. Now I know that I'm the one who, with my own hands picked up these drugs and with my own hand ingested these drugs. But the age that I started doing these drugs at 13 years old, was a direct result of the sexual abuse that I received from mussa. It's as if I really had no choice at that time in my life. When I started getting high, right out of the gate I was off and running. At 13 I was smoking weed, snorting cocaine and drinking alcohol. And I was doing these things in excess. The drugs made me feel like someone else, a different person than the sexually abused boy that I was now protecting and safeguarding from the cruel world that I live in.........
Along with "Container Diaries" another site popped up titled "Burn and Rot in Hell". Googling mussa's name brought me directly to this posting titled " This St. Francis Prep Sexual Abuse Survivor Wants You to Know His Story."

I read the story.

His story was my own story.

After reading it, I cried like an 11 year old boy would cry. Tears flowing over my cheeks as if a faucet was somehow attached to my eyes. The absolute tremendous force of vindication and relief came over me. Over the last twenty years when I had first told someone what had actually happened to me up until that day that I read that posting on Burn and Rot in Hell, I was always waiting for some other victim of mussa's to surface. Anytime there was anything about someone molesting some boy in a newspaper I would scan through the article looking for mussa's name. TV news stories I would wait to hear his name. Waiting and waiting for someone to validate my claims of sexual abuse from a man, a man of God, that went around preying on the youth of our community.

Let me go back to eighth grade. Once my family moved and school had started I found myself gravitating towards the kids who were getting high using drugs. I also was hanging out with the older guys by way of the four guys who coached my baseball team. For whatever reason these guys liked me and their friends liked me. So I would rotate between hanging out with the older guys and hanging out with the kids my own age. It was around this time that I was given my nickname that I would go by for the next 10 years: ZIGGY.

Danny was now Ziggy and that's exactly how I wanted it. I was able to put aside the hurt, confused boy and gain a false sense of self with Ziggy. Now I was this slick kid who would hang out with the older guys, do drugs, go to bars, out to the Hamptons, take road trips to rock concerts out of state. I hid Danny away. My last year at Holy Name I remember very few things about. That's probably because I wasn't there a lot. To this day I have no idea how I got away with all the time I took off from school. I would cut school a week or two weeks at a time. I would leave the house in the morning, go up to Rayray and Mickey's house and ditch school with everyone else who was ditching or just didn't go to school all together. When I did return to school I would bring a note that I had written, but I would forge my mother's signature using one of her cancelled checks and a Light Bright machine. The Light Bright machine would allow me to trace my mother's signature using just the lighted surface so it became transparent enough to see through. And my teacher would take it and accept it as if it was a normal thing to do. At no time did the school notify my parents of all of my absences and at no time did they question the validity of my notes from home. I might speculate that they had some kind of idea of what was going on from those un-authorized counseling sessions I was dragged out of class to go to. I believe they could have helped me then, they had to have known something and they had to have made the decision not to do anything about it.

Again it's only speculation. So my eight year was spent ditching school and getting stoned and getting into all sorts of trouble. This all being the direct result of a relationship I had with a person who was supposed to protect me.

One of the reasons that I started hanging out with the older guys was because they protected me. These guys were all in their 20's, and there were a lot of them. After a while, I became their mascot for lack of a better word. I had keys to some of their apartments where I could come and go as I pleased.

The other reason I was hanging out with these guys was because they gave me drugs. They thought it was funny or cute to see this tiny little kid smoking weed or snorting cocaine. I could go on for pages of some of the crazy things these guys did. But what mattered most to me at that time was being protected so no one would touch me again. And having the ability to gain access to drugs that would make me feel normal for the most part and take all those memories out of my head. The older guys provided me with those things. And there were truly good guys in that group, guys who tried to direct me in the right direction. And try to steer me away from the guys who were feeding me hard narcotics, thing was that I wanted those stronger drugs. I needed them to feel normal. Cocaine was the "non addictive drug" when I was first starting to do it in 1980. At least that's what everyone was saying. Well we all know that's the furthest thing from the truth......I spent my high school years like some sort of cool breeze kid. I was the one kid out of all the other kids in the neighborhood who the older guys liked and wanted me to hang out with them. School was just some inconvenience I had to deal with for eight hours every day. I was such a bad student that even if I tried to apply myself I would just get frustrated and give up. Every year I managed to have to go to summer school for two classes every summer even the summer after I graduated. Now I went to Catholic high school, and I had no interest in what the brothers had to say. At that point I hated school. Hated the whole institution . I was jaded. I couldn't see how important education was. How vital an education was. That's another thing mussa robbed from me. An education. Does this prick realize how much damage he has done all to satisfy some sick perversion? And the ones who protected him are just as culpable and responsible as he is. I even had to go to summer school AFTER I graduated. You can put that on the list as well. Robbed of every summer vacation from school.

After high school my Father got me a job as an ironworker. Dangerous job, yes. Well-paying job, yes. Did I keep the job, NO . My inability to to keep my mouth shut has cost me many jobs. My drug addiction has cost me many jobs, by the time I was 23 years old I had a very bad crack addiction. Whenever I feel threatened I get defensive right away. If I feel like someone is trying to get over on me or take advantage of me I feel the overwhelming need to stand up for myself and stop any transgressions.

My biggest regret in life was the job I lost that my father got me. I was in the local 3 electrician's union apprenticeship program. Unfortunately I was ill prepared for the classroom aspect of the job. I picked up the on the job training pretty easily. But the classroom stuff I just could not do. I was crippled from my early school experiences. I was never a good student after the abuse from mussa. I had no faith in the Catholic school education. Me just coasting through my school years did not benefit me whatsoever. I had no studying skills, no note taking skills and my attention span was that of a dog. I was so good at picking up my trade that my foreman while I was in the union gave me a job in his side company. His side business was the equivalent of a small business that someone would have. I was running jobs for him and I was barely able to hold it together because of my crack addiction. Again I would lose another job. But I learned my trade, and continued to learn it from guys with more experience than me. Tommy S., my coach from little league and my inductee into the older guys asked if I could take a look at some electrical work that his brother-in-law needed done at his business. At this time my addiction was full blown . I did have a tendency of cleaning up good. But I could only keep up that facade for so long, before it blew up in my face. Tommy's brother in law Marty G. caught me on my bounce back. I did some good work for him and he liked the work I did. With the work came money and money and me didn't last long. I was sleeping in the park before long and when Marty found out he took me into his home with his wife and newborn son.

Marty was the first person that I ever told about what mussa had done to me. Marty was a retired hero detective and is currently a politician. Marty looked out for me and in a big way! He ended up putting me on touch with Father John Harvey, a Catholic priest. He had an office in a church on the West Side of Manhattan on 34th street. He was very old, very firm and on his game.....He said to me one of his jobs for the church was taking care of their dirty laundry. Outside and inside the church, he told me he counseled nuns who were raped or assaulted by priests. Priests who were having sex with anyone from a parishioner or another priest. Whatever it is it came across his desk. I was very intimidated by him. But I told him what mussa had done to me. And he became very angry and said he was going to make them pay for that. At that time I was drinking and drugging, mostly drugging at that time. I was ready for what would turn-out to be a tune-up (in and out of detox/rehab).A chance to get off the street and clean up. Well Fr. Harvey told me he was going to have them send me to rehab. I thought that would be great, I wanted to stop. I always wanted to stop......a few days later I found myself up at Graymore , a large piece of property that the Catholic church owns in Garrison, NY. They have a retirement community of nuns, brothers and priests. Several graveyards and several churches. They hold religious retreats there and there is St. Christopher's Inn. At that time strictly a 19 day men's shelter and you could not have drugs in your system, and you must do the urine test when you get there. Alcohol abuse only. No druggies allowed.

Unbeknownst to me until I arrived, it's run by Franciscan friars. The last place I wanted to be was around these men in brown robes wearing sandles. I didn't trust them: case in point. The guy who did my intake was a rather large Friar Tuck fella. He got extremely close to me by rolling his chair right up to mine, our faces an inch apart and asked me "when your father's penis entered your mother's vagina would you ever have thought that you would have turned out the way you did?" First off the question makes no sense whatsoever. I couldn't counsel with myself at my conception. I believe he just said it to get his rocks off. That was what I concluded immediately after backing away from him.

After the 19 days they may "select" you to go to St. Joseph's rehab upstate by the Canadian border, also run by the Franciscan friars. I was having no part of it. Besides they knew about my allegations and were definitely giving me the cold shoulder at Graymore. I did the 19 day stay (tune-up) and went right back to the streets.

About this time I was offered a one way Greyhound ticket to Florida. Hurricane Andrew just destroyed southern Fla. So there was plenty of work for me there. So I traded in the grimy streets of Brooklyn for the white sands of Florida....Not such a good idea if you got a cocaine problem that you're trying to fix. Long story short. I ended up being sentenced to 3 years in a state penitentiary. After 18 months I was released and left Florida immediately.

Back to Brooklyn, back in the life. Many failed attempts at cleaning up. Joined the Navy only to be entry leveled discharged because of the level of drugs that were in my system. I also spent a year in Sunny California pretty much working for my Uncle Mike and staying with him and his wife and two little cousins. Mike was an amazing carpenter who made these beautiful door entries and bay windows by milling trees delivered off of trucks. Oh and we smoked a lot of pot. I was on the marijuana maintenance program. I wasn't smoking crack because I had no idea where to get it. I was living in Moreno Valley..... the armpit of America. Shit I was in Cali and I was living in the desert. After 9 months with Uncle Mike I hit the road and headed for the golden sands of Newport Beach working for an electrician who had a lot of famous clientele. I am notorious for cleaning up my act (I cleaned up good). Get a good job.......do real good at that job. Then destroy it by getting high and not going to work. And I would play this out time and time again. My employer would always take me back, give me multiple chance's til they just couldn't any more. Six months later I was back in Brooklyn sleeping on friends' couches until they were missing something and I was either gone or asked to leave. Drug addicts will rob you then help you look for whatever they robbed. A year later I would end up back in California for the next 7 years.

Again, for all the time I spent out in California , I would repeat the cycle of being completely destitute eating in soup lines and kitchens. Using drugs, unemployed to going in a program for a tune up getting my shit together to get a place of my own a good job only to repeat the cycle of starting to use drugs to losing everything. Repeat over and over. My inability to keep a job or apartment was due completely to my addiction. My way of punishing myself stuck in a cycle of insanity. I lived up and down the coast of California. San Francisco, Los Angeles, San Diego. I was always running away from myself. My life consumed by low self esteem and self doubt caused by a childhood of being a prisoner of my own self. Ziggy it turns out , was a manipulating drug addict who would do just about anything to get his next hit.

People who reached out to help would only have their hand slapped because I was not ready to stop. The messages that I received in my relationship with mussa has had a tremendous effect on the person I had become. Anywhere I turned to find help as far as being a survivor of sexual abuse was met with inexperience. Any counselor I went to in all of the rehabs I've been in all would respond with answers that would minimize the trauma I experienced. Or some even attempted to make excuses for mussa. On my second go at Graymore in 2002, St. Christopher's Inn had developed into thriving drug and alcohol rehab, and my counselor was a priest in the Franciscan order . Fr. Jim actually told me that he believes mussa was just trying to relate to me, trying to relive his childhood, because more than likely he was abused as a boy. ....So get this mussa was trying to play with me as if he was at my age because his childhood was most likely traumatized by some sort of sexual abuse by someone else......
well ......I have no tolerance for the abused to become the abuser. No way in hell would I ever put an innocent child into such a dark and isolated place . Why would someone, if sexually abused want to inject that horror on to someone else, let alone be a serial molester like I believe mussa is. To put dozens of people through that turmoil, send them off into a world of self hatred and doubt. A world of drug addiction and alcoholism.

I found a book titled "Victims No Longer" by Mike Lew. It's a book on child sexual abuse and surviving such an ordeal and the cause and effects of that abuse. That book gave me a lot of insight on my situation, the way I think and the things I have done to survive in my life that I carry with me every day. There was a section in the book that spoke of confronting your abuser and finding some healing and closure......way overrated. Confronting my abuser made things far worse than ever. Now I'm sure there may be some psychobabble bullshit that I was not emotionally prepared for such a confrontation, but frankly I was at the end of my rope. I was in search of help for many years and I was desperate for a solution. My needs were minimized in AA & NA, People would say shit like " you need to get over it" or "that shit happens to everyone" to the granddaddy of them all "what does that have to do with your drug problem" ....all actually quotes from people in those programs said to me. I needed, as suggested in those programs' literature, "outside help" and the professionals that I sought out weren't schooled on my plight and I sensed their inexperience on the subject. Or they were more concerned with the method of payment than anything at all I had to say.

So I took it upon myself to fix myself. I contacted the Head of the Franciscan order in Brooklyn from my tiny apartment in San Clemente , California . On the other end of the line I was received with resistance and attitude by Brother Thomas Grady. I told him about mussa molesting me while I was a young boy and the devastating effect that had on my life. He became very rude to me and started to, what seemed like, interrogate me on the reasoning and purpose for these allegations. Now you must remember, sexual abuse in the church was still at a whisper at this time. People who went to church didn't want to hear it and people who ran the church adamantly DENIED IT !!! So you can imagine what kind of predicament I was in and how much a pioneer I was in coming forward with no desire to be said pioneer. I told Grady I wasn't looking for anything but closure by this meeting I was trying to have with mussa and Grady treated me so badly and had an attitude toward me like I was the predator instead of the victim I truly was. So Grady reluctantly said he would set the meeting up for me at the time I would be home for Christmas. There were two stipulations, first Grady wanted me to go see a psychiatrist in Los Angeles. One that he would arrange and choose. I'm guessing he wanted to be sure i was a stable enough person with no bad intent. Not really sure what his reasoning was for me to be evaluated, whatever it was that he was or wasn't looking for, he was satisfied enough with the feedback from the shrink and I was given the ok to have my meeting with mussa. The second stipulation was when I addressed mussa with my accusations I was to begin each claim I had against him with .....Get this now....."AS I REMEMBER IT".....so for example....." As I remember it you put your hands down my pants while I was a passenger sitting next to you in your car " ...... or "As I remember it, you molested me in front of 17000 people at the KISS concert and got away with it". I agreed to this all the while knowing I was not going to follow such ridiculous ground rules.

So that Christmas I went to the Franciscan friars' headquarters on Remsen Street in downtown Brooklyn. I brought my younger sister with me, Eileen, who at the time was a school teacher. I remember the days leading up to the meeting having a lot of anxiety and being very nervous. The day of the meeting, Eileen and I were standing around the corner from the Franciscans' building. I was smoking a cigarette to kill some time and prepare myself mentally to what I was about to do. While we were standing there out of the corner of my eye , mussa walks right by us. Eileen's back was to him so she didn't see him. But I most certainly did. It had been over 20 years since I have seen this man who put my life into such turmoil and confusion. All the worry and reservations that I had in my mind about seeing him had immediately dissipated and left me. I turned to Eileen and said to her "this is going to be a piece of cake, he just walked by us." We watched as he walked ahead of us towards the Friar multi-million dollar Brownstone on Remsen St. in the exclusive neighborhood of Brooklyn Heights. Some vow of poverty, wouldn't you say? Coincidentally that's also mussa's current address. Eileen and I followed shortly behind him.

A few days earlier just after I arrived home , I went to see Grady. I have not met him up to this point, we talked over the phone and when we did speak he wasn't very nice to me to me, and meeting him in person wasn't any different. He wanted to see me to go over his ground rules and how this meeting was going to be done.

The meeting was a waste of everyone's time. We were greeted at the reception desk by Grady and I had introduced my sister Eileen who I told him I wanted her to be with me for moral support and the fact that she is an educator herself.

We entered a small room with four chairs of which one was occupied by mussa. For the first time in as many years I finally was able to look this man in the eyes and tell him what he did to me and what effect it has had on my life.. ....I spoke of specific events when he molested me, driving his car , the KISS concert, the sex education class we had inside his car while parked in Holy Name school yard. Told him how he molested me in dark movie theaters. The slow reaching over to put his hand on my knee and working his way up to my crotch and forcing his hand into my pants by aggressively pulling down my zipper to gain access to my private area. I told him how fucked up that made me feel and how fucked up my life was due to the abuse that I suffered.

mussa looked at me and told me that he was very sorry that I have these memories but as far as he is concerned that never happened what we had was good times together we horsed around, went to the movies, went to concerts and the Baseball Hall of Fame but never did he ever put his hands on me. I replied to mussa and said that I understand that he's lying because his boss is sitting right next to him, but he knows exactly what he had done to me at that point my younger sister Eileen spoke up and told musa that as far as she's concerned, as an educator and a school teacher what he did is one of the most cruelest things someone can do to a child. When you are trusted to nurture and protect someone only to destroy a child's life - he should be totally ashamed of himself. Again he acted as if we were totally out of our minds on what we accusing him of doing. Eileen and I just got up and left I didn't thank anybody, there was nobody to thank. I was not treated fairly by Brother Grady and even worse by mussa. Afterward I followed up with Grady and he told me that it was not humanly impossible for mussa to do what I said he did to me. I was scolded for making them take him out of school from his classes and his coaching and putting him into a therapeutic environment for a few weeks for evaluation.

Then they came to the conclusion that he just couldn't do this to anybody that was what I was told so here I was 20 years after the fact of being molested and I was being victimized again . I had nothing better to do on my Christmas trip back home then set-up and execute this meeting with these men. The hell with the Rockettes and the Christmas show, I wanted to falsely accuse mussa of violating me 20 + years earlier for my Christmas trip to NYC. The friars did however offer to pay for partial of any counseling or therapy. They offered me something like paying 30% of the cost, which to me at that time was worth nothing to me, I had no money to spend on therapy. But their offer of paying for some portion of therapy told me there that they felt my story had some truth to it, or they wouldn't have made that offer to me. So I was sent out the doors to continue of life of drug abuse for the next 10-15 years and which I guess they would hope I would just die from it and go away. But those days are over. And I always knew someday somewhere that someone else would come forward with a similar story as me. Everything I always read about lowlifes that prey on innocent children don't do it just one time. I even went to the Brooklyn District Attorney's office and filed a complaint on him. Even though the statute of limitations had run out, which I believe to be a bunch of bullshit especially when it comes to crimes against children. How was I supposed to get justice and come forward when the whole foundation of the abuse is based on shame and guilt. How do the lawmakers come to the conclusion that a child or an adolescent or a young adult can make such a decision to speak up about the abuse when there is nothing but shame and guilt associated with it all . Even to this day I still have to be very selective to who I tell this story to. Or if I badmouth the church to some old church lady who never misses a Sunday mass, people are so blind and in denial when it comes to these men. And the denial and the legal system is what keeps these men preying and not praying. After I googled his name about a year ago and the posting came up on Burn and Rot in Hell, I was sent into an emotional reaction both happy and very sad. FINALLY , its been 30 years since I've been waiting for someone else to come forward with same story that I had. I cried for an hour then I called my sister, and I called up my parents - finally I've had some vindication .

With this new information I actually thought the cat was out of the bag. mussa, from what I read in that posting, had finally admitted to these transgressions, the posting even said that mussa and the Franciscans even gave this guy checks. And he stated he had the canceled checks to prove it. The story was identical to mine, I just replaced hockey games with baseball hall of fame and movies . And I could also tell from the dates given in the account that I was a victim before him and also I could tell from the dates that I reported it before he did.

I had a lot of emotions dealing with this information. I was angry that, knowing I existed and had made similar claims, I was never notified by anyone to try and help me. I was angry about the money, and I was especially angry about how I was accused of wrongdoing and malicious intent when I sought help from these Christian men. So I decided to have another confrontation with mussa and I reached out to the current head of the order.This time I was treated more kindly and more with the atmosphere of understanding. I didn't have to jump through hoops to get to talk to mussa. I explained to Brother William Boslet the Superior General at the time of my past history with the order, how me and my sister had a meeting with mussa many years earlier and how dissatisfied and disappointed I was with the way I was treated and handled.

Bro. William had me come in first for a meeting with him. So I went to Remsen street to meet with him and he had another Brother, I forgot his name but I'm assuming it's some kind of legal person to sit in our meeting. And again for the God knows how many time, I told the story of me and brother joe mussa. From the look on both of their faces throughout the telling of my story told me he knew that mussa was a pedophile, and what I was saying he did to me as a child was true.

Brother William then informed me that mussa did not want to meet with me. That made me very angry. I was looking at this from a totally different angle. I actually thought that this man was willing to allow me to heal. I thought that because of the posting on Burn and Rot in Hell that he would of course be willing to meet with me and we would have a spirit of forgiveness. That healing would begin and we could get on with our lives.

I told Bro. William that that was bullshit, I said to him that he was his superior and he should tell mussa there is no option. He must take a meeting with me.

A phone call from Bro. William a few days later informed me the meeting was on. Shortly thereafter there we were again in the same building the same office and for the most part the same people . Hence Brother William and his associate. It was mussa , my sister Eileen and myself. I sat directly across from mussa and looked him squarely in the eyes. I had before me not this image of a man I looked at as a hero and role model that I had instilled in me from my days before the molestation . Nor did I have the man I was so fearful of telling no to and unable to muster courage to make him stop touching me. No, I had before me an aging overweight sad looking man. Somewhat hunched over as if the weight of the world was on him. And that is what I wish on him. That the guilt would crush him over the years. I don't know.

I took from my pocket a copy of the posting about him. I read it out loud for everyone in the room to hear and as much as I could, I kept direct eye contact with mussa. When I finished reading the blog posting, I turned to brother William and told him that the story

I read was identical to my story about my relationship with mussa. I then faced mussa and went over again, specifics of what he had done to me. I told him how he affected my life and how it still affects me today. And to my total disbelief he fucking denied doing anything to me. He remembered the trip to the Baseball Hall of Fame and he remembered hanging out with me at the mall, the movies and Burger King. Then he mentioned the Kiss concert. I just finished moments ago explaining the vivid memory of the guy standing in front of us watching him trying to get in my pants while I sat on his shoulders. mussa then did something that I found very telling. He raised his hands above his head and said he was not quite sure how he could have gotten into my pants while sitting on his shoulders. He wiggled his hands around and mimicked the molesting attempt. In my eyes it was a bizarre thing to do and it only served to make him look guilty. It was akin to OJ trying on the bloody gloves half-heartedly while making it look as if he was struggling to get them on. And that dumb look on Boslet's face. mussa had the same look on his pathetic face as well. He again denied me any closure or healing. The man who dedicated his life to helping mankind and to assist the suffering and helpless with love and understanding. A man who glorifies the lord in all he does, that's right , IN ALL HE DOES. A man who vowed to give service to the people of God. He is supposed to help heal the wounded, to bind up those who are bruised and to reclaim the erring. That's from the mission statement of the order of the Franciscan friars. I HAVE NO EXPERIENCE WITH SUCH BEHAVIORS. At this time I knew I was talking to a psychopath. I was again getting nowhere with this man or his colleagues. I looked this shell of the man I knew right into his eyes and asked "Have you ever molested a child before" he said "NO". Eileen chimed in and basically told him what a vile human he is to not acknowledge my pain and allow me closure. We got out of our seats and we left. Revictimized again by the men in robes pretending to be what they are not."

My only comment to Danny's story is this: We have to get these men off the street and we have to hold the people who protect them and insulate them from consequences accountable. We have to do it if we want to save our children.

We need the statute of limitations for child sexual abuse changed in New York. It's the only way.

CHAPTER THIRTY

THE LONGSHOTS: HERE WE ARE

It is here, in this last chapter, that I have to backtrack a little.

March, 2015 was a big month. It was the four year anniversary of the launch of BRH. I could not be prouder. This one little website gave the public something huge: an anonymous forum to send and receive information about child predators at schools.

The power of this surprised even me, and I didn't think anything could surprise me anymore. Almost four years to the day the first post went up, I was contacted by a young woman who was being sexually harassed at a well-known prestigious university in Brooklyn. She and two of her friends had been sexually harassed by the same teacher and they wanted to do something about it. This teacher, among other things, asked them if he could lick them, and sexually assaulted one of them.

She asked for my help, and I gave it. This is what I want for my future.

On March 25th, 2015, exactly four years after I was "terminated" from Prep, I got one of the biggest gifts of my life. The judge in Felicia Mooradian's breach of contract case against St. Francis Prep (regarding Assistant Principal Christopher Mendolia and former teacher Fernando Sicilia) handed down his decision regarding the school's motion to dismiss her lawsuit.

He let it through, despite huge obstacles and a longshot strategy created by Kevin Mulhearn and I.

The implications of this decision for students' rights were monumental. The Court said this:

> "The essence of the implied contract is that an academic institution must act in good faith in its dealings with students. The rights and obligations of the parties as contained in the school's bulletins, circulars, and regulations made available to the student become a part of this contract...Here, plaintiff's breach of implied contract cause of action is predicated on St. Francis Prep's alleged failure to comply with its obligations as set forth in the school's mission statement and faculty handbook. Specifically, the amended complaint alleges that St. Francis Prep breached its implied contract with plaintiff in which St. Francis Prep, its officials, and faculty were obligated by the terms of the St. Francis Prep mission statement and faculty handbook to:
>
> 1. treat students (including Plaintiff) with respect, integrity and dignity,
> 2. create a school environment filled with, inter alia, respect and integrity,
> 3. not intentionally expose students (including Plaintiff) to embarrassment, disparagement, or abusive language,
> 4. not use professional relationships with students (such as Plaintiff) for private advantage, and
> 5. not create, foster, or exacerbate conditions harmful to students' (including Plaintiff's) ability to learn, or to their health and safety.
>
> Accepting the allegations in the amended complaint as true, the court finds that plaintiff has sufficiently pleaded a cause of action for breach of contract against St. Francis Prep."

THIS IS HUGE. This means that any student who feels that St. Francis Prep (or any other private school) has broken any of its promises made in school literature may have a lawsuit for breach of contract against the school. The court validated a whole new way for students who feel that a private school has not lived up to its promises to sue. And, they have six years to do it (instead of three for negligence actions), since the statute of limitations for breach of contract is six years from when the breach occurred.

Felicia and I were ecstatic. But then Marla died six months later. Losing our key witness was a huge blow, even though Marla had left Felicia a copy of her documentary. Our options were limited, and in November, 2015, Felicia dropped her lawsuit involving Mendolia and Sicilia in exchange for Prep dropping its defamation suit against her.

However, if one longshot can come through, so can another. As of right now, Felicia's lawsuit involving Brother Ben is still alive in state court.

Now is a good time to mention this - one more case got a pass. Connie Lord and Chris Murphy were ask to testify at a Department of Education hearing regarding Rodney Alejandro. They will make sure he never teaches in New York State ever again.

For me, however, my Prep litigation song has been sung. In mid-May, the Federal Court of Appeals handed down its decision for my pending defamation claim appeal. Unfortunately, they affirmed the District Court's decision to dismiss it. They, like the District Court, held that Brother Leonard's statements about me in his January, 2013 letter were non-actionable statements of opinion.

You are probably wondering whether I was upset by this. The answer is no. I really only filed my lawsuit to prove a point: St. Francis Prep would be held accountable for thinking it has the unalienable right to crap on people. From now on, there would be a consequence for that.

That has always been the goal. Everyone who stepped forward wanted to bring the issues at Prep to light; we wanted to shine a big, bright spotlight on them, and we did.

My only regret is that I have not been able to recover compensation for victims like Connie Lord, whose life was ruined by what happened at St. Francis Prep, and who is at the mercy of the New York Legislature to open a window to the statute of limitations that would allow her to sue.

Right now, New York is one of only five states that has not eliminated or extended the statute of limitations on child sexual abuse cases. The statute of limitations continues to run at age 23.

The Child Victims Act (A.2872/S.63), sponsored by Assemblywoman Margaret Markey, D-Queens, would eliminate the criminal and civil statute of limitations for child sexual abuse crimes as well as establish a one-year window for victims to bring civil lawsuits against people or institutions in older cases.

California passed similar legislation in 2002, including the one-year window to file lawsuits for older crimes. More than 1,000 lawsuits, resulting in $1.2 billion in settlements by various dioceses of the Catholic Church, followed the passage of the law.

Specifically, Markey's bill provides that: "Sex crimes, particularly those committed against children, are among the most heinous and deeply disturbing in our society. They are crimes that leave life-long scars, multiple victims and require an all encompassing strategy to combat. Victims of childhood sexual abuse do not come to terms with their abuse until well into adulthood. Under current law they have no recourse."

The bill goes on to say "by eliminating the statute of limitations in childhood sexual abuse cases, victims of these horrific crimes will get their day in court and be able to seek the justice they have been denied."

The Catholic Church supports abolishing the statute of limitations for sex abuse cases going forward, however, does not support the one year window for instances in the past.

Of course they don't. They never will support opening themselves up to liability for their own negligence and inaction.

Until this bill is passed, this battle will still need to be fought another way.

It will need to be fought in print, on the screen, and in the streets. And, it will need to be faught tirelessly.

I'm game. *Are you?*

EPILOGUE

If you don't believe in miracles, I have some news for you. They happen. I say this without a shred of doubt in my heart. I have experienced too many on this journey to even consider believing otherwise.

In February, 2016, after four years of delving into the story behind former Franciscan Brother and St. Francis Prep principal Michael Moran, one of his victims contacted me.

John Gerrard was raped by Moran when he was a senior at St. Francis Prep in 1977. In case you have any doubts, yes, it was rape. John tried to push Moran off him, screamed "No!" repeatedly, but could not ward off the attack.

John is a retired New York City firefighter. Ron Howard modeled scenes in his movie "Backdraft" on footage of John exiting a burning building in Flatbush, Brooklyn. That fire left John with second and third degree burns, spinal injuries, and fourteen months of physical therapy to endure. That was the last fire he ever fought.

John now counsels prison inmates who are trying to turn their life around. He has had a long journey, and knows coming forward about what Michael Moran did to him is part of it.

In the practical scheme of things, what does John having the courage to come forward mean?

It means someone else will read this and know they are not alone.

It means someone else will find the courage to confront a situation they could not confront before.

It means there is one more voice clamoring for a change in the New York child sexual abuse statute of limitations, so that we can bring predators like Michael Moran to justice.

It means there is still hope.

WHERE TO GET HELP – RESOURCES

SNAP
(Survivors Network of those Abused by Priests)

www.snapnetwork.org

SNAP is the largest, oldest and most active self-help group for clergy sex abuse victims, whether assaulted by ministers, priests, nuns or rabbis. SNAP is a confidential, safe place for wounded men and women to be heard, supported and healed. SNAP works tirelessly to achieve two goals: to heal the wounded and to protect the vulnerable. The organization has more than 10,000 members and support groups meet in over 60 cities across the U.S. and the world.

BISHOPACCOUNTABILITY.ORG
(Documenting the Abuse Crisis in the Roman Catholic Church)

www.Bishop-Accountability.org

BishopAccountability.org aims to facilitate the accountability of the U.S. bishops under civil, criminal, and canon law. They document the debates about root causes and remedies, because important information has surfaced during those debates. They take no position on the root causes, and they do not advocate particular remedies. If the facts are fully known, the causes and remedies will become clear.

Road to Recovery Advocacy

www.road-to-recovery.org

Road to Recovery is a non-profit organization that offers compassionate counseling and referral services to survivors of sexual abuse. Launched in 2005 to provide direct assistance to victims of clergy sexual abuse, R2R has expanded its mission to include survivors of all sexual abuse.

Stop It Now!

www.stopitnow.org

Stop it Now! prevents the sexual abuse of children by mobilizing adults, families and communities to take actions that protect children before they are harmed. They provide support, information and resources to keep children safe and create healthier communities. Since 1992, they have identified, refined and shared effective ways for individuals, families and communities to act to prevent child sexual abuse before children are harmed - and to get help for everyone involved.

RAINN
(Rape, Abuse & Incest National Network)

www.rainn.org

RAINN (Rape, Abuse & Incest National Network) is the nation's largest anti-sexual violence organization and was named one of "America's 100 Best Charities" by Worth magazine. RAINN created and operates the National Sexual Assault Hotline (800.656.HOPE and online.rainn.org) in partnership with more than 1,100 local sexual assault service providers across the country and operates the DoD Safe Helpline for the Department of Defense. In 2015, the Online Hotline expanded to offer services in Spanish at rainn.org/es. RAINN also carries out programs to prevent sexual violence, help victims and ensure that rapists are brought to justice.

NATIONAL ALLIANCE TO END SEXUAL VIOLENCE

www.endsexualviolence.org

This alliance is a national advocacy organization representing state coalitions and local programs organizing against sexual violence and for survivors.

NOT ALONE – TOGETHER AGAINST SEXUAL ASSAULT
www.notalone.gov

NotAlone.gov includes information for students, schools, and anyone interested in finding resources on how to respond to and prevent sexual assault.

TALK ABOUT ABUSE TO LIBERATE KIDS
www.taalk.org

TAALK's mission is to reduce children's vulnerability to child sexual abuse and to support survivors through the healing process by creating awareness, education, support and healing programs and delivering them through local TAALK Chapters and partner organizations as well as locating programs and services from around the world and highlighting them through their media platforms.

NATIONAL CHILDREN'S ALLIANCE
www.nationalchildrensalliance.org

National Children's Alliance (NCA) is the national association and accrediting body for Children's Advocacy Centers (CACs). Formed in 1988, NCA has been providing support, technical assistance, and quality assurance for CACs, while serving as a voice for abused children for more than 25 years. A children's advocacy center is a child-friendly facility in which law enforcement, child protection, prosecution, mental health, medical and victim advocacy professionals work together to investigate abuse, help children heal from abuse, and hold offenders accountable.

DARKNESS to LIGHT
www.d2l.org

Their programs raise awareness of the prevalence and consequences of child sexual abuse by educating adults about the steps they can take to prevent, recognize and react responsibly to the reality of child sexual abuse.

APPENDIX B

SCREENSHOTS OF FACEBOOK MESSAGES FROM ANGEL AMORE

Exposing Child Sex Abuse and Corruption at America's Largest Private Catholic High School

Angel Amore

AND, Carol szostek is on match.com

Elizabeth Sorvillo
Hi
Thanks for the info, I had heard all those things but you reinforced it. I may send a text to my contact at Fox and see what happens. Please tell your friend my business partners and I talked at great lengths about the video before we posted it. It was a tough decision and I actually vomited from the stress and emotions around it. We needed to get across the gravity of the hypocrisy at the school, and we had to make it "newsy" and tangible. I feel somewhat vindicated now. It has and continues to be a long haul. Thanks for your support.

Angel Amore
you want hypocrisy? look into the Brothers Domenick and Ben situations. You might also want to look into Anthony Grimm

Elizabeth Sorvillo
I had heard some opinions about a couple of these guys, but never any stories.

Angel Amore
The story I heard was that a teacher saw pornographic images on a computer screen being used by and it was reported to pat mcGlaughlin. Nothing was done. A secretary in the office even sent a letter to the diocese about it and nothing was ever done

Angel Amore
Don't call it hypocrisy, call it what it is, a "selective view of the schools mission statement."

Socrates got his job because he played football

Mendolia is chairman of history because he's a jock as Pat M likes jocks as he was one and still lives by his glory days' of high school sports like Al Bundy.

Carol will retire this year for sure, now get pat mcglaughin: by the way, the teacher that reported to pat was

189

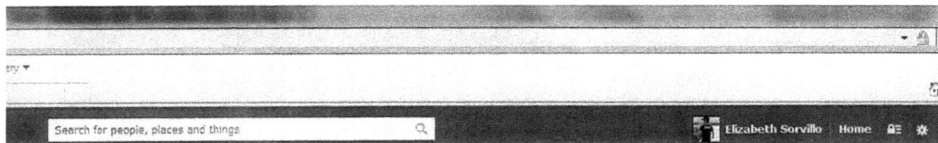

Angel Amore

+ New Message ⚙ Actions ▾

Elizabeth Sorvillo
Not sure how to go about the Pat annulment thing...so hard to prove this stuff...probably no records about ▮▮▮▮ and everyone will deny it. They will never fire ▮▮▮▮ since he has dirt on them. Do you know about Tom Nuzzi?

Angel Amore
I can ask my friend for details.

you're right though abuot ▮▮▮▮ and dirt: quite a few peole are still there just because they have dirt--that may be why Grimm is still there.

Elizabeth Sorvillo

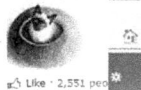

prep when he was fired in 1987. he tried to sleep with me for a year when I was there, was fired for stealing money from kids. then i met a graduate 15 years later, ▮▮▮▮▮▮▮▮ three of her friends. he went on to be a grifter in several school districts all across the country, harassing women and stealing money. you can google him.

Angel Amore

+ New Message ⚙ Actions ▾

Remember how ▮▮▮▮ left? Some kid that was his only failure went psycho and took every joke he said in class and used it against him .McGlaugin used it against him and he quit. Turns out she was a star softball player.. ▮▮▮▮ was a good teacher too, but I think he drank. ▮▮▮▮▮▮▮▮▮▮▮▮▮▮▮▮▮▮▮▮▮▮▮▮

You have a friend on FB that knows more about Ben that I do.

Elizabeth Sorvillo
Yeah, that friend is not going to give anything up because I am blacklisted at prep and he still works there. I know about ▮▮▮▮ he was a good teacher. the thing that bothers me most about Pat is that he is really dumb. It was always impossible for me to have a conversation with him about anything, basically.

Angel Amore
your FB friend is a former student at prep that Ben 'said things' to. She'll tell you everything

Elizabeth Sorvillo
ok. thanks. I will try to narrow it down.

Angel Amore

+ New Message   ⚙ Actions ▾

Elizabeth Sorvillo
can you tell me what age range my friend is in? I don't even know when br. ben was a teacher, that's the problem. I think he was there when I went there but other than that I don't know anything about him, even his last name. All I know is a couple of people over the years told me he is a jerk.

Angel Amore
ben was canned maybe the year you got there or perhas just before. As the story went, it was a student that is now a female college junior and member of your site and even commented on your BARIN FB page. Done in typical SFP fashion (he just left and the faculty was not told about it). I heard that he was still kept on by St Johns; he does yoga with SJU's womens volleyball team. You can be sure SFp never gave the heads up to Saint Johns.

Brother Dom kissed a boy as the story went but of course, he left on short notice for Rome. There was also a principal that was led out of the school in hand cuffs before enny took over

You shoud get in touch with mr baricelli. I bet he has all the dpe on everyone as i would think Mark Kroikowski ████████████████
████████████████████

I would think you'd want to shake the place up where to bishos has to get involved (like abortions etc)

Elizabeth Sorvillo
ok, thanks for the info. I have a better idea now. I was hoping all this would get the school on the bishop's radar, I know that is the school's only hope, I guess we shall see.

Elizabeth Sorvillo
what is br. ben's last name? I need a last name.

Elizabeth Sorvillo
I thought it was Ryann, but I asked her and she said Br. Ben left before she started school. She knew the story though, about his asking girls to hike up their skirts, etc. I am clueless now as to who it could be.

Angel Amore
Ask Felicia about Ben. She will give you the scoop. Do you have anyone inside? If you do you will be in great shape for dirt: there is a lot of anger inside SFP.

Ask people about the 2009 prom: Pat M never spoke to Armond nor went near her as she was there with some guy (Purifacato, Sughrue, Gambino, Ganci, and Kobayashi were there and saw it all--which proved to them the Pat M screwed her for her job; they would alll say it is

191

Controlled Burn:

Angel Amore

+ New Message   ⚙ Actions ▾

went near her as she was there with some guy (Puriracato, Sughrue, Gambino, Ganci, and Kobayashi were there and saw it all--which proved to them the Pat M screwed her for her job; they would alll say it is proof enough). Who does a 'casting couch' for a guidance job at SFP? A crazed woman from LI with capped teeth.

Get in touch with Maureen Gray. A black woman that used to teach there before your time there: according to my friend/source was referred to as a "NIGGER" by a religion teacher: ███████████

His boss, who approved of ███████████racism when she felt fit, ████ ██████used to recommend students go to Planned Parenthood (and that was not for pap screening or breast cancer screening, you know what it was for as much as I do). 2 and 2 together. If the bishop knew about that! How Catholic/Christian of Mrs ████

That department is poison for the school's "mission statement" and hypocrisy:
1 ███████████ and what I wrote (plus his██████████)
2 ███████████
3 ███████████who was kicked out of the seminary in Huntington (and Sally hired)

These are people that teach them about "God". I am not a believer but if I had had kids, I'd never allow THEM to be kids teachers

---

Angel Amore

+ New Message   ⚙ Actions ▾

Elizabeth Sorvillo
ok thanks. I will check it out as much as I can...esp. w/Felicia. Not surprised to hear any of it. I was at the 2009 prom, noticed the same thing!

Elizabeth Sorvillo
thanks
Ok, Felicia and I made contact. We are going to talk soon. I will do my best to get the bishop to step in. The school won't make it another two years with the current administration running it. I know it is Prep's only hope.

Angel Amore
I have gossip but of course it is not factual.You might find the boy Dom attacked as ███████ FB

Angel Amore
You can also dig into the religion department in that ████████ when she ran the department used to send students to planned parenthood (that will go over well with your bishop)

Angel Amore

+ New Message ⚙ Actions ▾

Elizabeth Sorvillo
ok thanks. I will see what i can find out..

Angel Amore
███████████████████████The porn on the comp was ███████ and NOT a classroom comp but a fac room on 2d floor library. Hes smarter than you think..... AND SFP people thinks you have someone inside (Sue Sparagna thinks its Andrea)

Elizabeth Sorvillo
Yeah, I bet they are shitting their pants over there!

Angel Amore
████████'s son is off to rehab
if asked, you can always claim you got your information from a teacher that told you Sue Sparagna told them (I don't know if you knew her

Elizabeth Sorvillo
I have to think about the best way to proceed. ██████████████████████ Yes, I do know Sue.

Angel Amore
True. No point I guess in going after ████████'s son given his issues. The school thinks that your site will just fade away

Angel Amore
Joseph Muller in the religion department maybe someone to go ask about SFP; Patrick McGlaughlin told Mary Ellen Bechtle he was willing to take a swing at him (which he did not which shows he IS a pussy) Ask him, just check privacy settings

Angel Amore
Abe Leston is regarded as the mole now

Elizabeth Sorvillo
I don't know how that could happen since he is the biggest suck up there and he wants mclaughlin's job so badly. what did they say to him? I was on vacation for a few days and I had time to think. I am going to go to the bishop. when did that incident w████████ happen? I need to get my facts straight. I will prob have a few more questions this week. I think I am going to call his office and explain who I am. felicia hasnt been back in touch so I will email her one more time.

Angel Amore
I mentioned what you said about leston and my source double checked and said you are right about him being an ass kisser. She said if he is the mole, they are even dummer than ever. What do you hope to accomplish with the bishop?

Elizabeth Sorvillo
I know, for them to even think he is the mole is so stupid, he is sooo into becoming an administrator there. They should realize he would never jeopardize that. Anyway, they need a whole new administration. I think the bishop needs to step in and make that happen. That would be ideal. Carolyn told me they always try to keep the goings on under the bishop's radar. I figure if I get it on his radar, knowing my media history, he won't have a choice but to do something.

Angel Amore

history, he won't have a choice but to do something.

Angel Amore

They also despise the bishop and bishops. you tell him about the ▊
▊ which dave ganci
witnessed. I saw a posting on BARIH and noticed some mentioned a
'mole'.

there are a dozen staff tipping you off. I assume that dean is the prime
suspect and if she retires this year, you know she was asked to call it
quits. You might also get some dirt from the Hawaii trip. Yo

Angel Amore

u know there is all sorts of dirt from that trip and since it is ted Jahn's
student paid annual free trip, ther eis no way he would disclose any
issues on the trip

b

student take and post photos.

Angel Amore

they have fired or forced retirement on teachers for trangressions much
less than what ▊ did: ▊ was forced to retire
because word was he had a serious gambling issue and the school
wanted to protect ▊. There was a teacher called Miss K
about 8 years ago that was forced to retire because her department
supervisor did not like her. There was an art teacher teacher a few
years ago, maybe 5, that was fired for hitting on students to (but brs
Ben and Domenick are still around). Word too is that ▊ had a
relationship with a boy at the prep who was ▊ assistant director of
student activities even after he graduated.

Elizabeth Sorvillo

Can you find out what year the ▊ thing happened so I have my
facts together? And if possible the name of the boy ▊ was involved
with? I am trying to be as accurate as possible in what I am going to
say. If I don't get anywhere with the bishop, I will try to see the
Cardinal. Yeah, I already thought about Hawaii, because I always hear
horrific Ted stories afterward. I will pay special attention to the photos
that go up on fb this week. thanks.

Angel Amore

The word was the ▊ walked into the 2nd floor faculty room of the
library with ▊ appointed "Assistant Director of Student Activities" in
June 2009, some college kid name Michael (my source said he thinks
the name was), and ▊ had porn on the computer. It was then
reported to pat Macglaughlin by both Sue Sparagna and Dave ganci.
The story was that Carl in the computer office then checked the
computers and found nothing but nobody believes that. The Bishop's
office received a letter on St Francis stationery soon after telling them
the same thing and nthing was done about it (the letter was nt signed
so the bishops office should not have taken it seriously).. That is part of
the reason why many suspect Andrea as the mole as being in the comp
department, she would over hear everything. You could always use Sue
Sparagna as a source as she is known as a blabber mouth. You can
write anything insane and say she told you that and nobody would say
it is not true. There is a also a rumor floating that Joe Muller of the
religion department is your mole as he had a recent fight with pat
MacGlaughlin and as he is not liked by the admin nor his own
department, they are thinking him. In other words they are targeting
him for firing.

Elizabeth Sorvillo

Ok, I am going to put my notes together this week and run it by a
friend to see how it all sounds when it is coming out of my mouth. I
want to be credible and not come across as a bitter, crazy person so I
have to really think about the best way to say things. Keep me posted if
anything else I need to know. Thanks.

Angel Amore

How did it go?

194

Angel Amore

You should also drop an email and friend request to [redacted].
He can give you some skinny on some SF shit . I think he even had an affair with [redacted]

Elizabeth Sorvillo
Ok, I will do that. I agree, I think he probably knows a lot. Thanks.

I still haven't gone to the bishop. I am trying to get someone to come with me and back up what I have to say. I think it will have more weight if there are two people. Maybe [redacted] will be able to help or suggest someone.

Angel Amore
What's new? There are rumblings now that Tony Grimm might be your mole and some people hope he is as he is such a weird man and many want to see him fired.

And what was that nonsense about pat mcGlaughlin being the hardest working man at SFP? he doesn't do a damned thing ther than try to relive his high school glory years

---

Angel Amore

I sent a message to [redacted] a few days ago and am waiting for a response. Yeah, I was there for that professional day and of course his son voted him "most calloused hands" for being such hard worker. I wanted to vomit. Of all the schools graduates attend, they had to do it at Iona where his kid goes. What a joke.

Angel Amore
It is stunning that they are still worship Pat Mac as he was a PE teacher. Rumor now says Mr K is your mole as he is angry [redacted] and [redacted] being passed over for chairperson of the department. Go after the religion department as they are the most hated department at St Francis:peg Bergin-Sementilli, Sue Vivona, and Sue Spraagna willl tell you everything

Elizabeth Sorvillo
I know, everyone has an issue with the religion department. It is so sad! Did they tell Mark K he [redacted] Is that why he's mad? I hope they [redacted]

Angel Amore
Mr K is pissed about not being chairman of the department as if his [redacted] would do it for him and pujak is pissed about living vicariously though his sons. bechtel is pissed around married to a man that no longer loves her and they all hate being catholic.No wonder you have issues with the religion department. Sue Sparagna is now pissed as she is going through menopause (as if anyone would

Elizabeth Sorvillo
Ha! Most of the people there have serious issues that require medication or therapy, lol.

Angel Amore
[redacted] was kicked out the seminary in Huntington for being gay and not a team player--so Sally Ryder hired him.You know he harasses students

Elizabeth Sorvillo
Yeah, I have seen him humiliate students many times. I thought he left the seminary. That is interesting that he was kicked out.

Do you know if Carolyn Szostek is retiring this year?

Angel Amore
+ New Message ⚙ Actions ∨

Elizabeth Sorvillo
Br. Mark had do much dirt! He told me all sorts of things that scared the crap out of me, a lot of the things you confirmed. Carol gave me a framed picture of the two of us. Who does that? I am contemplating making a dartboard out of it. Yeah, I may post pics on the blog when she retires, lol.

Angel Amore
You should make that picture as some sort of profile shot on BARJH.

You might want to take a trip to the Sly Fox Inn in Queens some satuday evening. Several secretaries party there and dance.You might get all sorts of info particularly after a few drinks in them.

Do you have any idea of who my source is? Just hoping I am covering the person's tracks for fear of the school.

I hope you don't

Elizabeth Sorvillo
I really have no idea. It could be anybody who has been there a while. I heard a lot of the things you told me in the four years I was there. So someone there a really long time I am sure would know everything, especially if they were liked and friendly. People love to spill the beans there because everyone is miserable. Thanks about the tip about Sly Fox, I may check it out.

Angel Amore
The Sly Fox is something of a hook up place too for singles and couples that are, shall we say, liberal in the mores department

Elizabeth Sorvillo
Ha ha! Too funny that the secretaries go there...wow, wild nights, lolol.

Angel Amore
I guess divorce does that to many

Angel Amore
Check their facebook pages, I bet they have pictures from bars that are the sly fox

I bet Carol scored with a 20 something at the Fox

Angel Amore
What did Barkley post that had to be deleted? I am intrigued and alo who was the guy that cheated schools back in 1986? I never herd that story

Elizabeth Sorvillo
I have no idea who it was! I can't tell from the email address. It could be anybody. I couldn't believe it! Somebody spilled the beans on Joe D. and all his people, and the person used last names and accused them of stealing, etc. The post said "you are all going down!" _____ Tom Nuzzi, Steve Hollis and Paul DeCurtis stole in 1986, it was called Sidgate. They were all gym teachers. They gave the kids inflated prices for school ski trips, and pocketed the extra money. I heard they gave Nuzzi a glowing letter of recommendation. He then went on a cross country spree. Google him.

Angel Amore
That is fucked up. Wasn't there also a history teacher fucking a student a few years ago and everyone was okay with that?

Angel Amore
Did you know that new SFP messsage board is a way for the school to get IP addresses of posters to see if they match up with BARJH posters?

Elizabeth Sorvillo
I don't even have the IP addresses of posters on my site. There is no way they can have the IP addresses. All I have is an email address of my posters.

Elizabeth Sorvillo
In other words, there is no way they can match up who posts on BRH with who posts on the school message board. They are using a scare tactic to make teachers afraid.

Angel Amore
I think they think someone is posting on the site from inside the school. As IF someone wuld be dumb enough to do that from a school computer. Then again, it is SFP.

Angel Amore

+ New Message   Actions ▾

Angel Amore
Carol has a "boy toy"

Elizabeth Sorvillo
Is it the same guy she was dating a couple of months ago or did she get a new younger guy?

Elizabeth Sorvillo
I am actually the one who had put her on match.com because she was so friggin lonely. I wrote her profile for her and made her password and everything. Then she latched on to the first guy she went on a date with and started sleeping with him after only a few weeks. She didn't even like him, found him boring, and was embarrassed of him. But that didn't stop her from screwing him, lol. How did you hear about him? Did she bring him to the teachers' thing they have after graduation? He is an ex-cop.

Angel Amore
let's put it this way: my source is very 'liberal' sexually and finds others that are. There are a handful of lifestylers at SFP. You can tell by who their partner, gf/bf is, or spouse. I think you need to hit Sly Fox a few Saturday's. That is something of a give away. The 'mole' which I don't know whether or not you have, or how many, is actually a secretary in Joseph Disomma's office as they regard themselves as 3rd class memebers of the SFP 'community" and want payback

Angel Amore
try sly fox on the break on parent-teacher night and see who is there....connect the dots

Elizabeth Sorvillo
Ok I will go and see what happens. hopefully no one will throw a chair at me lol

Angel Amore
Ms K, ████████, was fired by Sally Ryder for personal reasons but SFP pretended she retired (get in touch with her).....

Elizabeth Sorvillo
My best friend at prep when we were in high school married a guy named ████████. Is this woman's first name Claudia? I lost touch after college. I need a first name. I am def going to the Sly Fox that night with my partner and a good friend. What time do they usually show up there?

Angel Amore
I think the teacher was named barbara but I am not sure. I think the adult lifestylers would be there after 10. I wonder if CS ever did any of that: I can see her doing something lie that too, swinging

Angel Amore
any luck at sly foxx?

Elizabeth Sorvillo
It is tomorrow night.

Angel Amore
Did you have any luck getting in touch with ████████?

Elizabeth Sorvillo
I sent him a facebook e but he never answered me. It's ok. I have a contact who knows the bishop and he told me that will be a dead end

Controlled Burn:

Angel Amore ✛ New Message ⚙ Actions ▼

Elizabeth Sorvillo
I sent him a facebook e but he never answered me. It's ok. I have a contact who knows the bishop and he told me that will be a dead end anyway. The bishop knows a lot but won't draw more attention to it. Apparently the people in his inner circle call him "the ▆ prince." Isn't that f'in scary! There are other ways. The user Barkley who posted all that stuff about joey diamonds and his crew and used full names has been active on the site recently. I have a feeling he/she is up to something.

Angel Amore
He didn't respond to you? I would have thought he would as he was essentially fired. Forgive me, he quit on his own like the ones who 'retire'. I think he might have went to law school too so he may not be the type of man to put things in writing.

Want me to try to get his # for you? I guess you can hit places he hangs out at like eating at portofino in Forest Hills, the diner over next to st johns on union tpke, I saw him at BlueBay on 2 fridays in the past 2 months, and a former student said he hits Classica pizzeria on Union Turnpike fairly regularly with his wife. No I am not stalking him I just know a few things from over the years and run into students all the time (they tell everything always). ▆ must have all the dope as he was friends with everyone.

The bishop is on the side of the school admins and always will be: SFP admins brag about their ability to quash things in the media. notice how you were ONLY on Fox 5? it was not just clergy involved in the sex scandals but everyone. police who went to the schools kept hush as did media people that went to the schools and parents never believed it either. Ask about the fire some bum set in the cafeteria about a decade ago. It never made any news agency. I understand too that the bishop was despised by the people in his own diocese. look it up and connect dots

Elizabeth Sorvillo
I gave ▆ my number in case he wanted to call instead of writing...he never answered me at all. I think everything is going to work out over the summer...I just have a feeling prep won't be happy when the new school year starts. I do believe wheels are in motion, you have to trust me. By the way, joey d sent ▆ to pay my business partner a visit. We were threatened about posts. In the meantime, they confirmed that joey diamonds = joe d at prep.

Angel Amore
What is CS'ss phone number and address? I think I am going to try to get some action from her so I can put her pics on my "conquest" wall. I'll bet I can even get her to do some serious kink shit too: then I can mail you action shots of her getting rammed. I'll show that widow who's "Dean of Discipline"

Elizabeth Sorvillo
She is very conservative, scarily so. Sorry.

Angel Amore
trust me: I've managed to get it on with all sorts. My hunch is that she is gullible and a pro player like me can get her

Elizabeth Sorvillo
I am only one of 3 people at school who had her phone number, so she would know if I gave it out to anyone. She is done anyway, now that she has to retire. There are bigger fish there and hopefully the seeds were planted so they get fried. There are too many people there who are pissed at the admins...something's gotta give.

Angel Amore
Do you know where she hangs out? I am serious: I am gonna get to brag how "I fucked carol szostek". Once they g over 50 and are single, wmen just dont care anymore. They give it up at the drop of a hat (as did a few sfp secretaries)

198

Angel Amore

+ New Message · ⚙ Actions ▾

Elizabeth Sorvillo
She goes to Robert Moses to play golf every saturday in the summer. I think the course is the last field there. She really doesn't have a regular place that she eats. Her boyfriend is probably attached to her hip now, as she is so needy and so is he. She also goes to that field at robert moses (the third field on the left) about 3 times during the week. She sits to the right of the concessions about 50 feet from the water. Always the same spot. That's her most regular activity. Her other regular activities are getting her hair and nails done, but I don't know where.

Angel Amore
looks like I will have to bust out my very snug swimwear (D&G mind you) and start hitting Robert Moses. She sees me tanned & toned with a "Hey Carol! Is this your beach spot? I've been coming here for years and never saw you"......start the 70s porn music

thanks

Angel Amore
I noticed that BARJH has been a little quiet of late. Has news from SFP decreased? I guess it would considering it is summer though

Elizabeth Sorvillo
The insurgents who send me cryptic messages sometimes said that they have another route in mind...haven't heard anything in a while so I am assuming they are up to something.█████ got back to me, finally, and said that everything he knows was posted on the site already.

Angel Amore
OK I assume when school starts up we will be getting some quality shit from your insurgents. I look forward to it. ☺

Elizabeth Sorvillo
Ha I hope so. The last thing I heard is that Joe D. is shitting his pants.

Angel Amore
I am suprised that ██████ had nothing to say: I think he is 'playing nice' as he knows all sorts of shit about the school and the religion department. Ask him about Mark K, peg Bergin (the grape vine said they had a 'thing' going on), tony grimm, leo pujack, and sally rider. Hit the school where it pretends to be. Catholic? When it suits them

Angel Amore
Ask him about the cafeteria fire

Elizabeth Sorvillo
Yeah, he was all like "I am so surprised about Carol! He was not into sharing anything. Instead he said "he felt he was a good teacher" but got railroaded by a guidance counselor. I remembered that after he said it, it was Gerilyn Coccia. She hated his guts. She's Carol's new best friend, since it's not me anymore.

Make your conquests public. I would love to know who at Prep. I'm the gay chick and I was probably the most conservative one there, lol. Married women there with kids hit on me.

Angel Amore
Gerilyn Coccia hated his guts? Wow! I always thought the 2 were friends as they used to be always chatting. You think she was setting him up? I have Carol in my crosshairs: after I conquer her, I'll post her pics.

I am a bit shy about going public with those pictures. Could I be leaving myself open for a law suit?

Elizabeth Sorvillo
From my research for my website, NY doesn't have a right to privacy law. Pictures might be risky but a list of names would be ok. And If anyone gave you a hard time you say, "I have pictures". I think Gerilyn def. set him up. She was the counselor for the kid he had the "incident" with that got him fired. He emptied the girl's purse in class and used the F word. After he emptied the purse, he said something like "Now she's all fucking pissed at me." Gerilyn ran with the kid to Pat's office.

By the way, Gerilyn is the one who hit on me.

Angel Amore
Gerilyn hit on you? Word always was she was a lesbian (she is 'butch' looking). I guess she set him up as he was more 'popular' than her. He was a nice guy and saw the good in people so I'd bet he doesn't have a clue he was set up. I woud bet Pat M was part of that too (and even lenny). I am sure there was more than just Gerilyn Coccia involved. I bet if you told him that he was set up, he'd spill the beans to you

Elizabeth Sorvillo
Maybe I'll do that. He said he only checks FB messages like every 3 months, that's why it took him so long to get back to me.

Gerilyn asked me out like 20 times, would call me at night when she had crisis her husband could have handled, and even came into my classroom in front of students sat behind me on my desk, put her arms around me and kissed me on the neck - and not in a "friendly" way. Carol and I talked about it a million times, Gerilyn had no self control where I was concerned. She was out of her mind - threw caution to the wind and would act out.

I know she wants the Deanship, she's been waiting for it. That's why she pushed her way into Carol's life.

Angel Amore   + New Message   ⚙ Actions ▾

Elizabeth Sorvillo
It was really bad, my girlfriend was gonna kick the shit out of her - calling me crying at all hours of the night when her husband is standing right there.

Angel Amore
Can you blame her for hitting on you? You're very pretty. She was that blatant? In front of the students? How repressed! Crazy. By not coming out she is being unfair to many people like her kids and husband. Typical of the sexually repressed and of course she wants the deanship as I bet she wishes she had a big penis

Elizabeth Sorvillo
Yeah, Carol even said she's a big lesbo, lol. I think she wanted to do Carol, I knew she had a thing for older women, that's why I was surprised she hit on me. She absolutely was out of her mind where I was concerned. It was a problem at work, then became a problem at home. Carol told me to keep a lid on it because they were friends. Thanks for the compliment ☺

Angel Amore
SFP is a real swinging place: the dean fucking guys after her hubby dies, a guidance counselor going for women even though she is married and has kids, a playin' religion teacher, 2 gay religion teachers, a sex crazed AP whose wife dumped him for another woman and then banged Robin, etc. I am defintely going to nail Carol and then send pics to Gerilyn! HA HA HA!

Elizabeth Sorvillo
Good luck, lol.

Elizabeth Sorvillo
where do i look
to see the pics?

Angel Amore
are you on AIM? My SN is EatinMuf

Elizabeth Sorvillo
No I am not even sure what AIM is, lol.

Angel Amore
AOLs Internet Messenger

Elizabeth Sorvillo
ok i will take a look

Elizabeth Sorvillo
I got to your Aim page,

Angel Amore

I emailed [redacted] and told him I was a former student. I didn't realize I spelled his name wrong all this time. Like he said to you he said he didnt know anything that was not really public knowledge and already on burnandrotinhell. He did say "I always preferred not knowing stuff so I could answer honestly if asked". He said he was "surprised" that Gerilyn hated him as he thought they always got along and felt somewhat "betrayed" by her. He also said the religion department always talkied bad about her and he even defended her. He also said . her 'friends' Mary Ellen Bektle and Mr K said the nastiest stuff about her as well as against Maureen Gray. He said he was not surprised by the "disingenuity" at SFP. He also said that when he resigned, Bektle gave him a bad review as a teacher which he did not sign and never spoke to anybody in that department again. He also said pat Macgackin never once asked him about it. I kind of fet bad for him as they called him a bad teacher and he was tops

Elizabeth Sorvillo

He def was a good teacher. He was all the kids' favorite. Gerilyn would do anything for money and power. She was extremely two-faced. She and that horrible [redacted] girl [redacted] that whole thing against [redacted] It was just a matter of time. Gerilyn thought she would get points for exposing a teacher's bad classroom practices. Gerilyn was trying to frame Robyn and get her fired because Robyn hates Gerilyn. So Gerilyn decided she would investigate Robyn and found out Robyn's husband stole their daughter's identity and racked up bills in her name. He was arrested for fraud and it was in the newspaper. Gerilyn showed me the article. Robyn once told me Mary Ellen's husband was in a bit of trouble when he tried to dabble in politics - some news came out about him, but she didn't say what. Any idea what that was?

Angel Amore

Who is [redacted] Another teacher? It sounds like Ms Coccia is a very sick person. [redacted] was a harmless sort of guy, why would anyone have anything against him other than being a nut? I recall Royn's husband and the ID theft thing but as is typical of the prep it was hushed up but I do recall Coccie being angry that robyn got the job and she was passed over (maybe she should have fucked pat). I think mary ellen's husband ran for some sort of county seat and lost the primary but that is all I ever heard. That and he was in charge of the Baricelli divorce

Angel Amore

Sorry, I realized that [redacted] was the softball player. My impression is that [redacted] wants to move on and put SFP behind him. I feel bad for him as he did not deserve what he got nor see it coming. You should email him again and give him the dope n Gerilyn. I'd bet if he felt betrayed, he'd give up everything. Ask him about his relationship with Gambino

Elizabeth Sorvillo

I don't want to bug [redacted] again just yet. Honestly, from what I have heard, my gut feeling of what could happen in Sept. is that either there will be a whole new administration or the school will close. Maybe your friend who teaches there should put feelers out for a new job so he or she doesn't get caught without options.

Angel Amore

My source said the school is doomed to a prolonged death as are 90% of catholic high schools. DC and Stella maris closed to no fanfare and then the famed Rice HS in Manhattan. Between the sex scandal pay offs, mismanagement, a deep seated want of failure (the older people want it to fail so their replacements can not do a better job than them), and complacency ("we've always done it this way"), they are fucked. prep likes t think it competes against Molloy and others but today they are competing for students that chose those smaller, specialized high schools in the public system (Prep would never admit that). The school will get continually worse until it becomes CTK and finally collapses.

My friend said as far as the word is, the administration next year is the same: even CS is to return. No changes (basically proves his theory)

Elizabeth Sorvillo

Wow, that's interesting. I guess we'll see what happens in September. It sounds like your friend has a handle on it, so that's good. I just wanted to give a heads up because from what I've heard, another news story could be coming that would be way worse than any bad publicity they got from my website.

Join our mailing list!

http://cliikin.com/join/26

www.ingramcontent.com/pod-product-compliance
Lightning Source LLC
Chambersburg PA
CBHW071119280326
41935CB00010B/1056